Digital Citizenship in Africa

The Digital Africa series explores how digital technologies have opened new spaces for the exercise of democratic rights and freedoms in Africa, as well as how repressive regimes have used digital technologies to diminish, or remove those rights. The series foregrounds vital new research from East, West and Southern Africa, that combines empirical rigor with theoretical sophistication in order to offer new, more nuanced perspectives on the interactions between digital technology and social life on the continent. In so doing, it offers an important, in-depth corrective to existing studies of the relations between digital technologies and social and political power, studies that have overwhelmingly focussed on the Global North.

Each volume is co-edited by the series editor in collaboration with an established scholar in the field, and each features comparative and rich case studies authored by emerging and established African scholars involved in the African Digital Rights Network. Thanks to contributors' diverse disciplinary and professional backgrounds, each chapter offers uniquely practical suggestions for policy, practice and further research.

Titles include:

Digital Citizenship in Africa: Technologies of Agency and Repression
Digital Disinformation in Africa: Hashtag Politics, Power and Propaganda

Digital Citizenship in Africa

Technologies of Agency and Repression

Edited by

Tony Roberts and Tanja Bosch

ZED

LONDON · NEW YORK · OXFORD · NEW DELHI · SYDNEY

Zed Books
Bloomsbury Publishing Plc
50 Bedford Square, London, WC1B 3DP, UK
1385 Broadway, New York, NY 10018, USA
29 Earlsfort Terrace, Dublin 2, Ireland

BLOOMSBURY and Zed Books are trademarks of Bloomsbury Publishing Plc

First published in Great Britain 2023

A catalogue record for this book is available from the British Library.

A catalog record for this book is available from the Library of Congress

ISBN: HB: 978-1-3503-2446-6
PB: 978-1-3503-2445-9
ePDF: 978-1-3503-2448-0
eBook: 978-1-3503-2447-3

Series: Digital Africa

Typeset by Deanta Global Publishing Services, Chennai, India
Printed and bound in Great Britain

To find out more about our authors and books visit www.bloomsbury.com and sign up for our newsletters.

To John and Auriol Roberts
for nurturing a love of reading and study

Contents

Illustrations

Figures

Tables

Contributors

Kiss Abraham is a feminist civil-society activist, researcher and journalist. Known for his political cartoons and graphic art, Kiss is a member of the Media Institute of Southern Africa and a founding member of the Zambian Social Forum, the African Regional Social Forum and the African Digital Rights Network. Kiss is passionate about creating civic space, the use of art in civic action, and promoting dialogue on development issues. Kiss established the organizations Knowledge and Information Systems for Social Innovation in 2003 and the New Zambian online platform in 2010. Kiss wrote *The Names in Your Address Book Are Your Social Network for Advocating Women's Rights* (2009) and *Sex, Respect and Freedom from Shame in Women & ICTs in African and the Middle East* (2014). With Sam Phiri, he co-authored the *Zambia Digital Rights Landscape Report for the African Digital Rights Network Report Digital Rights in Closing Civic Space* (2021).

Sandra Ajaja is a feminist tech activist who holds an undergraduate degree in Electrical and Electronics Engineering (Nigeria) and a master's degree in Gender and Development from the Institute of Development Studies (UK), and is completing an MBA at Syracuse University (USA). Having experienced gender inequality in accessing education and technology opportunities, Sandra founded Fempower Africa, a social enterprise that is expanding diversity in the technology space in Africa while channelling resources to female tech talent and technology entrepreneurs on the continent. Fempower Africa has become a platform for over 20,000 women to access mentorship and training to develop world-class technical skills and capabilities. This work has resulted in Sandra winning several international awards, including the Mandela Washington Fellowship, a Diana Princess of Wales award and a Commonwealth Scholarship Award.

Felicia Anthonio heads the #KeepItOn Campaign at Access Now, a global campaign of over 290 organizations that fights against internet shutdowns. Before joining Access Now, she was a Programme Associate at the Media Foundation for West Africa (MFWA) where she coordinated the African Freedom of Expression Exchange (AFEX), a continental network of free-expression organizations in Africa. Felicia led the AFEX's campaigns and advocacy work on freedom of expression, including the safety of journalists, access to information and internet freedoms and digital rights with a particular focus on policy reforms that are inimical to the enjoyment of freedom of expression (offline and online). She is a 2019 Fellow of the African Internet Governance School (AfriSIG). She holds a master's degree in Lettres, Langues et Affaires Internationales from l' Université d'Orléans, France, and holds a bachelor of arts degree in French and Psychology from the University of Ghana.

Tanja Bosch is an associate professor of media studies and production in the Centre for Film and Media Studies at the University of Cape Town, South Africa, where she also holds the position of Deputy Dean of Research and Postgraduate Affairs. She teaches journalism and multimedia production, social media, radio studies and research methods at undergraduate and postgraduate levels. Dr Bosch has published widely in the field of radio studies in South Africa; and is emerging as a leading African academic, publishing in the area of social media activism, with her work on #RhodesMustFall and #FeesMustFall and other hashtagged campaigns. Her book *Social Media and Everyday Life in South Africa* (2021) follows up her journal publications on 'Using online social networking for teaching and learning: Facebook use at the University' and 'Twitter activism and youth in South Africa: The case of #RhodesMustFall'. Tanja is the chair of the African Digital Rights Network.

Atnaf Brhane is a co-founder of Center for the Advancement of Rights and Democracy (CARD) and a digital rights activist based in Ethiopia. In 2012, he cofounded the blogging collective Zone9 Bloggers and conducted extensive social media campaigns on rule of law and freedom of expression. In 2016, the collective accepted awards from Reporters Without Borders, HRW, Martin Ennals and CPJ. In 2014, Atnafu was arrested, related to his activism work, and was imprisoned for eighteen months. From 2018 to 2019, Atnafu was Digital Integrity Fellow at Open Technology Fund and worked with human rights defenders and human rights organizations in Ethiopia on creating awareness in digital literacy and security. He cofounded the Network for Digital Rights in Ethiopia. He co-authored the *Ethiopia Digital Rights Landscape Report for the African Digital Rights Network* and *On Selfies and Hashtags: The Patterns and Antidotes of Disinformation during Armed Conflict in Ethiopia* (forthcoming).

Mavis Elias is the holder of degrees in Civil Engineering (Namibian University of Science and Technology) and a master's in International Development (Institute for Development Studies, UK). She is a social entrepreneur, philanthropist, mentor and public speaker. Mavis is the founder of the EM Love Foundation, a Namibian charity, and co-founder of Ehaveco Events, which focuses on women empowerment initiatives that help individuals and businesses realize women's full potential. Mavis is a director of Namibia's One Economy Foundation. Mavis is also a radio presenter at Radiowave and occasionally serves as master of ceremonies, having hosted the Namibia Music Awards and other prestigious events. She is a Vivid Philanthropist Award winner (2015), a Queen's Young Leader Award (2018), Women in Business and Governance Award (2019) and a Chevening Scholar. Mavis is an award-winning blogger, a columnist for Monochrome and the *New Era* newspaper.

Yohannes Eneyew is a PhD candidate and teaching associate at the Faculty of Law, Monash University in Australia. His project looks at how an appropriate balance should be struck between freedom of expression and the right to privacy on the internet under the African human rights system. Recently, he was a visiting researcher at the Law and Technology Research Group, Faculty of Law, Ghent University. Prior to this, he was a lecturer of law at the School of Law, Bahir Dar University in Ethiopia, where he was teaching and researching on Media Law and Human Rights. He holds a Master of Laws (LL.M) in International Human Rights Law (University of Groningen), LL.M in Public International Law (Addis Ababa University) and a Bachelor of Laws (LL.B) from Wollo University. His research interest spans the areas of internet freedom, intermediary liability, African human rights law, international human rights law and TWAIL.

Nanjala Nyabola is a writer and researcher. A Rhodes Scholar, Nanjala holds an MSc in Forced Migration, an MSc in African Studies from the University of

Oxford and a J.D. from Harvard Law School. She has held numerous research and practice fellowships and is currently a non-resident fellow at the Stanford University Digital Civil Society Lab, the Overseas Development Institute, and the Centre for Human Rights and Global Justice at New York University. At the time of writing, she was a PhD candidate at King's College, London. Nyabola has written extensively about African society and politics, technology, international law and feminism for academic and non-academic publications. Her journalism includes work for *Al Jazeera, Foreign Affairs, Foreign Policy*, and the *Guardian*. She is the author of *Digital Democracy, Analogue Politics: How the Internet Era Is Transforming Kenya* (2018), *Travelling While Black: Essays Inspired by a Life on the Move* (2020) and *Strange and Difficult Times: Notes on a Global Pandemic* (2022). She serves on the boards of Access Now and the International Fund for Public Interest Media.

Francis B. Nyamnjoh is professor of anthropology at the University of Cape Town. He holds a BA and an MA from the University of Yaounde, Cameroon, and a PhD from the University of Leicester, UK. He joined UCT in 2009 from the Council for the Development of Social Science Research in Africa (CODESRIA), where he served as Head of Publications from July 2003 to July 2009. He has also taught sociology, anthropology and communication studies at universities in Cameroon and Botswana. His books include #RhodesMustFall: Nibbling at Resilient Colonialism in South Africa; *Negotiating an Anglophone Identity*; *Rights and the Politics of Recognition in Africa*; *Africa's Media, Democracy and the Politics of Belonging*; *Insiders and Outsiders: Citizenship and Xenophobia in Contemporary Southern Africa*; and *Mobile Phones: The New Talking Drums of Everyday Africa*. Dr Nyamnjoh has published widely on globalization, citizenship, media and the politics of identity in Africa.

Ayobami Ojebode holds a PhD in development communication from the University of Ibadan, Nigeria. He teaches development communication with special focus on the media and political, cultural and social development. In 2007, Dr Ojebode was a visiting research fellow at the University of Oxford (2007) where he studied media coverage of minority ethnic groups in Nigeria. In 2008, he was visiting researcher at the College of Communications, the Pennsylvania State University, US, researching the Nigerian mass media and was a fellow in Leiden (2010) completing his work on the former guerrilla pressmen. His publications include the articles 'Media Diversity With and Without a Policy: A Comparison of the BBC and Nigeria's DBS', 'Beyond Tweets and Screams: Action for Empowerment and Accountability in Nigeria – the Case of the #BBOG Movement' and the Nigeria country report in 'Digital Rights in Closing Civic Space: Lessons from Ten African Countries' (2021).

Babatunde Ojebuyi is a full-time lecturer in the Department of Communication and Language Arts, University of Ibadan, Nigeria. Babatunde holds a BA, an MA and a PhD from the same department at the University of Ibadan. Ojebuyi's teaching and research interests cover media studies in the areas of media theories, media and ethics, and new media. He has written books and published well-researched articles in reputable local and international journals. His publications include *Media Literacy, Access and Political Participation among South African Black Youth* (2015), *Mobile Phone Use for Agribusiness by Farmers in Southwest Nigeria* (2016) and *We Are Not Parasites: Intergroup Differentiation in the User-Generated Content of Nigerian News Media* (2019).

Oyewole Oladapo is a lecturer in the Department of Communication and Language Arts at the University of Ibadan, Nigeria. He received his doctoral degree in 2018 from the University of Ibadan. His doctoral thesis examined variations in online and offline audiences' deconstruction of newspaper representation of Nigeria's unity. Oyewole's areas of interest include media and development, protests and politics on social media, and media and identity. He has authored and co-authored book chapters and articles in both local and foreign journals. His publications include the Digital Landscape Report on Nigeria for the African Digital Rights Network report 'Digital Rights in Closing Civic Space: Lessons from Ten African Countries' (2021).

Marjoke Oosterom is a research fellow at the Institute for Development Studies (IDS) in the UK. She holds a PhD from IDS and has a background in comparative politics and development studies. Her research concentrates on how experiences of violence and conflict affect forms of agency, citizenship, and everyday politics and governance. Her specific expertise is on youth politics and youth agency in response to insecurity and violence, and politics in the informal economy. Marjoke has studied experiences of citizenship and agency among internally displaced persons (IDPs) and refugees in conflict settings, and their interactions with humanitarian actors and forms of public authority. She is involved in the Action for Empowerment and Accountability program in fragile settings, and she has also worked on IDS projects on changing civic space. Her publications include 'Gender and Fragile Citizenship in Uganda: The Case of Acholi Women' and 'What Does Closing Civic Space Mean for Development? A Literature Review and Proposed Conceptual Framework'.

Sam Phiri is a senior academic at the University of Zambia where he heads the Department of Media and Communication Studies. His research focuses on national politics, political communication and political organizations and parties. His projects include 'Research in Communications: Focus of Mass Communication Teaching at the University of Zambia' and 'Person Not Profit – An Africanist Approach to Corporate Social Responsibility Theory'. His publications include the 'Zambia Digital Rights Landscape Report' (with Kiss Abraham), the African Digital Rights Network report 'Digital Rights in Closing Civic Space' (2021); 'Media Development Aid and the Westernisation of Africa: The Case of the Open Society Initiative for Southern Africa' (2016), 'Political Dis-Empowerment of Women by ICTs: The Case of the Zambian Elections' (2011) and 'Youth Participation in Politics: The Case of Zambian University Students' (2019).

Tony Roberts is a research fellow at the Institute for Development Studies (UK). After a period as lecturer in Innovation Studies at the University of East London, Tony founded and led two international development agencies working in Central America and Southern Africa. After he stood down as Chief Executive of Computer Aid International, he completed a PhD in the use of digital technologies in international development. After a postdoc at the United Nations University, in China, Tony joined the Digital research team at IDS where his research focuses on digital inequalities, digital citizenship and digital rights. He is a co-founder of the African Digital Rights Network (ADRN). He has edited a section of the SAGE Handbook on Participatory Digital Research Methods and the ADRN publications 'Digital Rights in Closing Civic Space: Lessons from Ten Countries' and 'Surveillance Law: A Review of Six African Countries'. His publications and blogposts are available on his website: appropriatingtechnology.org

Foreword

Francis B. Nyamnjoh

To speak of citizenship and belonging in whatever form is to imagine and construct a community of shared interests, responsibilities and aspirations. One is, and becomes, a citizen through relationships with others, institutionalized relationships in one form or another, guided by codes of conduct, democratic and contested. No institution – however carefully thought through from the outset – is perfect, hence the need to embrace incompleteness. Seen through the prism of incompleteness, citizenship is a permanent work in progress in a world of physical and social mobility of people and ideas, thanks to ever-evolving material and digital technologies of self-activation and self-extension. There is power in incompleteness as a lens to perceive life and live our creative ingenuity. Creating and institutionalizing productive, dynamic and inclusive citizenship requires constant awareness and embrace of our shared and universal reality of incompleteness in being, in action and through the technologies of self-extension that our creative ingenuity brings about.

It is productive to see citizenship in terms of the various technologies of extending ourselves to enable us to function in our society and world, to be recognized and validated by multiple instances of legitimation of our existence and being. Citizenship, in this sense, gives us a stamp of approval and judicial and political legitimacy. The fact of contributing – materially, morally and spiritually – entitles us to benefit from the community of which we are part. Citizenship is expected to mitigate the challenges of functioning as if one were living in splendid isolation. We seek citizenship to be supported and to feel supported by the cultural, political and economic communities with which we identify through relationships, shared memories, commitments and responsibilities. The communities (be these small scale or large scale, ethnic or nation state) that bestow citizenship would hardly be fulfilled or sustained in their aspirations for completeness (however illusory) without the support of its citizens. Thus, within the framework of incompleteness, power is fluid and flexible, and accessible to both institutions and individuals, who can use material and digital technologies at their disposal as a check on one another against excesses.

For anyone remotely familiar with the tendency among airlines to reward loyalty and regularity through frequent flyer programmes, and with the practice among big tech companies to limit access and ownership to digital contents by introducing expiry dates to subscriptions, one can ill-afford to take citizenship (digital or otherwise) for granted. The hierarchies of being and belonging that characterize our communities and the world at large make citizenship and the visibility we seek through it hierarchical and unstable. Availability of citizenship in principle must not be conflated with affordability. Just as digital subscriptions can expire and be withdrawn from those without the purchasing power to maintain them, so too can digital (and other forms of) citizenship. Similarly, like the potential for frequent flyer visibility and privileges, citizenship is something that is available to all and sundry in principle but can seem elusive even for those who have earned it. This, it could be argued, makes a game of citizenship, even when belonging and its entitlements for all and sundry ought not to be in question in a world of incompleteness in motion. One cannot rest on one's laurels as a citizen.

There are bounded societies or communities in which thoughts, beliefs and behaviour are rigidly prescribed, monitored and controlled, and in which conventional channels of communication are dominated by the privileged and the powerful. In such societies, the creative and innovative avenues for empowering the sidestepped and the marginalized made possible by new technologies (such as the internet, the cell phone and the smartphone) hold great promise for freedom and democracy as truly inclusive, participatory pursuits. And since democracy cannot be taken for granted, every open society or community has the potential to relapse into boundedness.[1]

At the heart of this book are questions of citizenship explored through the nexus of digital technologies as magic enablers and multipliers, or, quite simply, *juju*.[2] Put together by Tony Roberts and Tanja Bosch – two foremost researchers

---

[1] Nyamnjoh (2022).
[2] Nyamnjoh (2019).

on the everyday creative appropriation of digital media across Africa – this book makes a compelling and richly substantiated case on the important role of digital technologies in the crystallization of citizenship in Africa. It is a major addition to the growing number of studies on the catalytic role of digital technologies in the pursuit of democracy and social justice on the continent.[3] The book brings together a broad range of detailed and insightful case studies from various African countries and regions on digital activism and the makings of digital citizenship for social categories. Of importance in the analysis are categories informed by factors such as race and ethnicity, culture and religion, geography, class, gender, and sexual and intergenerational relations. These are important angles of reflection and research, the intersections of which hold great promise for nuanced complexity. The case studies articulate how feelings of repression, suppression and oppression by the status quo and the powerful and privileged have pushed Africans – either collaborating or in their individual capacity – to seek complementary channels of expression for their collective or individual aspirations for recognition and representation, and through those channels, to forge local and global solidarities.

The research explored is an agenda-setting contribution to a meaningful conversation on the nature and possibilities of citizenship and the role those digital technologies could play in facilitating or inhibiting the potential for citizenship. Nevertheless, as the book rightly highlights, digital opportunities do not come unaccompanied by opportunism. The reality of economic, political and cultural inequalities and the resilient unevenness of the playing fields, even in the digital sphere, ensure this. Thus, in Africa, while digital connectivity has proven enormously beneficial, especially in its capacity to fuel the resolve of ordinary people in their everyday struggles against authoritarian states and the whims and caprices of dictatorships in various guises and disguises,[4] it has also negatively impacted the very democracy it purports to promote.[5] These contradictions are not confined to Africa. In the United States, for example, Tom Nichols, himself a regular consumer of social media, faults digital hyper-connectivity for 'destroying the culture and habits of a democratic society' by 'making us angrier, more narcissistic, more

---

[3] Nyabola (2018).
[4] Nyabola (2018), Nyamnjoh and Brudvig (2016).
[5] Mutsvairo (2016), Nyamnjoh and Brudvig (2016).

isolated, more selfish, and less serious as citizens'. He finds the flooding of social media users with 'unfathomable amounts of data' counterproductive to liberal democracy, as it leaves users with very little time to chew and digest, reason and reflect with the required patience, tolerance and perspective that are virtues of good democratic practice.[6]

Another constraint is the sheer power of social media platforms to put reality together and impose hierarchies of visibility narrowly configured to satisfy the logic and desire for profit. If platforms can be said to confer citizenship, the very same platforms – as the example of Donald Trump's de-platforming on Twitter and Facebook and Christopher Wylie[7] before him demonstrate – platform citizenship can be withdrawn at the whim and caprice of the platform provider. It is citizenship shackled by the diktats of the provider. What the platforms have done (whether Facebook or Twitter) is to appropriate what used to be instances in a society where one could create what we might call 'prominence' or 'visibility'. Being socially visible and even attaining celebrity status had conventional institutional settings that were in the public domain. We knew what to do or where to go for cultural capital or social capital. You had to work, and you often went from word of mouth, then through various traditional media and conventional media, the publishing industry and so on. The trajectory was clear. However, with social media, algorithms can thrust a complete nonentity into the limelight overnight, with the press of a button. Those of us who are generous with our online friendship must have experienced that the 'likes' we generate do not necessarily match the number of friends we have accumulated on Facebook, for example. You might have 1,000 Facebook friends, and when you create a post, you expect at least a significant number of your friends to react to it, but often, all you are able to harvest is a paltry 10 likes, 50 at most or maybe 100 (when it's a good post).

'What happened to the 1,000 friends I had?', you are bound to find yourself asking. It is because the algorithms are created in a way to take attention away when you cannot be commercialized, when you are not a commercial entity. When you are not a sensation and not 'agent provocateur' enough to attract advertising, you may not quite blossom even within the limited range of our

---

[6] Nichols (2021).

[7] The whistle-blower of the now-defunct Cambridge Analytica firm that sought to influence the outcome of the 2016 US elections by mining and weaponizing the data of millions of Americans in collusion with Facebook. He was de-platformed on Facebook.

social media silos. Algorithms are programmed to prioritize the commercial interests of the platform providers. If you are just a very predictable, mundane type of user with no gravitas, you are unlikely to attract visibility. On the other hand, somebody might post something less salient than your post, but who has all the gravitas in terms of sensationalism and all the likelihood that they will not attract that many views or likes, and then before you know it, they have gone viral. They have appropriated through these apps a function that used to be more generously distributed around society, although depending on one's background, one's class and so on, you fell short, or you came closest. These platforms are not just enablers in a positive sense of the word. If you are fighting repression and constriction of voices, the platform providers must increasingly be questioned, just as we question other instruments of control, like the state and government. Corporate authoritarianism must not escape critical interrogation, simply because of evidence that corporations allow for some measure of trickle-down munificence.

Challenges to the crystallization of digital citizenship highlighted by the authors in this book include the advantageous position that colonial languages continue to enjoy to the detriment of endogenous languages in Africa; the frustrating resilience of repressive governments and states in their adaptability to the changing technological landscape, and capacity to develop ever new techniques of monitoring and controlling the otherwise fluid and transgressive digital technologies, and to curb the enthusiasm of nationals and communities drawn to such technologies in unprecedented ways; the ability of patriarchy to limit the rewards of the digital mileage covered in promoting a feminist agenda for citizenship; the hard zero-sum realities of states determined to flex their muscles as bounded communities vis-à-vis the determination of those caught betwixt and between borders to salvage lives and livelihoods and militate for flexible citizenship with the help of digital technologies; and the double-edged nature of ethnic and religious identities that simultaneously facilitate and frustrate digital mobilization and citizenship. The authors make a critical point in reminding the reader that accessibility to digital technology and digital citizenship is a necessary but not sufficient condition for citizenship in all its complexity and nuance.

Just as technologies prop us up, they can also deflate us, often without warning. They are as many forces of liberation as they are tools of repression and suppression. Just as we can use them to enhance meaningful citizenship in our lives, the very same technologies can be adopted and adapted by states, governments, and economic and cultural elites (among others) to police freedoms and limit inclusion. Thus, the positive role of digital technologies must not be taken for granted. On offer by digital technologies are not just applications for liberation and empowerment of ordinary people but also specially designed spyware and malware for no other purpose than to serve the interests of repressive forces. This is a warning to us that even as we embrace the technologies, we should not be too effusive or too euphoric about the possibilities. We need to be constantly alert, as well, to the dangers of the lure and allure of technological innovations.

Even though the potential of digital platforms to enable and empower is not in doubt, algorithms are configured to confirm the biases of platform consumers and not to challenge them. The customization which platforms engage in is much more a form of surveillance, behavioural control and crystallization of biases than it is about liberation, knowledge and inclusivity. A consequence of such coercive conformity is the formation of epistemic bubbles that corrupt a shared sense of reality and encourage a spiral of silence that stifles diversity and objectivity with prescriptive and dictatorial insistence on conformity. When this happens, those entrapped in 'the bubble will perceive themselves to be engaging in vigorous contestation and criticism – unaware that what they are doing is confirming and re-confirming their shared biases'.[8]

Although as users of digital platforms, we love the feeling of being in control, and to think of ourselves as immune to manipulation or cognitive biases, the reality is that algorithms are excellent at targeting and soaking us in content to keep us clicking within our silos, echo chambers, bounded communities or bantustans à la apartheid-era South Africa. This creates an illusion of choice that seeks to blunt our critical instincts as users to the monitoring and filtering processes going on in the background. As Christopher Wylie reminds us, without privacy, 'our power to decide who and how we want to be' – the power to grow and to change as we see fit – is lost, and with it our ability to be tolerant and to accommodate our creative diversity as humans.[9]

It is thus an irony that the algorithm potential for big tech companies to embrace and promote incompleteness, interconnections and conviviality is not

---

[8] Rauch (2021).
[9] Wylie (2019).

being fulfilled by social media operators. As corporate entrepreneurs driven by commercial considerations, social media operators are more interested in curbing the enthusiasm of users for genuine freedom and networking than in fostering inclusivity across frozen divides and rigid hierarchies of citizenship, being and belonging to shared spaces and places beyond the narrow confines of identity silos, echo chambers and filter bubbles. For digital media to effectively contribute to the growth of a more inclusive model of citizenship would require algorithms that challenge our biases and propensities for selective perception and seek a balance among economic, political, cultural and social considerations.

Bibliography

Mutsvairo, B. (2016) *Digital Activism in the Social Media Era*, London: Springer Nature.

Nichols, T. (2021) *Our Own Worst Enemy: The Assault from Within on Modern Democracy*, Oxford: Oxford University Press.

Nyabola, N. (2018) *Digital Democracy, Analogue Politics: How the Internet Era Is Transforming Politics in Kenya*, London: Bloomsbury Publishing.

Nyamnjoh, B. (2022) *Incompleteness: Donald Trump, Populism and Citizenship*, Bamenda, Langaa.

Nyamnjoh, F. and I. Brudvig (2016) *Mobilities, ICTs and Marginality in Africa: Comparative Perspectives*, Cape Town: HSRC Press.

Nyamnjoh, F. B. (2019) 'ICTs as Juju: African Inspiration for Understanding the Compositeness of Being Human Through Digital Technologies', *Journal of African Media Studies*, 11 (3): 279–91.

Rauch, J. (2021) *The Constitution of Knowledge: A Defense of Truth*, Chicago: Brookings Institution Press.

Wylie, C. (2019) *Mindf*ck: Cambridge Analytica and the Plot to Break America*, New York: Random House.

Acknowledgements

This book could not have been produced without the inspiration and active support of many activists and scholars who have guided us by their example or helped us review this text. The book is a product of the African Digital Rights Network, and special thanks go to founding members Anand Sheombar, George Karekwaivanane, Juliet Nanfuka and Koketso Moeti. At the Institute of Development Studies, Amy Cowlard and Jasmin Morris have ably steered the ship, and we are indebted to the generous support and reviewing expertise of Becky Faith, Kevin Hernandez, Pedro Prieto Martin and Karishma Banga. Our colleagues Rosie McGee and John Gaventa provided kind and incisive feedback on the introduction. Thanks are also due to Olivia Dellow and Nick Wolterman at Zed Books for their patience, encouragement and forbearance.

Introduction

Spaces of digital citizenship in Africa

Tony Roberts and Tanja Bosch

Digital citizenship, put simply, is the use of mobile and internet technologies to participate in civic and political life. African citizens increasingly use digital technologies including mobile phones, the internet and social media to interact with their social, economic and political environments as digital citizens. This digital citizenship is enabled by the new action possibilities afforded by digital technologies to instantly share text, images and video with millions of people locally and globally. Digital technologies enable citizens to form groups, share experience and information, without dependencies on establishment media or political institutions. However, access to digital devices, connectivity and the digital literacies needed to make effective use of these opportunities is not evenly distributed. Notwithstanding this inequality of access, digital technologies are being used by millions across Africa to engage in new forms of civic engagement and political participation.

Although there is a growing body of literature on activist use of social media in Africa (Mudhai et al. 2009; Ekine 2010, Frére 2011; Mutsvairo 2016; Willems and Mano 2017; Dwyer and Molony 2019), there is very little existing research that focuses explicitly on digital citizenship in Africa. This leaves open important questions about how the widespread use of digital technologies is affecting the nature of African citizenship, how it is enhancing or impeding engagement in different forms of citizenship and the extent to which it amplifies the power of citizens, the state and private companies. This book makes a modest contribution to addressing this under-researched area by providing the first collected edition of case studies from across the continent on digital citizenship in Africa. It aims to build bridges between media studies, citizenship studies, development studies and African studies.

In this research project we set out to understand the continuities and discontinuities between citizenship and digital citizenship in Africa and how the positive openings it generates are now being constrained by forms of digital authoritarianism and surveillance capitalism (MacKinnon 2011; Zuboff 2019). While digital technologies have often been characterized as enabling democratic openings in Africa, scholars are now also documenting their use in new forms of digital repression (Choudry 2019; Feldstein 2021). Old antagonisms familiar from the offline world are now emerging in online spaces, often evident as contestation between various forms of digital citizenship and digital authoritarianism (Mudhai 2009; Roberts and Bosch 2021). The aim of this book is to illuminate this dynamic through a range of case studies from different African countries viewed through the lens of digital citizenship. A deeper examination of core elements of digital authoritarianism will be the focus of the next two books in this series: *Digital Disinformation in Africa* and *Digital Surveillance in Africa*.

In our previous work with colleagues at the African Digital Rights Network we analysed how citizens from ten different African countries made creative use of digital technologies to open up new civic space online (Roberts and Mohamed Ali 2021). In each country we also documented the growing range of repressive uses of digital technologies to close down online civic space (Roberts et al. 2021). The use of digital technologies has undoubtedly enhanced people's ability to collectively organize and to make rights claims to government and other powerholders, but the state has gradually gained influence over digital spaces and is becoming adept in its use for social control (Nyabola 2018; McGee et al. 2018; Hintz et al. 2019). All of our digital acts, mobile calls, payments, likes and retweets leave digital traces that enable state and corporate surveillance, targeting, manipulation and control. The increasing trend of state-ordered surveillance, online disinformation and internet shutdowns represents new forms of digital authoritarianism that shrink the space for democratic citizen engagement (Freedom House 2018; Mare 2020).

In this book we argue for an understanding of digital citizenship as an active process, in which citizens use mobile and internet technologies to take part in the social, economic and political life of communities of which they are a part. Each chapter analyses a different episode of active digital citizenship to extend our understanding of distinctive aspects of digital citizenship in Africa. Each episode of digital citizenship featured in the book involves citizens using digital technologies to influence policies, claim rights or hold governments to account. Collectively, the authors investigate how mobile and internet technologies are being used both *positively* by citizens to expand democratic space online and *negatively* by states to shrink or shut down that civic space. Not all countries in Africa are covered in this collected edition; anglophone countries predominate. We hope to encourage other researchers to write about digital citizenship in other countries. The Digital Africa series itself will include more lusophone and francophone countries in future collected editions.

This introductory chapter first outlines key understandings of the concept of *citizenship*, and specific African conceptions of citizenship, which we use as a foundation for conceptualizations of *digital* citizenship in Africa. The book is not centrally concerned with citizenship in the sense of a status bestowed by states on individuals; it is instead concerned with the active process of civic and political engagement irrespective of official status. We are also concerned with how citizens access and make active and effective use of digital technologies in civic engagement and political life. Authors place each case study in historical and political context to understand how structural factors shape digital citizenship. We are interested in the specific affordances that digital technologies provide for African citizenship and in the affordances they provide for digital authoritarianism. Once we have established this theoretical framework, the remainder of this introduction briefly outlines the contributions of each chapter, showing how authors illuminate our understanding of the dynamic and contested spaces for digital citizenship in Africa. Each chapter illustrates how the use of digital technologies is being employed both to enlarge and to shrink the available space for digital citizenship.

Conceptions of citizenship

Definitional debates about citizenship have implications for our understanding of digital citizenship. We therefore begin with a review of the debates about citizenship and African citizenship, before moving on to explore digital citizenship and digital citizenship in Africa.

Citizenship has been widely contested at both a definitional and conceptual level. Many scholars distinguish between liberal, republican and communitarian conceptions of citizenship. Liberal conceptions of citizenship see it as a status bestowed upon individuals by the state, providing them with rights, with the role of the state being to protect the ability of individuals to pursue their own self-interests. Republican conceptions of citizenship see it as a set of obligations individuals have to participate in government – a process of active civic engagement in policy debates, decision-making and elections. Communitarian conceptions of citizenship emphasize community affiliation rather than individual rights or obligations to the state, arguing that the social relations and loyalties that people have as part of sub-national groups are often more meaningful and practically significant than abstract rights and distant political processes. As we will argue, this communitarian perspective resonates with some African conceptions of citizenship that emphasize the importance of ethnic, religious or language groups above affiliation to the state.

Citizenship does not occur in a vacuum; it is expressed in spaces and places (Jones and Gaventa 2002), and the specific historic, cultural and power relationships of those spaces inevitably shape the temporal and situated meaning and practices of citizenship in those places. This makes the situated study of citizenship in particular geographies and within specific groups essential to a full understanding of digital citizenship in Africa.

Active citizenship

One aspect that is contested in the literature is whether citizenship is better understood as a status bestowed upon an individual by the state and to which rights and obligations are attached or as an agency-based process of participation in political and civic life. Narrowly and legally defined, citizenship involves the entitlement to carry a passport or national identity document, which brings associated entitlements such as the right to vote and associated obligations such as respecting laws and norms. However, such legal-political definitions of citizenship are, in practice, constantly being challenged and renegotiated due to globalization, migration and when countries join or leave economic and trading blocs. It is also now affected by the advent of online communities and platforms that enable borderless online commerce, employment, education and politics. Gaventa (2010) suggests that neoliberalism and globalization increasingly frame citizens as passive consumers, users and beneficiaries and instead argues for a conception of citizens as active producers and rights-bearers. This view recognizes the colonial and exclusionary origins of liberal and republican practices of citizenship but instead asserts everyday practices of citizenship that express relatedness, belonging, solidarity and demands for dignity, right and social justice (Nyamu-Musembi 2006; Gaventa 2010).

Marshall defined citizenship as 'a status bestowed on those who are full members of a community' (1950: 28). By defining citizenship in relation to membership of a 'community' rather than a nation state, it becomes possible to conceive of citizenship of various collectives on local or global scales based on affiliations including (but not limited to) those of proximity, culture, values, gender, ethnic group, class, caste or religion. People are generally members of more than one such community. However, Marshall's account of citizenship places insufficient emphasis on the processes necessary to attain and defend it. The rights that we have are themselves the outcome of ongoing active citizenship such as the women's suffrage, civil rights and labour rights movements, as well as the contemporary #MeToo, #BlackLivesMatter and #ENDSARS movements. Jones and Gaventa (2002) argue that to be meaningful, any conception of citizenship should carry with it a conception of rights. Lister (2003) defines this form of active citizenship as the process of bringing neglected issues into the public realm in acts of rights-claiming.

Nyamu-Musembi (2006) also argues for the need for citizenship to focus on actors' agency, pointing out that such 'actor-orientated perspectives are based on the recognition that rights are shaped through actual struggles informed by people's own understandings of what they are entitled to'. A focus on citizenship as an ongoing *process* and not just the *product* of state decisions positions people as active participants in the ongoing project of exercising, defending and claiming rights rather than as passive recipients of status bestowed by the state. From this perspective, the #hashtag campaigns and digital openings/closings considered in this book can be seen as examples of such active citizenship processes involving the exercise, defence and claiming of rights.

From this perspective, Naila Kabeer (2005) argues, the history of citizenship can be viewed as the history of struggle over how it should be defined and who and what it includes or excludes. Definitions of citizenship consign 'certain groups within a society to the status of lesser citizens or of non-citizens, and on the struggles by such groups to redefine, extend and transform "given" ideas about rights, duties and citizenship. They therefore help to shed light on what inclusive citizenship might mean when it is viewed from the standpoint of the excluded' (Kabeer 2005: 1). As the case studies in this book illustrate, citizenship is a double-edged sword that can be used to both include and exclude, and can be used as means of resistance or discipline 'Citizenship is frequently used to exclude "outsiders" through the drawing and policing of boundaries of citizenship and residence . . . [this] does not invalidate citizenship's use as a progressive political and analytical tool' (Lister 2003: 8).

In principle, every citizen enjoys the same citizenship rights and entitlements. In practice, access to these entitlements is uneven, in ways that are often structured along familiar dimensions of (dis)advantage, including gender, ethnicity and class. Achieving these rights and entitlements is not automatic, especially for disadvantaged communities. The ability to exercise, defend and expand these rights depends on an ongoing process of active citizenship.

Conceptions of African citizenship

The earlier conceptions of citizenship draw primarily from academic debates in the Global North. African scholars provide alternative conceptions of citizenship essential to understanding digital citizenship in Africa and of particular relevance for this volume. Ekeh (1975) claims that the colonial context of African politics informs its distinct conceptions of citizenship. He argues that citizenship acquires a variety of meanings depending on whether it is conceived in terms of what he refers to as the primordial public or the civic public. The primordial public is the indigenous moral order of communal identity and obligations, and the civic public is the idea of a nation state involving rights and national taxes that were originally imposed under colonialism and later institutionalized by local elites in constitutions and political settlements following independence. In relation to the primordial public, Ekeh (1975) argues that African citizens have moral obligations to contribute and perform duties at the level of extended family or ethnic group in exchange for the intangible benefits of identity and the psychological security of belonging. Ekeh argues that the structure of the civic public is different and amoral. 'A good citizen of the primordial public gives out and asks for nothing in return; a lucky citizen of the civic public gains from the civic public but enjoys escaping giving anything in return whenever he can' (Ekeh 1975: 108). These two elements of African citizenship are distinct from Western conceptions.

More recently, in *Citizen and Subject*, Mamdani (1996) analyses the colonial roots of African citizenship, arguing that during occupation, a white colonial elite of settlers were 'citizens' privileged politically, economically and culturally, while the colonized Black majority were devalued 'subjects'. Mamdani argues that the lives of white citizens were shaped by modern law, religion and formal employment, while the lives of Black subjects were shaped by customary law, beliefs and the informal economy. Mamdani argues that civic power in post-colonial Uganda was deracialized but not detribalized, with the result that rural Ugandans remained subject to the power of customary law and loyal to their ethnic-religious group rather than to national law and universal citizenship. Writing about citizenship in the post-independence period, Ayoade (1988) analysed some of the socialist, one-party and president-for-life political settlements, concluding that many were 'states without citizens', that is, members remained subjects rather than citizens as they lacked the ability to use citizenship to exercise constitutional rights and effectively secure state responsiveness to their needs and priorities.

Nyamnjoh (2006) argues that the dominant Western literature tends to emphasize universal 'civic' citizenship and rights at the expense of 'ethnic' conceptions of citizenship, 'thereby downplaying the hierarchies of inclusion and exclusion informed by race, ethnicity, class, gender and geography that determine accessibility to citizenship in real terms' (Nyamnjoh 2006: 237). He argues that universal conceptions of citizenship are premised on a denial of existing hierarchies and inequalities of citizenship which 'insiders' impose on 'outsiders'. Nyamnjoh (2006) argues that 'There has been too much focus on "rights talk" and its "emancipatory rhetoric", and too little attention accorded to the contexts, meanings, and practices that make citizenship possible for some and a far-fetched dream for most'. Nyamnjoh's work provides a more situated analysis of citizenship and draws attention to the processes by which different ethnic and gendered hierarchies of citizenship are constructed and reproduced in Africa.

To resolve these tensions Nyamnjoh suggests the introduction of 'flexible citizenship' (2006: 241). Nyamnjoh argues that political elites scapegoat immigrants as the reason for economic hardship. 'Citizens are made to believe that their best chance in life rests with reinforcing the distinction between them and . . . blaming migrants for their failures' (2006: 241). Like Flores and Benmayor's (1997) study of Latino citizenship and feminist research (Lister 2003; Yuval-Davis and Werbner 1999), Nyamnjoh's research begins by identifying those who are excluded from citizenship and then taking their standpoint to understand how citizenship is unevenly experienced and contested. He writes that 'There is a clear need to reconceptualize citizenship in ways that create political, cultural, social and economic space for excluded nationals and non-nationals alike, as individuals and collectivities'. Such inclusion, he argues, 'is best guaranteed by a flexible citizenship unbounded by race, ethnicity, class, gender or geography, and that is both conscious and critical of hierarchies' (2006: 239).

These conceptions of African citizenship, from Ekeh and Mamdani to Ayoade and Nyamnjoh, in which affiliation to ethnic group predominates over nation state, are a feature of several chapters in this volume, most notably the chapters on Ethiopia and Nigeria.

Cultural citizenship

Another relevant and related conceptualization for this volume is the notion of cultural citizenship which combines active citizenship concepts with a form of ethnic citizenship. The term 'cultural citizenship' was coined by Latino scholars in the United States to articulate their experience of second-class citizenship in their own countries (Flores and Benmayor 1997). Their work examines the role that culture plays in citizenship and the role of active citizenship in shaping culture. In their research, 'cultural citizenship' refers to the agency of persons (whether formally classed as citizens or undocumented 'non-citizens') in processes or practices that assert their human, social or cultural rights. This includes political demands for equity, inclusion and full participation, but the authors also include everyday cultural practices that play a part in producing social and cultural identity in their definition of cultural citizenship:

> Cultural citizenship can be thought of as a broad range of activities of everyday life through which Latinos and other groups claim space in society and eventually claim rights . . . the motivation is simply to create space where the people feel 'safe' and 'at home', where they feel a sense of belonging and membership . . . the right to control space and to establish community is a central one. (Flores and Benmayor 1997: 15–16)

Flores and Benmayor chose to work with groups that were excluded from effective citizenship, and they focused on episodes of contestation where excluded groups were claiming space, producing identity, making rights claims and demanding to be heard. Their claims were often counter-hegemonic and met by opposition: 'creating social space and claiming rights can be oppositional and can lead to powerful redressive social movements . . . through these movements new citizens and new social actors are emerging, redefining rights, entitlements, and what it means to be a member of this society' (Flores and Benmayor 1997: 276).

Yuval-Davies and Werbner (1999: 2) highlight the fact that many communities are more passionately attached to their ethnic group than to their nationality, arguing that 'communities that privilege origin and culture thus tend to foster much deeper passions than those organised around notions of citizenship'. They define citizenship as much more than simply the formal relationship between an individual and the state; rather, it is 'a more total relationship, inflected by identity, social positioning, cultural assumptions, institutional practices and a sense of belonging' (1999: 4). The perspective represented in their edited collection and a special edition of *Feminist Review* (No. 57, 1999) presents understandings of citizenship that recognize how gender, nationality, religion, ethnicity, 'race', ability, and age mediate the construction of citizenship and determine access to entitlements and capacity to exercise independent agency. They conclude that despite its gendered history and tendency to exclude non-citizens, the concept of citizenship has potential value for a progressive politics that expands agency, rights and autonomy, if reimagined from a feminist perspective and in alliance with the labour movement and other disadvantaged groups (1999: 28–29).

Concepts of digital citizenship

The conceptualization of digital citizenship we present in this volume builds upon the concepts of citizenship described earlier. This section reviews the concepts of digital citizenship that we find most useful for interpreting how mobile and internet technologies are being used to participate in civic and political life in Africa.

Digital citizenship, put simply, is the process of participating in civic life using digital tools or in online spaces. Different digital tools and online platforms afford citizens different possibilities for civic action. Unlike citizenship, digital citizenship cannot be framed as a status bestowed upon individuals by the state. A person does not need permission from the state to become a digital citizen. Any citizen who makes active use of mobile and internet tools in their social, economic and political interactions is taking part in digital citizenship. They do, however, need to have access to digital tools, connectivity and digital literacies which are unevenly distributed; and because the majority of digital citizenship takes place on corporate social media platforms which can (and do) ban individuals, it is increasingly private corporations rather than the state who hold the power to enable and limit digital citizenship. Digital citizenship may or may not involve participation in formal politics, though not all online activity can be considered citizenship. Determining the parameters of what constitutes digital citizenship is contested as the following sections make clear.

We begin this section by reviewing the literature on the issues of digital access and digital affordances that are fundamental to digital citizenship. We then review definitions of digital citizenship, active digital citizenship and African digital citizenship before reflecting on the critical questions on digital citizenship in Africa that are answered in the case study chapters included in this volume.

Digital access to citizenship

Digital citizenship is predicated on access to digital technologies, connectivity and to the technical and civic skills needed to use them in social and political life. These issues of equitable access to technology are pertinent in all the countries studied in this volume. Significant digital divides exist between continents, between countries within Africa and between different demographic groups within each country (Norris 2001; Mutula 2008; Van Dijk 2020). For example, access to the internet is at 95 per cent penetration in Nigeria and at 85 per cent penetration in Kenya, but it is less than at 20 per cent penetration in more than twenty African countries (statista.com 2021). Around the turn of the century, the digital development literature included a substantial focus on these 'digital divides' or uneven technology access within and between countries (Norris 2001; Castells 2002; Baskaran and Muchie 2006; Van Dijk 2006; Fuchs and Horak 2008; Unwin 2009).

Increasingly, this research goes 'beyond access' to examine the other necessary conditions to translate access into effective use (Gurstein 2003). Within any population, understanding the dimensions and dynamics of access to digital technologies is a matter of empirical investigation to establish exactly who enjoys availability of digital devices, for whom connectivity is affordable and who has the necessary awareness, abilities and agency to make effective use of digital technologies in civic life (Roberts and Hernandez 2019). Empirical investigation frequently shows that digital access is often delimited along intersectional lines. Women, and especially low-income rural women, are often the least connected (Ikolo 2013; Carboni et al. 2021). The case studies in this volume on Namibia and feminist digital citizenship in Nigeria analyse technology access to show the gendered hierarchies of digital citizenship.

Digital affordances for citizenship

Theoretically, the concept of affordances is often used to assess how different digital technologies make possible different social action. Originally used by Gibson (1977) to refer to the action possibilities suggested to the viewer by an object such as a handle, Norman (1988) appropriated the term to refer to those aspects of a technology that *invite, allow or enable* particular action possibilities for the user. Hutchby (2001: 444) reminds us that the affordances of technologies are only potentialities by defining affordances as 'aspects which frame, while not determining, the possibilities for agentic action in relation to an object'. From this perspective it has been argued that social media has useful affordances for enabling citizens the action possibilities of immediate global communication and the ability to create online spaces to self-organize, influence opinion at scale and project policy alternatives (Tufeki 2017; Earl and Kimport 2011). The use of affordances to analyse which technologies invite which action possibilities has become a feature of the digital development literature (Roberts 2017; Faith 2018).

Early literature emphasized the positive action possibilities afforded by digital technologies to enhance citizen voice and agency. Research documented how communities and issues that are under-represented in the establishment media, political parties and civil society could gain traction through networked organization (Benkler 2008; Shirky 2008). As each new generation of digital technology was appropriated for civic engagement, the empirical literature grew. This included, for example, studies on the use of SMS text messages in digital activism (Okolloh 2009; Ekine 2010), humanitarian action (Meier 2015; James and Taylor 2018), social media protest (Tufekci 2017; Egbunike 2018), civic technology (de Lanerolle et al. (2017), citizen-led accountability initiatives (McGee et al. 2018) and everyday digital citizenship (Bosch 2021).

Over this period, the early cyber-optimism of those who championed the digital as a means to reinvigorate citizen engagement (Negroponte 1995; Katz 1997) became tempered by the cyber-pessimism of those concerned by deepening divides, algorithmic discrimination and digital surveillance and disinformation (O'Neil 2016; Eubanks 2017; Hernandez and Roberts 2018; Noble 2018; Benjamin 2019). More recent scholarly attention has also focused on how the use of digital technologies reflects and reproduces existing exclusions and inequalities (O'Neil 2016; Eubanks 2017; Hernandez and Roberts 2018; Benjamin 2019) and how repressive governments are deploying technologies and tactics to close down online civic space (Oladapo and Ojebode 2021; Karekwaivanane and Msonza 2021). A new cyber-realism may now be emerging that provides theoretical tools able to analyse both the positive opportunities and negative consequences of digital citizenship (Isin and Ruppert 2015; McGee et al. 2018; Hintz et al. 2019; Roberts and Mohamed Ali 2021).

Digital citizenship defined

In the educational studies literature, digital citizenship involves a concern with teaching students to become safe and responsible online citizens. This literature is largely focused on how to teach and measure student competencies in online etiquette, safety and the development of the skills necessary to enable learners to become online citizens (Ribble et al. 2004; Jones and Mitchell 2015; Nickel et al. 2020). This agenda is sometimes extended to include building the competencies of parents, teachers and the wider community (Bearden 2016). In some cases, the scope of digital citizenship in educational studies extends beyond concerns to developing students' digital literacies to include political literacies such as lessons in aspects of civic engagement and participation in democratic processes (Ribble 2015). In general, the media studies and citizenship studies literature are less concerned with the conformist issues of online etiquette and responsible digital citizenship and are predominantly focused on the reformist role of digital technologies in activism to influence social change.

Mossberger, Tolbert and McNeal (2008: 1) define digital citizenship as 'the ability to participate in society online'. Inclusion, civic participation and economic opportunity are their three metrics of the ability to participate online and, therefore, of digital citizenship. They define digital citizens as 'those who use technology frequently [daily], who use technology for political information to fulfil their civic duty, and who use technology at work for economic gain' (2008: 2). To the extent that digital technologies thus facilitate inclusion, participation and economic opportunity, the authors, concerned with the US experience of digital citizenship, argue that the internet is essential to citizenship in the information age. Like other early literature on digital citizenship, they are generally optimistic about the potential benefits of digital technologies for social inclusion, civic participation and economic opportunity. Their research showed that voter turnout and economic opportunity were positively correlated with internet use, and they saw the potential for increased internet access to foster an increasingly informed population and increased civic engagement and economic growth. However, despite their optimistic outlook, their findings showed that affordable access and literacy skills are preconditions for benefiting from internet access. Their analysis showed that contrary to what was hoped, as internet access expanded, 'gaps based on race, ethnicity, and social economic status are not disappearing' (2008: 121), leading them to conclude that 'Social inequalities such as poverty, illiteracy, and unequal educational opportunities, prevent all Americans from enjoying full participation online and in society more generally' (2008: 157).

Active digital citizenship

Although much of the digital citizenship literature has been concerned with the important issues of technology access, digital literacies and effective use, a distinct strand of scholarship has focused on active digital citizenship: the use of digital technologies to make claims in relation to the state (Ekine 2010; Tufekci 2017; Ojebode and Oladapo 2018; Bosch 2021; Karekwaivanane and Monza 2021). Isin and Ruppert (2015: 44) argue that 'what makes a subject a citizen is the capacity for making rights claims' and that becoming digital citizens involves making rights claims through the internet. They argue that by performing rights claims (through speech acts), a person becomes a citizen and that by making rights claims online they become digital citizens. Isin and Ruppert (2015) adopt an active conception of digital citizenship arguing that 'digital citizenship is best defined and understood through people's actions, rather than by their formal status of belonging to a nation-state and the rights and responsibilities that come with it'.

This logic puts human agency at the centre of the analysis of citizenship. In legal-political analysis, rights (and internet access) are gifts bestowed upon passive citizens by the state. From this perspective, citizens are passive beneficiaries of rights that are bestowed upon them already fully formed by powerholders. Conversely, from the agency-based perspective of Isin and Ruppert, people can make claims to rights that do not yet exist or to rights that exist in theory but not in practice. They argue that it is the very agency of humans that is necessary to (re)create and (re)produce rights and citizenship through the processes of imagining them, digital speech acts to demand them and legal process to code them into law. It is through their digital acts of rights-claiming that people create the spaces for digital citizenship that contribute to processes of reform and transformation.

Isin and Ruppert (2015) argue that all digital acts take place in physical space by embodied citizens, but that they are qualitatively different from non-digital citizenship in several regards. First, they are not bounded by the borders of the nation state; a viral campaign can engage thousands of people in multiple nation states simultaneously. Second, digital acts are not bound by the same conventions of physical space; online communities have their own norms and conventions. Acts of digital citizenship cannot easily be contained within existing 'borders and orders' and are not necessarily limited to the boundaries of the nation state but beyond to cyberspace (2015: xiii). By creating online spaces, digital citizens are able to develop new online norms and conventions in further acts of digital citizenship.

Isin and Ruppert (2015) go on to study particular types of digital citizens (citizen journalists, hackers, open-source activists) to analyse the novel digital acts and conventions of these new civic actors in creating openings of online civic space. They also look in detail at closings of online civic space such as digital filtering, surveillance and tracking. They argue that both openings and closings result from the (cyber)space of power relationships between online citizens and online conventions. In their analysis, digital citizenship and digital surveillance are not independent of each other but are part of the same ongoing contestation, in which breaking, calling out and contesting digital conventions (regulatory practices, algorithmic practices, etc.) is a new and increasingly important site of civic engagement to shift power. According to Isin and Ruppert (2015: 180), to conclude that digital rights can be delivered by laws alone 'is to neglect that the daily enactment of rights in cyberspace is a necessary but not sufficient guarantee. Conversely, to think that the daily enactment of rights in cyberspace is the guarantee of freedom is to neglect that without inscription, enactment would not have its performative force.' This combination of online and offline action is a theme of several of the case study chapters in this book.

Hintz et al. (2019: 20) characterize digital citizenship as everyday cultural practices, social media exchange and economic transactions mediated by the platform economy and define digital citizenship as the 'performative self-enactment of digital subjects' (2019: 40). They distinguish their approach by conceptualizing digital citizenship as constituted as much by the actions of the state and corporate actors as by citizen agency. They note that 'the overarching focus in studies of digital citizenship is on users' action and digital agency' (2019: 31), including how people enact themselves as digital citizens (Isin and Ruppert 2015), and their effective use of digital access and literacy to enhance civic engagement (Mossberger et al. 2008) and to 'democratise civic and political participation and facilitate social inclusion' (Vivienne et al. 2016: 8). The cumulative effect of this, they argue, is that 'the concept of digital citizenship has an intrinsic connection with citizen empowerment' (Hintz et al. 2019: 31). 'Digital media, it is claimed (explicitly or implicitly), have allowed us to raise our voices, be heard in social and public debate, and construct our role in society. This implies a democratizing trend in state–citizen relations, and therefore a power shift towards citizens' (Hintz et al. 2019: 31).

However, Hintz et al. argue that digital citizenship studies also need to explore the ways that digital citizenship practices are limited and constrained by the digital practices of states and corporations in the context of what Zuboff (2015) has termed 'surveillance capitalism'. The idea that social media facilitates corporate surveillance and the commodification of all digital acts 'complicates dominant narratives celebrating social media platforms as sites for pleasure and play, as well as tools to be used for liberating purposes by a host of progressive social and political actors' (Hintz et al. 2019: 9). This idea that digital citizenship is constituted not only by the agency of citizens but also by the actions of the state and corporations is central to the understanding of digital citizenship explored in this book.

State surveillance and disinformation

For many scholars of digital citizenship, a key turning point in the study of digital citizenship was the Cambridge Analytica scandal and Snowden revelations, which revealed the full extent of state and corporate engagement to the detriment of open democratic spaces online. The Cambridge Analytica scandal revealed how political parties were using Facebook surveillance to construct data profiles of citizens to covertly target them with content designed to manipulate their beliefs and voting behaviour (Cadwalladr and Graham-Harrison 2018; Nyabola 2018). Cambridge Analytica worked on the 2013 election in Kenya as well as on the 2016 Brexit referendum and Trump election. The Snowden revelation provided a torrent of evidence that the US, UK and South African governments were among those conducting mass surveillance of citizens' mobile and internet communications – far exceeding their legal powers. The research that followed these media stories showed that states were making systematic use of mobile and social media surveillance to spy on citizens (Cadwalladr and Graham-Harrison 2018; Van Zyl 2016; Bosch and Roberts 2021). Governments classified as both authoritarian and liberal democratic were found to have engaged in extensive surveillance of their own and foreign citizens and in manipulation of electoral processes in ways that violated constitutional rights to privacy of communication and that impinge on the space for digital citizenship (Nyabola 2018; Cadwalladr and Graham-Harrison 2018; Zubóff 2019).

Evidence that states and corporations were tracking and recording digital citizenship caused some reorientation of research priorities and prompted a more critical stance from researchers and activists. Hintz et al. (2019) argued for a new realism about digital citizenship that was neither utopian nor dystopian, echoing earlier warnings from Mudhai (2009), Mare (2018) and Nyabola (2018) about the encroachment of the state into the digital social sphere.

The pervasive collection of citizens' mobile and internet communication by state security forces and by corporations, including Facebook and Cambridge Analytica, has quickly become a routine feature of civic life causing Hintz et al. to note that 'Digital citizenship is shaped by the increasing normalization of such monitoring' now that 'The tools that we use to enact and perform our citizenship are hosted by a small set of commercial platforms, provided by a highly concentrated business sector' (Hintz et al. 2019: 35). This inflection point has resulted in an emerging body of literature on digital citizenship that is much more critical than the majority of early studies and which now includes investigation of the multi-million dollar market supplying technologies to government agencies across the African continent for use in illegal surveillance of citizens (Roberts and Mohamed Ali 2019; Roberts, Mohamed Ali, Farahat, Oloyede and Mutung'u (2021)) as well as the power relationships reflected in what Freedom House (2018) have called a descent into digital authoritarianism (MacKinnon 2011; Freedom House 2018; Mare 2020; Roberts and Bosch 2021).

African digital citizenship

Oyedemi (2020) usefully builds on Mossberger et al.'s access-based definition of digital citizenship, arguing that in an increasingly digital world, access to the internet and the skills needed to make practical use of access have become important for effective participation in society. Oyedemi defines a digital citizen as 'someone with regular and flexible access to the Internet, the skills to apply this technology, and a regular use of the Internet for participation and functioning in all spheres of the society' (Oyedemi 2020: 244). Oyedemi also moves the discussion about digital citizenship beyond access and use to include the issues of rights, equality and social justice. He argues that the use of the internet has become crucial for inclusive citizen participation in the economy and in social and civic life, and for the enrichment of democracy. He discusses at length how the internet has become a key resource for individuals to participate more effectively in the economic, social, cultural and political life of the community. By extension, he argues that citizenship is hampered if some people are unable to participate in society based on their lack of access. The key elements in Oyedemi's (2020) theory of digital citizenship are the ability to access and the skills to regularly and flexibly use the internet, the policies to make this possible and the issues of equitable access and inclusive participation, rights and social justice.

Emmanuel Chijioke Ogbonna (2018) provides a rare comparative analysis of digital citizenship across several African countries. Ogbonna focused on examples of digital citizenship enacted through social media in Tunisia, Egypt, Libya and Algeria before an in-depth analysis of Nigeria. Using examples including the viral #BringBackOurGirls campaign, Ogbonna argues that citizens who were previously excluded from the political sphere have found in social media an effective platform for information sharing, rapid communication, coordination and mobilization that allows citizens to bypass established political mechanisms. Ogbonna analyses the situated historical, political and sociocultural factors, including those that shape and limit digital citizenship. He concludes that while social media aids group formation and 'expands participatory space to corners hitherto shielded and previously unconnected' (2018: 42) and can contribute to deposing regimes, the 'fractured social order' cannot be mended by digital citizenship alone. The deeper structural challenge of creating sustainable power-sharing mechanisms remains even when regimes change and Ogbonna wants to see digital citizens move beyond protest to offer a 'viable policy pact' that addresses the root causes of Africa's socio-economic problems, including the weaponization of ethnic divisions by powerful elites to accumulate resources.

In her study of the 2015 #FeesMustFall campaign in South Africa, Tanja Bosch suggests that we see the social media platform Twitter as 'an emergent space of radical citizenship' (Bosch 2016: 170). She illustrates how citizens from different gender, class and ethnic backgrounds who would not otherwise readily coalesce were able to come together on Twitter and use the affordances of the digital platform to make rights claims for social justice that mobilized opinion across the country and globally. For young South Africans who are largely disengaged from mainstream political parties, Twitter and the #FeesMustFall campaign made possible a form of 'participatory citizenship'. In the same volume, Viola C. Milton (2016) also considers the kind of digital citizenship being forged in a campaign to save public broadcasting in South Africa organized by the SOS Coalition. The coalition's online activities provided a platform for a range of actors to make claims and present policy proposals for the future of South Africa's public broadcasting including a range of legal, financial and technical concerns. Twitter was used to share information, mobilize opinion, organize offline protests and influence policy outcomes. The paper provides a glimpse into digital citizenship as an active practice that was successful in opening parliamentary hearings to the public and influencing policy.

There is an emerging literature on African digital citizenship that considers the role of ethnicity (Egbunike 2018) or cultural citizenship (Bosch 2021). Drawing on the citizenship literature, there is scope to consider African digital citizenship using the unbounded, flexible, hierarchical and multidimensional and overlapping forms of citizenship proposed by Ong (1999), Lister (2003), Isin and Wood (1999) and Nyamnjoh (2006). In approaching digital citizenship in Africa, the state may be an important reference point, but it may not be the most important aspect of citizenship. From these emerging perspectives, it is clearly possible to conceive of African digital citizenship as reflecting distinct and specific cultural, ethnic, religious or gender belongings or interests that may be national or sub-national in character. The ethnic element of digital citizenship in Africa is clearest in the case study chapters from Ethiopia and Nigeria.

This perspective resonates with the work of Isin and Wood (1999), who argued that the internet will present the possibility for new forms of politics and citizenship due to the disruption of the monopoly of nation state power and the foregrounding of new digital rights issues including digital access, privacy and surveillance. Isin and Wood envisage digital citizenship as a method for enhancing existing forms of citizenship by using digital tools to increase information sharing, civic participation, transparency and accountability. However, they also express concern about the use of technologies of surveillance and biometric identification, citing early examples of biometric ID being used to govern citizens' access to social welfare and government services, and to moderate human behaviour. Isin and Wood concluded that technological citizenship was not only about the agency issues of 'how to harness new technologies for new forms of political enactment [but also] about how to limit the uses of technology that encroach upon civil and political rights' (Isin and Wood 1999: 159).

Critical perspectives on digital citizenship in Africa

Our initial literature review clarified that existing digital citizenship research focuses primarily on the Global North and predominantly uses conceptual lenses derived from the same geography. Most of the existing literature emphasizes the positive use of social media in enabling new possibilities for activism. We were motivated to conduct this project by a concern to better understand under what conditions it is possible to harness the positive affordances of digital technology for citizenship and social change. However, we were also motivated to understand the negative affordances of digital technologies for surveilling digital citizens, closing online civic space and otherwise limiting citizenship. This reflects Hintz et al.'s (2019) point that digital citizenship is constituted both by citizen agency and by the actions of the state and corporations. We were also concerned to capture the wider environmental factors (Ogbonna 2018) that shape the space for digital citizenship in Africa. This required more critical analysis than we found in the existing digital citizenship literature.

In his analysis of digital citizenship in Africa, Ogbonna (2018) reminds us that however useful social media is in providing new opportunities for citizen engagement in civic life, online activism is not a sufficient condition for transformational social change. Even if social media activism does play a role in regime change, the institutional, economic and political environment is likely to mean that change in political leadership at the top is insufficient to translate into the desired social, economic and political change. Although regime change was achieved in Tunisia and Egypt this has not led to the kind of transformational social change that digital activists called for. Mindful of this sober reality, the authors in this volume situate their analysis in the relevant political, economic or social context to illustrate the continuities and discontinuities of colonial and post-independence realities.

In embarking on this project we were also motivated to better understand the extent to which digital citizenship in Africa was specifically digital and/or specifically African. Is online digital citizenship in Africa in any way different from offline citizenship in Africa? Do the affordances of digital technologies produce new forms of citizenship? Is digital citizenship in Africa different from digital citizenship elsewhere? Put otherwise, we wanted to interrogate – What is African about digital citizenship in Africa and what is digital about digital citizenship in Africa? Producing case studies from a range of African countries provided us with the possibility to learn whether the distinct colonial and post-colonial realities of African nations were reflected and reproduced in emerging forms of digital citizenship. We hoped that the case studies would also allow us to understand how the intersecting gender, ethnic and rural/urban power relations were mirrored or shattered by the migration of civic participation to online spaces.

Our previous work with the African Digital Rights Network has given us a keen interest in understanding more about how the space for digital citizenship was being opened and closed in each country. We wanted to understand more about the interrelationship of digital citizenship and digital authoritarianism: How do states respond to effective digital citizenship and how do digital citizens respond to effective digital repression? Although uptake of mobile and internet technologies has been rapid across Africa, access to digital technologies, digital connectivity and digital literacies has not been even or universal. As a result, we also were mindful to investigate what factors either block access to digital technologies altogether or prevent those with access from translating it into digital citizenship. The case studies contained in this book illuminate these questions.

Chapter summaries

The chapters in this book employ a range of case studies and theoretical reflections to extend the understanding of digital citizenship in Africa presented earlier. The authors of each chapter investigate how mobile and internet technologies are being used to both expand and limit digital citizenship in countries across the continent. Each chapter features a distinct episode of contestation played out in digital space or using digital tools, drawing on different understandings of the concepts of digital citizenship discussed earlier, to interpret empirical examples of digital citizenship in the countries they have studied. Their recommendations for policy, practice and further research provide guidance for governments, civil society and academics alike.

In Chapter 2, Ojebode, Ojebuyi, Oladapo and Oosterom examine how ethnic-religious divisions can constrain or expand the space for digital citizenship in Nigeria. The authors illustrate how digital citizenship can be used to either unite citizens across ethnic-religious fault lines to confront injustice or divide them along ethnic-religious fault lines. They use two case studies, the #ENDSARS protests, which went viral globally and forced government action, and the #PantamiMustGo campaign, which divided citizens and extinguished pressure for change. The authors use the concept of resilience to describe how community members respond and recover from external shocks and show how citizens use digital media in ways that can either strengthen or weaken social security and resilience. They use this framing to show how the #ENDSARS movement confronted the state to promote citizen security and inclusion, while dynamics in the #PantamiMustGo campaign were such that it undermined resilience. These two campaigns of digital citizenship had very different outcomes: the #ENDSARS movement expanded the space of digital citizenship by building solidarity across ethnic-religious fault lines to secure concessions from the state; while the digital citizenship in the #PantamiMustGo campaign mobilized entrenched polemic positions that benefited the status quo.

In Chapter 3, Brhane and Eneyew explore digital citizenship in Ethiopia using the Zone9blogger and the #LetOurVoicesBeHeard campaigns. They draw on the work of Mamdani (1996) and Nyamnjoh (2006), who have argued that ethnicity is as important as nationality in African conceptions of citizenship. The authors construct their own understanding of Ethiopian digital citizenship, which they argue has been shaped by the country's ethnic hierarchy. The chapter shows how, in the period prior to 2005, the government provided an enabling environment for digital citizenship, which saw a rapid expansion of blogging and digital civic engagement, but after electoral losses in 2005, the government dramatically closed civic space, arrested critical bloggers and imposed a series of internet shutdowns. As the Oromo/Amhara protests increased between 2015 and 2017, oppressed ethnic groups made increasingly sophisticated use of a range of digital technologies to make rights claims on the Tigrayan-dominated government. The incoming Abiy government of 2018 implemented many reforms, including media freedoms and releasing prisoners critical of the previous government, but also implemented many internet shutdowns to constrain the space for digital citizenship.

In Chapter 4, Anthonio and Roberts examine how authoritarian states are using internet shutdowns to limit digital citizenship especially during elections and protests. It is the success of digital citizenship making rights claims that results in states implementing internet shutdowns. It is often only when states feel threatened by citizen action that they react with internet shutdowns to curtail digital citizenship. The authors use case studies from Ethiopia, Nigeria and Uganda to illustrate the diverse forms that internet shutdowns are now taking, the factors that motivate them and how they affect digital citizenship. The unintended impacts on the economy and national reputation are assessed alongside a range of new forms of digital citizenship developed to evade internet shutdowns as well as to monitor, mitigate and manage their effects. The authors show how the space for digital citizenship is a site of ongoing contestation. Internet shutdowns close the space for digital citizenship, but they are always partly evaded and never permanent – so the space of digital citizenship is always in permanent flux.

In Chapter 5, Ajaja uses the concept of cyberfeminism to extend our understanding of feminist digital citizenship in Nigeria, addressing a gap in the existing literature. The author explores the factors that contribute to the significant increase in women's digital citizenship in Nigeria. By analysing the case studies of #BBOG and #ENDSARS through a unique conceptual framework, three factors are identified as increasing feminist digital citizenship: increased rights violations, increased access to digital technologies and the safety afforded by online spaces for feminist digital citizenship. The opening of digital spaces allowed feminists to organize, rehearse resistance and provide leadership for both online and offline campaigns. This incidence of African feminist digital citizenship took the form of agency-based rights-claiming to demand accountability and government action to end social injustices. The author argues that the resulting form of feminist digital citizenship was qualitatively different from and significantly more successful than the street demonstrations that preceded it and which failed to secure government action. It is argued that digital spaces were central to enabling feminist voice and leadership to develop outside of offline patriarchal civic spaces and that digital communication tools enabled their rights-claiming #hashtag campaigns to reach a global audience unmediated by patriarchal media channels. The chapter shows that constraining structures of patriarchy limited women's citizenship but that increased technology access and solidarity across gender and ethnic divisions rapidly expanded the space of digital citizenship and secured concessions from the state.

In Chapter 6, Phiri, Abraham and Bosch analyse digital citizenship in Zambia to document how activists have used digital tools creatively to expand the space for digital citizenship alongside an expanding series of technological, legal and policing efforts to constrain the space for digital citizenship. The authors focus on three case studies using the theoretical frame of dromology to argue for a conception of rights-claiming citizenship constituted by the exercise of performative actions and struggles with the state over the control of digital space. This chapter argues that the space for digital citizenship is contested on three fronts which the authors explore in turn: technologies, tactics and laws.

In Chapter 7, Elias and Roberts analyse the emergence of digital citizenship in Namibia ahead of the November 2019 elections and assess its relevance for political accountability. The chapter focuses on the use of electronic petitions and social media to open up digital spaces for citizenship not dominated by legacy media and gerontocratic politicians. The investments made in social media campaigns by the main political parties in the election suggest that they judged this new digital public sphere to be increasing in importance. Despite increased mobile internet access, digital citizenship was only possible for 30 percent of the population at the time of the election. Namibian digital citizens used social media platforms to call the government to account for its record on youth unemployment and state corruption. Although the use of social media technologies amplified digital citizens' claim-making in online space, they had only limited success in translating this increased 'voice' into the 'teeth' necessary to secure accountability. Online petitions and campaigns around voting machines did not produce any response from the government. However, two weeks before the election, WikiLeaks released 30,000 files exposing a ten-million-dollar corruption scandal dubbed #FishRot on Twitter. The combination of mainstream media and digital citizenship resulted in the resignation of the Minister of Justice and the Minister of Fisheries. Digital citizenship will be more significant in Namibia's next elections in 2023 and 2027. The outcomes will not be determined by technology, but they will amplify the agency and potential of digital citizens and political parties alike.

In Chapter 8, Nanjala Nyabola calls for a decolonisation of the language of digital citizenship. She reminds us that the academic and policy debates about digital rights and citizenship take place predominantly in colonial languages, so those speaking African languages are excluded and silenced. This epistemological violence is evidenced by the overwhelming dominance of English on the internet platforms, journals and other media that host digital rights debates. Nyabola provides deep reflections on the historical and political construction of colonial language domination in Africa and on the internet alongside the dynamic and fertile evolution of indigenous languages, dialects and slang. The largest and fastest-growing African language is Kiswahili, with eighty-two million speakers, yet there are no words for key digital rights terms like 'data protection' or 'surveillance', making it practically impossible for millions of people to make rights claims in their own language about issues shaping their digital lives. The chapter shows how digital citizenship is effectively constrained by colonial structures and provides a practical example of decolonisation in which Kiswahili speakers literally change the terms of the debate.

Conclusion

This book provides the first compilation of case studies of digital citizenship in Africa. We hope that other scholars will build on this modest start by adding new case studies from countries not represented in this first edition. The book provides the most comprehensive analysis to date of digital citizenship in Africa and the implications of citizen agency, access and affordances as well as state and corporate enabling and constraints. This section draws some tentative conclusions and recommendations.

Digital citizenship in Africa is distinctive by virtue of its distinct history, political settlements, institutions and cultural specificity. Its colonial legacy, post-independence politics and the cultural distinctiveness of ethnic, religious and language composition in African countries are reflected in specific forms of digital citizenship. The rich case studies and critical analysis provided in this volume show that it is not possible to copy an understanding of digital citizenship from the Global North and paste it uncritically onto any African country.

Based on the lessons from the Nigerian case study, we argue that not all digital citizenship is progressive or desirable. If we define digital citizenship without a normative dimension – as any online civic engagement – then digital acts calling for the violation of the rights of other ethnic groups, genders or sexualities would qualify as digital citizenship. For this reason, we argue for a normative definition of *transformative digital citizenship* that goes beyond signifying any online political or civic engagement to include an explicit commitment to social justice and human rights. To this end, we define transformative digital citizenship as the use of digital technologies in an active process of claiming rights and the pursuit of social justice.

Our second key point derived from the case studies in this project, is that digital citizenship in Africa is a contested terrain in constant dynamic flux, due to the agency of multiple actors and competing interests. All spaces are comprised of power relationships, and digital spaces are no exception. The spaces in which digital citizenship in Africa takes place, open and close in proportion to the agency of citizens and structures of constraint and opportunity. Arising from the analysis of this dialectic, a number of recommendations arise for policy, practice and further research. For governments, funders and civil-society organizations, decisions about whether to invest in structures of opportunity or structures of constraint are critical policy choices. The main lesson for practice is the need to engage proactively in creating and expanding online civic space.

Finally, we argue that digital citizenship needs to be constantly exercised, defended and extended, or it may be lost. Citizens have increasing access to digital technologies, but this access is stratified by a range of barriers that create digital divides between citizens and either enhance or restrict a person's capability for digital citizenship. Citizens who have access to digital technologies need to make effective use of them in acts of citizenship that help open up wider spaces for digital citizenship. If they do not, the space is likely to shrink or be shut down.

Further research is necessary in countries not represented in this first edition, as well as studies to identify additional factors impinging on the scope of transformational digital citizenship in Africa. As the two Nigerian chapters illustrate, the experience of digital citizenship varies not only between but within countries and over time. This fluidity of digital citizenship over space/time is a significant finding emerging from this study and supports Nyamnjoh's contention (in the 'Foreword' of this volume and elsewhere) that more flexible concepts of citizenship are required. It also suggests that future research on digital citizenship in Africa needs to be contextually situated. Future studies should seek to understand more about the implications of digital citizenship in Africa taking place on platforms owned by foreign multinationals. As the data captured by social media platforms, mobile phone companies and state agencies are increasingly used to calculate and channel access to social protection payments and government services, future research attention will need to be directed at 'algorithmic citizenship'. This volume is guilty of an overemphasis of social media in digital citizenship; future research should include the role of other digital technologies such as civic tech, radio and participatory video in digital citizenship.

Bibliography

Ayoade, J. A. (2019) 'States Without Citizens: An Emerging African Phenomenon', in D. Rothchild and N. Chazan (eds), *The Precarious Balance*, 100–18, London: Routledge.

Baskaran, A. and M. Muchie (2006) *Bridging the Digital Divide: Innovation Systems for ICT in Brazil, China, India, Thailand and Southern Africa*, London: Adonis & Abbey Publishers Ltd.

Beardon, S. (2016) *Digital Citizenship: A Community-Based Approach*, London: Sage.

Benjamin, R. (2019) *Race After Technology: Abolitionist Tools for the New Jim Code*, Cambridge: Polity Press.

Benkler, Y. (2008) *The Wealth of Networks*. New Haven, CT: Yale University Press.

Bennett, W. L. and A. Segerberg (2012) 'The Logic of Connective Action: Digital Media and the Personalization of Contentious Politics', *Information, Communication & Society*, 15 (5): 739–68.

Bosch, T. (2016) 'Twitter and Participatory Citizenship: #FeesMustFall in South Africa', in B. Segerberg (ed.), *Digital Activism in the Social Media Era*, 159–74, Newcastle: Palgrave Macmillan.

Bosch, T. (2021) *Social Media and Everyday Life in South Africa*, Oxon: Routledge.

Bosch, T. and T. Roberts (2021) *South Africa Digital Rights Landscape Report*, Brighton: Institute for Development Studies.

Cadwalladr, C. and E. Graham-Harrison (2018) 'Revealed: 50 Million Facebook Profiles Harvested for Cambridge Analytica in Major Data Breach', *The Guardian*.

Carboni, I., N. Jeffrie, D. Lindsey, M. Shanahan, and C. Sibthorpe (2021) GSMA Connected Women: The Mobile Gender Gap Report 2021, London: GSMA, accessed 12 October 2021.

Castells, M. (2002) *The Internet Galaxy: Reflections on the Internet, Business, and Society*, Oxford: University Press on Demand.

Choudry, A. (2019) *Activists and the Surveillance State: Lessons From Repression*, London: Pluto Press.

de Lanerolle, I., M. Walton, and A. Schoon (2017) *Izolo: Mobile Diaries of the Less Connected, Making All Voices Count Research Report*, Brighton: Institute for Development Studies.

Dwyer, M. and T. Molony (2019) *Social Media and Politics in Africa*, London: Zed Books.

Earl, J. and K. Kimport (2011) *Digitally Enabled Social Change*, Cambridge, MA: MIT Press.

Egbunike, N. (2018) *Hashtags: Social Media, Politics and Ethnicity in Nigeria*, Lagos: Narrative Landscape Press.

Ekeh, P. (1975) 'Colonialism and the Two Publics in Africa: A Theoretical Statement', *Comparative Studies in Society and History*, 17: 1. doi: 10.1017/S0010417500007659.

Ekine, S. (ed.). (2010) *SMS Uprising: Mobile Activism in Africa*, Cape Town: Pambazuka Press.

Eubanks, V. (2017) *Automating Inequality: How High-Tech Tools Profile, Police and Punish the Poor*, New York: St Martin's Press.

Faith, B. (2018) 'Gender, Mobile, and Mobile Internet: Maintenance Affordances, Capabilities and Structural Inequalities: Mobile Phone Use by Low-Income Women', *Information Technologies & International Development*, 14: 66–88.

Feldstein, S. (2021) *The Rise of Digital Repression: How Technology Is Reshaping Power, Politics, and Resistance*, Oxford: Oxford University Press.

Flores, W. V. and R. Benmayor (eds). (1997) *Latino Cultural Citizenship: Claiming Identity, Space, and Rights*, Boston: Beacon Press.

Freedom House (2018) *Freedom on the Net 2018: The Rise of Digital Authoritarianism*, Washington DC: Freedom House.

Frére, M. (2011) *Elections and the Media in Post-Conflict Africa*, London: Zed Books.

Fuchs, C. and E. Horak (2008) 'Africa and the Digital Divide', *Telematics and Informatics*, 25 (2): 99–116.

Gaventa (2010) 'Seeing Like a Citizen?: Re-Claiming Citizenship in the Neoliberal World', DRC Working Paper 346, Brighton, Institute for Development Studies. https://opendocs.ids.ac.uk/opendocs/handle/20.500.12413/12551.

Gibson, J. (1977) *The Theory of Affordances in Perceiving, Acting, and Knowing*, eds. Robert Shaw and John Bransford, London: Oxford University Press.

Gurstein, M. (2003) 'Effective Use: A Community Informatics Strategy Beyond the Digital Divide', *First Monday*, 8 (12). https://journals.uic.edu/ojs/index.php/fm/article/view/1107.

Hernandez, K. and T. Roberts (2018) *Leaving No One Behind in a Digital World*. K4D Emerging Issues Report, Brighton, UK, Institute of Development Studies.

Hintz, A., L. Dencik, and K. Wahl-Jorgensen (2019) *Digital Citizenship in a Datafied Society*, Cambridge: Polity Press.

Hutchby, I. (2001) 'Technologies, Texts and Affordances', *Sociology*, 35: 441–456.

Ikolo, V. (2013) *Gender Digital Divide and National ICT Policies in Africa*, IGI Global. https://www.igi-global.com/chapter/gender-digital-divide-national-ict/68483.

Isin, E. and E. Ruppert (2015) *Being Digital Citizens*, Lanham: Rowman & Littlefield International.

Isin, E. and P. Wood (1999) *Citizenship and Identity*, London: Sage.

James, E. and A. Taylor (2018) *Managing Humanitarian Innovation: The Cutting Edge of Aid*, Rugby: Practical Action Publishing.

Jones, E. and J. Gaventa (2002) *Concepts of Citizenship: A Review*, Brighton: Institute of Development Studies.

Jones, L. and K. Michell (2015) 'Defining and Measuring Youth Digital Citizenship', *New Media & Society*, 18 (9): 2063–79.

Kabeer, N. (2005) *Inclusive Citizenship: Meanings and Expressions*, London: Zed Books.

Karekwaivanane, G. and N. Msonza (2021) 'Zimbabwe Digital Rights Landscape Report', in T. Roberts (ed.), *Digital Rights in Closing Civic Space: Lessons From Ten African Countries*, 43–60, Brighton: Institute of Development Studies, accessed 12 October 2021.

Katz, J. (1997) *Birth of a Digital Nation, Wired Magazine*, April 1997, accessed 12 October 2021, https://www.wired.com/1997/04/netizen-3/.

Kemp, S. (2021) Data*Reportal – Zambia 2021*, DataReportal. https://datareportal.com/reports/digital-2021-zambia.

Lister, R. (2003) *Citizenship: Feminist Perspectives*, London: Palgrave Macmillan.

MacKinnon, R. (2011) 'China's Networked Authoritarianism', *Journal of Democracy*, 22 (2): 32–46.

Mamdani, M. (1996) *Citizen and Subject: Contemporary Africa and the Legacy of Late Colonialism*, Princeton: Princeton University Press.

Mare, A. (2018) 'Baba Jukwa and the Digital Repertoires of Connective Action in a "Competitive Authoritarian Regime": The Case of Zimbabwe', in B. Mutsvairo (ed.), *Digital Activism in the Social Media Era*, 45–68, Newcastle: Palgrave Macmillan.

Mare, A. (2020) 'Internet Shutdowns in Africa: State-Ordered Internet Shutdowns and Digital Authoritarianism in Zimbabwe', *International Journal of Communication*, 14: 4244–63.

Marshall, T. H. (1950) *Citizenship and Social Class*, Cambridge: Cambridge University Press.

McGee, R., D. Edwards, C. Anderson, H. Hudson, and F. Feruglio (2018) *Appropriating Technology for Accountability: Messages From Making All Voices Count*, Brighton: Institute of Development Studies.

Meier, P. (2015) *Digital Humanitarians*, New York: CRC Press.

Milton, V. C. (2016) *@SOS_ZA_#SABC: Civic Discourse and the Negotiation of PSB Principles, in Mutsvairo, B. (ed) Digital Activism in the Social Media Era*, Newcastle: Palgrave Macmillan.

Mkandawire, H. (2016) 'The Use of Facebook and Mobile Phones to Report Presidential Election Results in Zambia', *African Journalism Studies*, 37 (4): 81–99.

Mossberger, K., C. J. Tolbert, and R. S. McNeal (2008) *Digital Citizenship: The Internet, Society, and Participation*, Cambridge, MA: MIT Press.

Mudhai, O., W. Tetty, and F. Banda (2009) *African Media and the Digital Public Sphere*, New York: Palgrave Macmillan.

Mutsvairo, B. (2016) *Digital Activism in the Social Media Era*, Newcastle: Palgrave Macmillan.

Mutula, S. M. (2008), 'Digital Divide and Economic Development: Case Study of Sub⊠Saharan Africa', *The Electronic Library*, 26 (4): 468–89.

Negroponte, N. (1995) 'The Digital Revolution: Reasons for Optimism', *The Futurist*, 29 (6): 68.

Nickel, S., P. Craven, C. Lovitt, and J. Davies (2020) *Garfield's Guide to Digital Citizenship*, Minneapolis: Lerner.

Noble, S. (2018) *Algorithms of Oppression*, New York: New York University Press.

Norman, D. (1988) *The Design of Everyday Things*, New York: Basic Books.

Norris, P. (2001) *Digital Divide: Civic Engagement, Information Poverty, and the Internet Worldwide*, Cambridge: Cambridge University Press.

Nyabola, N. (2018) *Digital Democracy, Analogue Politics*, London: Zed Books.

Nyamnjoh, F. B. (2006) *Insiders and Outsiders: Citizenship and Xenophobia in Contemporary Southern Africa*, Council for the Development of Social Science Research in Africa, London: Zed Books.

Nyamu-Musembi, C. (2005) 'An Actor-oriented Approach to Rights in Development', *IDS Bulletin*, 36 (1): 41–51.

Ojebode, A. and W. Oladapo (2018) 'Using Social Media for Long-Haul Activism: Lessons From the BBOG Movement in Nigeria', Utafiti Sera Research Brief Series, Partnership for African Social & Governance Research, accessed 12 October 2021.

Okolloh, O. (2009) 'Ushahidi, or "Testimony": Web 2.0 Tools for Crowdsourcing Crisis Information', *Participatory Learning and Action*, 59 (1): 65–70.

Oladapo, O. and A. Ojebode (2021) 'Nigeria Digital Rights Landscape Report', in T. Roberts (ed.), *Digital Rights in Closing Civic Space: Lessons From Ten African Countries*, Brighton: Institute of Development Studies, accessed 12 October 2021.

O'Neil, C. (2016) *Weapons of Math Destruction: How Big Data Increases Inequality and Threatens Democracy*, London: Penguin.

Ong, A. (1999) *Flexible Citizenship: The Cultural Logics of Transnationality*, Durham: Duke University Press.

Oyedemi, T. D. (2020) 'The Theory of Digital Citizenship', in J. Servaes (ed.), *Handbook of Communication for Development and Social Change*, 237–55, Singapore: Springer.

Ribble, M. (2015) *Digital Citizenship in Schools*, Arlington: International Society for Technology in Education.

Ribble, M. B., G. Ross, and W. Tweed (2004) 'Digital Citizenship: Addressing Appropriate Technology Behavior', *Learning & Leading With Technology*, 32 (1): 6–9.

Roberts, T. (2017) 'Participatory Technologies: Affordances for Development', in J. Choudrie, M. Islam, F. Wahid, J. Bass, J. Priyatma (eds), *Information and Communication Technologies for Development. IFIP Advances in Information and Communication Technology*, vol. 504, 194–205, New York: Springer.

Roberts, T. and T. Bosch (2021) *Digital Citizenship or Digital Authoritarianism in OECD Development Co-operation Report 2021: Shaping a Just Digital Transformation*, Paris: Organisation for Economic Cooperation and Development. https://www.oecd-ilibrary.org/sites/ce08832f-en/1/3/2/9/index.html?itemId=/content/publication/ce08832f-en&_csp_=17c2a7153f8f3e72e475ec60ee15c40c&itemIGO=oecd&itemContentType=book.

Roberts, T. and K. Hernandez (2019) 'Digital Access Is Not Binary: The 5 "A"s of Technology Access in the Philippines', *Electronic Journal of Information Systems in Developing Countries*. https://onlinelibrary.wiley.com/doi/full/10.1002/isd2.12084.

Roberts, T. and A. Mohamed Ali (2021) 'Opening and Closing Online Civic Space in Africa: An Introduction to the Ten Digital Rights Landscape Reports', in T. Roberts (ed.), *Digital Rights in Closing Civic Space: Lessons From Ten African Countries*, Brighton: Institute of Development Studies. https://opendocs.ids.ac.uk/opendocs/bitstream/handle/20.500.12413/15964/Kenya_Report.pdf?sequence=12&isAllowed=y.

Roberts, T., A. Mohamed Ali, M. Farahat, R. Oloyede, and G. Mutung'u (2021) *Surveillance Law in Africa: A Review of Six Countries*, Brighton: Institute of Development Studies. https://opendocs.ids.ac.uk/opendocs/handle/20.500.12413/16893.

Shirky, C. (2008) *Here Comes Everyone: The Power of Organising Without Organisations*, New York: Penguin.

Statista.com (2021) Share of Internet Users in Africa as of December 2020, by Country, accessed 12 October 2021.

Tufekci, Z. (2017) *Twitter and Tear Gas: The Power and Fragility of Networked Protest*, New Haven: Yale University Press.

Unwin, T. (2009) *ICT4D: Information and Communication Technologies for Development*, Cambridge: Cambridge University Press.

Van Dijk, J. (2006) 'Digital Divide Research, Achievements and Shortcomings', *Poetics*, 34 (4–5): 221–35.

Van Dijk, J. (2029) *The Digital Divide*, Cambridge: Polity Press.

Van Zyl, G. (2016) ' "Sockpuppet" Twitter Accounts Used in #HandsOffGuptas Information War', *Fin24*. https://www.news24.com/Fin24/sockpuppet-twitter-accounts-used-in-handsoffguptas-information-war-20161111.

Vivienne, S., A. McCosker, and A. Johns (2016) 'Digital Citizenship as Fluid Interface: Between Control, Contest and Culture', in Anthony McCosker, Sonja Vivienne, and Amelia Johns (eds), *Negotiating Digital Citizenship: Control, Contest and Culture*, 1–18. London: Rowman & Littlefield.

Willems, W. and W. Mano (2017) *Everyday Media Culture in Africa*, London: Routledge.

Yashar, D. (2005) *Contesting Citizenship in Latin America*, Cambridge: Cambridge University Press.

Yuval-Davis, N. and P. Werbner (1999) *Women, Citizenship and Difference*, London: Zed Books.

Zuboff, S. (2015) 'Big Other: Surveillance Capitalism and the Prospects of an Information Civilization', *Journal of Information Technology*, 30 (1): 75–89.

Zuboff, S. (2019) *The Age of Surveillance Capitalism: The Fight for the Future at the New Frontier of Power*, London: Profile Books.

2

Ethno-religious citizenship in Nigeria

Ethno-religious fault lines and the truncation of collective resilience of digital citizens: The cases of #ENDSARS and #PantamiMustGo in Nigeria

Ayobami Ojebode, Babatunde Ojebuyi, Oyewole Oladapo and
Marjoke Oosterom

Introduction

Nigeria has the largest number of internet users (about 136 million) in Africa and the sixth largest in the world (National Bureau of Statistics (NBS) 2020). Though not all internet users are 'digital citizens' – a term we will unpack later in the chapter – all digital citizens are internet users. Therefore, the large number of internet users gives a hint as to the large number of digital citizens in Nigeria. Nigeria is a multi-ethnic and multi-religious society with a history of acrimonious politics and events running along its ethno-religious cleavages (Otite 1990). How this ethno-religious multiplicity impacts citizenship and citizen claim-making has been the subject of many studies (Ekeh 1978; Osaghae 1990; Ukiwo 2003; Egwu 2004; Osaghae and Suberu 2005; Çancı and Odukoya 2016). However, the question of whether digital citizenship is also affected by the pressure of these cleavages remains largely unanswered. Sharply divided along the regional lines of North and South and the major ethnic lines of Hausa-Fulani, Igbo and Yoruba, Nigeria presents a good opportunity for exploring the nature of digital citizenship that is produced in an ethno-religiously diverse context.

Digital citizenship has been understood in at least three different ways: being involved in acceptable and ethical conduct in the digital space

(Hollandsworth, Dowdy and Donovan 2011); being able to use and actually using the opportunities for development and growth in the digital space (Choi and Kim 2018); and being active citizens making civic demands and contributions and holding governments accountable using digital technologies (Hintz, Dencik and Wahl-Jorgensen 2017). Digital citizenship studies have proceeded along these lines, examining the presence of ethics and etiquette in online activities, if (and how) educational institutions were fostering digital citizenship and the practice of or obstacles to active digital citizenship from a socio-political perspective.

However, one important aspect of citizenship that has been neglected in the study of digital citizenship in Africa is the place of ethno-religious loyalties and affinities (Ekeh 1975; Ndegwa 1998) in people's enactment of their digital citizenship. Whereas most Africans see themselves as citizens of their countries, their ethnic and religious loyalties often play a strong role in their sense of belonging and experiences of citizenship (Oosterom 2016) – and, consequently, in their expressions of citizenship through social and political action.

Furthermore, ethno-religious fault lines in Africa have been the source of mobilization and different forms of collective action, some of which have been harmful, such as electoral violence and inter-ethnic and inter-religious violence. This debate has not sufficiently been addressed for the digital realm – an important space for expression and for enacting citizenship. The internet and social media are important spaces where people can mobilize for digital action. Digital campaigns and movements constitute one example of mass digital action. While some of these movements promote inclusive citizenship, other forms of action can undermine citizens' unity of purpose in times of digital campaigns or even promote violence.

Such actions run along ethnic or religious divisions or, what we choose to describe as fault lines, do have the tendency to undermine collective citizen action. A fault line is a divisive issue capable of causing negative consequences – a line along which, metaphorically speaking, an eruption could occur. With reference to social and political collective action, fault lines might weaken the ability of citizens to present a united front, thus limiting the efficacy of such actions.

In this chapter, we reflect on the following question: Do ethno-religious fault lines undermine digital citizens' collective resilience by which is meant their ability to collectively mount pressure for change? We are particularly interested in citizens' ability to muster collective resilience that crosses religious and ethnic fault lines in polarized contexts such as Nigeria. While some studies of digital activism and digital citizenship show that citizens do unite around a cause, mount pressure for change and record some measure of success (Olorunnisola and Martin2013; Aina et al. 2019); others show that citizens are often so sharply divided that protests are matched with counter-protests (Lee 2018; Beattie, Zhang and Thomas 2020; Colpean 2020). In what situations do digital citizens tend to unite around a common goal and in what situations do they break into opposing factions? To what extent do ethnic-religious unity or divisions determine the effectiveness of collective digital citizenship in Nigeria?

This chapter analyses two protests that involved large-scale digital action: the #ENDSARS movement and #PantamiMustGo protest, analysing Twitter data in both instances. The analysis focused on the extent to which tweets promoted ethno-religious divisions and incited violent action and thus undermined digital citizens' unity or promoted unity of purpose by calling for non-violence and making claims on the state to protect citizen security. We also address the different outcomes of digital action: while the government conceded to #ENDSARS, it made no concessions in the case of #PantamiMustGo.

The case studies: #ENDSARS and #PantamiMustGo

In October 2020, a group of young people began an online protest against the excesses and cruelties of a special unit of the Nigerian police force known as the Special Anti-Robbery Squad (SARS) (Punch 2020). The movement began online but soon spread offline and became arguably the best organized and focused street protest in Nigeria's (recent) history. The movement's original request was for the government to disband SARS and compensate victims of its brutality. Within a week, the online and offline pressure mounted by protesters forced the government to abolish SARS and to promise wider reforms within the police force (Ayitogo 2020). However, the protest was hijacked by violent hoodlums resulting in deaths and widespread looting and destruction (Daka 2020). The government later deployed armed security personnel to quell the protest at the Lekki Toll Plaza in Lagos, resulting in what the protesters branded

#LekkiMassaccre (Samuel 2020). Despite this, #ENDSARS, which trended on Twitter in Nigeria and other countries (*The Guardian* 2020), was an important example of activism that obtained an immediate positive response from the government.

In the second example, in April 2021, an online news outlet published a report accusing Mr Isa Pantami, Nigeria's Minister of Communications and Digital Economy, of support for and affiliation with terrorist Islamist groups. This was picked up by many other outlets and went viral. Videos and audios of Mr Pantami's sermons and speeches in support of the terrorist groups emerged just as did #PantamiMustGo, with citizens calling for his resignation. However, a counter-hashtag and offline group emerged, stating that the campaign against Pantami was anti-North and anti-Islam, and asking all Muslims to rise in support of the minister. #PantamiMustStay thus trended alongside #PantamiMustGo, with each garnering over 100,000 tweets within a few days (Premium Times 2021). Unlike #ENDSARS, #PantamiMustGo did not yield the desired result, as the federal government stood behind the minister and dismissed the protesters as unserious and idle.

Both #ENDSARS and #PantamiMustGo-#PantamiMustStay present an opportunity to explore the nature of digital citizenship in a highly polarized nation and to tease out the obstacles to the collective resilience of digital citizens.

Connecting digital citizenship to collective resilience and security

In this section, we connect the scholarship on digital citizenship to the concept of resilience in critical security studies, which analyses the range of self-protection strategies and social institutions developed by communities to respond to ongoing insecurity and violence and/or its aftermath. Sousa et al. (2013: 247) define community resilience as 'positive collective functioning after experiencing a mass stressor, such as a natural or human-made disaster'. Scholars researching community resilience emphasize social relations, interactions and processes through which resilience develops, highlighting that these are shaped by power dynamics, and that individual and community resilience are entwined (Blewitt and Tilbury 2014; Brown 2016; Vertigans and Gibson 2020).

Vertigans and Gibson's (2020) study with youth in Kenya's largest informal settlement, Kibera (Nairobi), shows how people emphasize their social and reciprocal relationship to neighbours and the wider community, which offers a sense of belonging, pride and hope – important resources for their individual coping. Similarly, a qualitative study in a disadvantaged township in South Africa showed how youth demonstrated a propensity towards altruism and felt a 'strong sense of both individual and community responsibility to transform social conditions' (2020: 252). Specifically, in relation to responding to political violence, scholars have emphasized factors that operate within the relationship between individuals and their communities, like involvement in school, work and also political struggles (Sousa et al. 2013: 244), and connectedness to and acceptance by the community (Cortes and Buchanan 2007).

Some have emphasized the need to explore people's own understanding of risk and what *they* consider as resources for resilience at the community level (Mosavel et al. 2015). In her book on community resilience in contexts of cyclical, inter-communal violence in Nigeria's Plateau state and in Indonesia, Krause (2018) connects individual to community-level resilience. She argues that the analysis needs to focus on how people perceive a conflict situation to understand their responses (Krause 2018: 69), and how social learning and previous experiences influence perceptions. She highlights the role of *human agency* in communities – notably formal and customary (religious) leaders who have legitimate authority to persuade community members and (youth) groups not to respond violently to threats (for instance, when riots could spread from neighbouring areas, or when gangs or violent groups from other areas provoke a fight). These leaders establish rules and informal institutions for violence prevention, help resolve disputes inclusively and can effectively repress deviant individuals (Krause 2018: 75). She notes that institution-building *among* community leaders is important to maintain social control, which facilitates communication and information exchange, and also signals credibility of violence prevention efforts (Krause 2018: 75.).

In addition to the role of leaders and institutions, Krause (2018) highlights the importance of two other social processes that build resilience: depolarization of social difference and creating a cross-cleavage identity; and engagement with armed actors to negotiate neutrality, refuse collaboration and gather intelligence as part of conflict-prevention efforts (Krause 2018). Krause's book thus highlights the interactions between various social groups and actors but particularly leaders. The issue of online action presents a new dynamic that is not addressed in Krause's book, because it may involve interactions between people that do not live in the same geographical areas, outside of established relationships between community leaders and citizens. Yet the processes of depolarization and creating divisions might be strongly influenced through digital action and social media.

The role of digital action and social media is relatively new in the field of critical security studies. It has been explored for its role in spreading hate speech and inciting violence, as well as promoting peaceful action and protest (Roberts and Marchais 2017). Digital action has also been linked to coping and resilience-promoting tactics – for instance, among vulnerable refugee communities (Udwan, Leurs and Alencar 2020). Connecting social media action to expressions of active citizenship and peace-building, Oosterom, Pan Maran and Wilson (2019) demonstrate how youth in a conflict-affected region of Myanmar, where ethnic militia clash with the state military, were actively screening disinformation that was spread online and posting counter-messages. They strongly believed this could help stop rumours and de-escalate tensions to maintain the peace. These examples illustrate that digital action can both promote or undermine resilience by inciting violence and becoming part of conflict dynamics. Digital action can reinforce the identities of members of a political community, deepening social divisions (Udwan et al. 2020). It is, therefore, the nature of digital action and expressions that need to be explored. The cases selected for this chapter represent these two possibilities. As we will show, #ENDSARS took on the state to promote citizen security and inclusion, while dynamics in #PantamiMustGo were such that it undermined resilience. Since online expressions are also forms of claim-making and hence part of active citizenship, we now turn to the conceptualization of citizenship and digital citizenship.

Citizenship and ethno-religious mobilization

From both historical and political perspectives, citizenship has remained a contested notion (Carens 2000; Dagnino 2005; Hunter 2016; Lonsdale 2016; Kligler-Vilenchik 2017). Therefore, given its controversial nature, it is extremely difficult to ascribe a one-size-fits-all definition to the concept.

For instance, Hunter (2016) has argued that there has been serious tension between how historians and social scientists have conceptualized citizenship. While social scientists have axiomatically submitted that colonial states were characterized by a dichotomous status of subjecthood and citizenship – suggesting clear discrimination between the majority of the population and a privileged minority given full legal rights – historians have held a converse view. However, for the sake of clarity and contextualization, it is expedient to attempt some descriptions of citizenship and explicate their implications for collective social actions, civic norms and practices (Kligler-Vilenchik 2017) such as ethno-religious mobilization in contemporary society.

Citizenship has commonly been defined according to three dimensions. First, it refers to the 'membership of a political community', whereas the second and third dimensions of 'legal status' and 'political agency' refer to the rights, entitlements and obligations that come with this membership (e.g. Cohen 1999; Carens 2000; Kymlicka 2000; Lister 2003; Kabeer 2005). The legal status is defined by the citizens' political, civil and social rights where citizens are seen as the legal persons free to act according to the law and seek protection by the law. The second dimension sees citizenship as a political action where citizens actively participate in the political institutions of their society, while the third dimension considers citizenship as belonging to a political community that provides some unique identity. Similarly, Lokot (2020) explains that based on its traditional definition, citizenship is seen as a special personal status based on one's legal belonging to a sovereign nation state. Citing Waters (1989), Lokot further explains that apart from the fact that citizenship confers certain rights and obligations as derived from the laws or normative frameworks, the traditional idea of citizenship closely connects to ideas of territory, belonging and identity.

As evident in the foregoing definitions, the concepts of legal status, political agency and identity as the characteristics of citizenship have implications for social cohesion and the enactment of civic norms and practices. Citizenship is also about inclusion and exclusion: formal institutions such as laws but also informal institutions like social and gender norms create hierarchies in citizenship or the extent to which substantive citizenship is genuinely enjoyed (Lister 2003; Nyamnjoh 2007). In particular, ethnic and religious minorities may formally have equal rights, while discriminatory norms and practices restrict their substantive citizenship. As argued by Nyamnjoh (2006), even in many African countries, including Nigeria, with liberal democracy and global consumer capitalism, the problems of identity politics and ethnic citizenship still manifest. In such circumstances, while most nationals can claim their legal citizenship, some groups, because of their ethnic identities or stereotypes, consider themselves or are regarded to be less authentic claimants of legal citizenship and its privileges. In other words, citizenship in many African states is characterized by cultural discrimination and social dichotomy. This trend could be exploited by the political elite to weaken the strengths of digital citizenship and prevent citizens from uniting to promote a nation-building agenda.

In a country where the formal and informal institutions that underpin a notion of citizenship cause the exclusion of certain social, ethnic or religious groups, as the case in China, such groups might take collective action that would resist their exclusion or marginalization by the state and society (McCarthy 2000). McCarthy further argues that such activism, apart from being 'a means of asserting minorities' rightful place in the contemporary Chinese body politic', could also 'cement cross-national ethnic and religious identities, thereby consolidating the material and ideological resources that make anti-state behaviour more feasible' (McCarthy 2000: 107). In situations where members of different ethnic, social, political or religious groups are permitted to enjoy the privileges and rights of substantive citizenship, they would be encouraged to participate in mobilization for nation-building, while the converse holds for a situation where there is discrimination or preferential treatment of the members of a social group.

Nigeria is a good example of how the conception of citizenship along ethno-religious identity and sentiments has generated anti-state mobilizations and divisions among citizens themselves (Udeagha and Nwamah 2020). As Alao (2020:21) asserts, the ethno-religious segmentation of Nigeria has ignited inter-group contentions whereby the various ethnic and religious groups, especially Christians and Muslims, are perennially 'mobilized and militarized' along these ethno-religious alignments. And, unfortunately, these rivalries have constrained the national integration efforts of different administrations over the years. It has been established that ethnic sentiments provide frames that the political elite could use to appeal to a group of citizens and unite them against other groups. This is confirmed by a Nigerian study by Ojebuyi and Lasisi (2019), which reveals that the majority of online readers in their responses to news stories about Nigeria's unity were found to be attracted to readers from their own ethnic group but highly hostile towards other readers who belonged to different ethnic groups. In Kenya, as in Nigeria, ethnicity is 'a powerful conditioning factor of political subjectivity, rights, membership, and opportunities for political participation as well as for the inter-relationship between these components' (Balaton-Chrimes 2016:16). This trend of ethnic citizenship could also manifest in digital citizenship and activism where an ethnic appeal could divide the citizens and prevent them from achieving a collective agency against social oppressions. Egbunike (2018) confirms this, arguing that politics and ethnicity are sensitive and connected topics in Nigeria, and when taken to social media, where citizens have space to unleash hate speech, these topics could further divide a country already battling with bruised unity.

Digital citizenship, ethno-religious cleavages, violence and tension

Mossberger, Tolbert and McNeal (2008) define digital citizenship as the qualities that a person is expected to have as a responsible member of the digital community. One of those qualities is the regular and effective use of digital technologies either for negative purposes such as self-destruction or for positive objectives such as self-actualization, political participation, education or civil mobilization (Musgrave 2015). Mossberger (2009) further popularized the concept of digital citizenship by conceptualizing it as how citizens explore and use the large volume of political information and an array of opportunities available online. Therefore, digital citizens are those individuals who use the internet frequently because they have access and motivation and possess certain practical and digital skills and the educational proficiencies to perform online activities such as searching, using the information on the web, and interacting with other members of the cyber community (Mossberger 2009; Breindl 2010; Hicks 2017). Although digital citizenship is a universal concept, there still exist some inherent contextual characteristics that distinguish the definition of African digital citizenship from the global or Western definitions. As explained by Hunter (2016), one of the major features of the colonial states was stratification into subjecthood and citizenship which suggests some degree of social inequality and dichotomy. Interestingly, the post-colonial African states have continued to preserve these indices of dichotomy such as identity politics and ethnic citizenship as indicators of colonial legacy (Mamdani 1996, 2001) that have characterized digital citizenship in the sub-Saharan African states. Digital citizens use the internet for different purposes such as economic gain, political participation and general information to fulfil some civic duties, norms and practices (Mossberger et al. 2008; Kligler-Vilenchik 2017). Even though the internet holds the potential to provide social equity and empowerment of minority and marginalized or disadvantaged citizens (Hernandez and Roberts 2018, Mehra, Merkel and Bishop 2004), the digital factors – access, competence and motivation – identified by Breindl (2010) constitute a major challenge to digital citizens as these digital factors encourage active minorities, who are already privileged, to be over-represented in cyberspace compared to the disadvantaged group, who have lesser access, agency and competence to enjoy the digital benefits (Hernandez and Roberts 2018). Therefore, as it is incontestable that the emergence of digital citizenship has significantly enhanced the process of citizens' engagement in democracy, it is glaring that the rise of e-society has also created some levels of dichotomy and inequalities, especially with the emphasis on access to the internet, competence and motivation as the basic requirements for fair and inclusive involvement in civic duties through cyberspace.

Socio-demographic factors such as gender, religion, ethnicity and education influence how citizens use the internet to participate in politics (Baker-Bracy 2004; Campbell 2006; Pontes, Henn and Griffiths 2019) and enjoy other digital dividends such as 'remote access to health and education information, financial inclusion and digital pathways to economic and political empowerment' (Hernandez and Roberts 2018: 1). This is because the digital citizenry is also a subset of the traditional citizenry and the two groups are bound to share some normative characteristics such as exhibition of ethno-religious loyalties and sentiments (Udeagha and Nwamah 2020). Consequently, as citizens use digital technologies for political participation and other civic duties, the social and ethno-religious cleavages, tensions and violence that play out in real life also manifest in digital life. Musgrave's (2015) position gives credence to this reality as the author asserts that real life is digital life, arguing that we are now in a generation when boundaries between real life and digital life are becoming increasingly indistinct.

Literature underscores the importance of framing in mobilizing citizens (Benford and Snow 2000). Frames that resonate with people motivate them to join and stay on in a movement, just as frames that run contrary to deeply held beliefs and biases can evoke opposition. Injustice, human rights, security and safety, and democracy frames are generally likely to attract more people than those appealing to narrower and small-group interests (Benford and Snow 2000; Oriola 2021).

Methodology

We set up a query on Tags at https://tags.hawksey.info/get-tags/ to collect #ENDSARS tweets over thirty-nine days, from Monday 19 October, the day before the deadly shootings of #ENDSARS protesters at the Lekki Toll Plaza in Lagos, to Thursday 26 November 2020. Tags is an open-access Google Sheets-based site for archiving tweets from Twitter.

The query retrieved 85,465 tweets. We set up another query to collect tweets related to the Pantami saga. That query ran from Friday, 16 April to Thursday, 2 May 2021, to retrieve 121,432 tweets over sixteen days. Our datasets are only a fragment of the tweets generated in relation to the two protests, especially #ENDSARS, which trended in many countries across the world. Nevertheless, the randomness with which Tags retrieves tweets assures some degree of representativeness, as two queries set up on Tags at the same time, using the keyword, retrieved different sets of tweets. The two datasets were analysed separately using a combination of Notepad++ 7.9.5 and Ant Conc 3.5.9 (Windows). We complemented the analysis of tweets with a review of news stories from mainstream media and news blogs to track government responses to the two cases.

An initial exploration of the retrieved tweets revealed use of multiple hashtags in both datasets. We focused the first stage of our analysis on the hashtags contained in the entire 206,897 tweets retrieved. We ascertained the extent to which the hashtags were related to the focus of the two cases of citizen actions and how often each hashtag was used. We then focused the analysis on the twenty most popular hashtags used in each case. With 65,047 hashtags, the first 20 hashtags in the Pantami corpus constituted 79.5 per cent of the total 81,852 hashtags. In the #ENDSARS corpus, they constituted 77.1 per cent, with 127,423 out of the total 165,277 hashtags.

In the Pantami corpus, all the hashtags that were used to promote the call for the resignation of the minister were coded as 'pro-resignation'; those that were used to mobilize against the call for resignation were coded as 'anti-resignation'; while those that were used by protesters on both sides were coded as 'anti- and pro-resignation'. Hashtags that called attention to issues other than the Pantami saga were coded as 'other civic issues'. Those that campaigned for the breakaway of a section of the country were coded as 'secessionist'. In the secessionist category were tweets that called for the re-creation of Biafra, a defunct state whose breakaway from Nigeria resulted in the country's thirty-month civil war between 1967 and 1970. Hashtags with a focus different from the aforementioned were coded as 'unrelated' while the remaining hashtags were grouped under the label 'others'. Classification of the hashtags used in the #ENDSARS corpus followed the same process. The hashtags that aligned with the goal of the protesters were coded as 'pro-#ENDSARS'; those against it were coded as 'anti-#ENDSARS'; while those that were used to both ends were coded as 'pro- and anti-#ENDSARS'. Hashtags with a focus different from the aforementioned were coded as 'unrelated', while the remaining hashtags were grouped under the label 'others'.

Next, we examined the nature of actions and opinions contained in the tweets for the following issues:

We were interested in actions such as inciting or facilitating confrontational action, inciting violent action, promoting or facilitating peaceful action (such as calling for peace and dialogue), reporting and denouncing violence or justifying violence. We were interested in these because they are the antithesis of collective citizenship action. We mapped the tweets for opinions expressed on issues such as good governance, rights to security, right to protest and freedom of speech. To uncover ethno-religious fault lines in the citizen actions, we examined the tweets for the presence of words that define national politics of ethnic and religious identities in Nigeria. Those words are North and South, the country's two regions; Hausa and Fulani, the two major ethnic groups in the North; Igbo and Yoruba, the two major ethnic groups in the South; and Christian and Muslim, the two major religions in the country. First, we used the keywords function of AntConc 3.5.9 to isolate the tweets that contained the keywords. For confirmation, we used the search function of Notepad++ 7.9.5 to explore the keywords and got the same outcomes. Next, we read the tweets containing the keywords to understand the goal to which they were used to pursue in tweets. During the qualitative reading of the tweets, sample tweets were purposively selected for illustration purposes. In this case, as it is in the hashtag analysis, the keywords were not mutually exclusive; multiple hashtags and keywords were used in a single tweet. The units of analysis used were thus hashtags and keywords.

Based on this analysis, we examined the outcomes of the two cases of citizen action to make inferences about the resilience of digital citizenship in Nigeria.

Using social media data raises some ethical issues, especially in contexts where the civic spaces have been found to be shrinking (Roberts 2021). Many governments have demonstrated a high degree of intolerance of free speech and public criticism, especially those expressed on social media platforms. This is the situation in Nigeria too, with legislative efforts being made to control the use of social media (Oladapo and Ojebode 2021). Specifically, after the #ENDSARS protests of 2020, there were reports of police arrest and brutality against young people who had on their mobile phones trails of having participated in the protests. There were also reports of confiscation of national passports and refusal of the right to travel out of the country simply because of having participated in #ENDSARS protests (Akinwotu 2020). Given these realities, we decided to back-check a portion of the tweets in our datasets. We found that some users had deleted the tweets from their timelines. While we could not be sure of the reasons for this, we could not rule out safety and security concerns. As a result, we decided to anonymize the tweets we quoted in this chapter. As an additional measure of protection, we presented only paraphrases of tweets that contain views that were critical of government positions on the two issues analysed. Lastly, to avoid inadvertent disclosure of the identity of the users, we engaged in minimal quotations, citing only portions of tweets that were found relevant to our discussions. It is also noteworthy that there were positive developments after the initial clampdown on the protesters. The government set up a panel of inquiry in the affected states, which led to cessation of #ENDSARS-related arrests.

Issue consistency in #ENDSARS and Pantami tweets

The hashtags used in the #ENDSARS tweets were mostly focused on the objective of the activism, which was for government to end police brutality. Table 2.1 presents a summary of the focus of the hashtags.

As Table 2.1 shows, three hashtags pursued the protesters' primary demand to end SARS (#ENDSARS 48,389; #ENDSARSImmediately 4,748; #ENDSARSNow 1,493). Four hashtags sought an end to police brutality and demanded reform of the Nigerian police (#EndPoliceBrutalityinNigeraNOW 4,031; #EndPoliceBrutalityinNigera 2,600; #ReformTheNigeriaPolice 2,564; #EndPoliceBrutality 1,398). Three hashtags demanded good governance (#EndBadGovernmentinNIGERIA 6,655; #EndBadGovernanceinNIGERIA 6,035; #EndBadGoveranceInNigeria 1,434). Another three hashtags sought the release of an arrested protester (#FreeEromzy 2,185; #FreeEromz 2,177; #FreeEromosele 2,169). Two hashtags protested the alleged shootings

Table 2.1 Focus of Hashtags Used in #ENDSARS Protest

Hashtag	Focus	Frequency	Total
#ENDSARS	Pro-ENDSARS	48,389	122,746
#SoroSokeGeneration	Pro-ENDSARS	24,454	
#EndBadGovernmentinNIGERIA	Pro-ENDSARS	6,655	
#EndBadGovernanceinNIGERIA	Pro-ENDSARS	6,035	
#LekkiMassacre	Pro-ENDSARS	5,324	
#ENDSARSImmediately	Pro-ENDSARS	4,748	
#SideWithNigeria	Pro-ENDSARS	4,034	
#EndPoliceBrutalityinNigeraNOW	Pro-ENDSARS	4,031	
#EndPoliceBrutalityinNigera	Pro-ENDSARS	2,600	
#ReformTheNigeriaPolice	Pro-ENDSARS	2,564	
#FreeEromzy	Pro-ENDSARS	2,185	
#FreeEromz	Pro-ENDSARS	2,177	
#FreeEromosele	Pro-ENDSARS	2,169	
#SoroSoke	Pro-ENDSARS	1,970	
#ENDSARSNow	Pro-ENDSARS	1,493	
#EndBadGoveranceInNigeria	Pro-ENDSARS	1,434	
#EndPoliceBrutality	Pro-ENDSARS	1,398	
#LekkiMassaccre	Pro-ENDSARS	1,086	
#sanwoolu	Pro- and anti-ENDSARS	2,134	
#tuesdayvibe	Unrelated	2,543	
Others	Sundry issues	37,854	
Total		**165,277**	

of unarmed protesters (#LekkiMassacre 5,324; #LekkiMassaccre 1,086). The protesters used one hashtag to project their ideological orientation (#SoroSokeGeneration 24,454); one hashtag to invite others to speak up against police brutality and other issues (#SoroSoke 1,970); one hashtag to express patriotism to Nigeria (#SideWithNigeria 4,034); and one hashtag to evaluate the role of a major political actor in the shooting of unarmed protesters (#sanwoolu 2,134). Only 1 unrelated hashtag featured among the first 20 (#tuesdayvibe 2,543, a generic hashtag with which Nigerian Twitter users share experiences which make their Tuesdays pleasurable). In summary, the hashtags that demanded an end to SARS constituted 42.9 per cent; those that projected the protesters' ideological orientation 19.2 per cent; those that demanded an end to bad governance 11.1 per cent; those that demanded an end to police brutality and called for police reform 8.3 per cent; those that called for the release of an arrested protester 5.1 per cent; those that appraised the shooting of protesters 5.0 per cent; those that expressed patriotism to Nigeria 3.2 per cent; those that appraised the role of a major political actor in the shooting of protesters 1.7 per cent; those that invited other actors to speak up in support of the cause of the protesters 1.5 per cent; and those that were unrelated, 2.0 per cent.

Contrarily, we found that the first twenty most-used hashtags in the Pantami tweets focused on diverse issues, many of which are not directly related to the central focus of the activism. Table 2.2 summarizes the focus of those hashtags.

As Table 2.2 shows, 5 hashtags (n = 29,316) focused on demanding the resignation of Isa Pantami from the office of the Minister of Communications and Digital Economy. Opposing that call were 4 hashtags (n = 20,732). Besides the two groups of hashtags, we found 1 hashtag that was used by users on both sides of the divide (n = 598).

Besides those that focused on the Pantami issue, we found five hashtags that extended the activism to other civic causes (#BuhariMustGo 3,521, calling for the resignation or removal of President Muhammadu Buhari; #RevolutionNow 2,392, promoting a protest convened by Omoyele Sowore, a presidential candidate of Action Alliance Congress in the 2019 presidential election; #ENDSARS 2,171, appealing to the popularity of an October 2020 protest against police brutality; #impeachbuhari 739, calling for the impeachment of President Muhammadu Buhari; and #ArrestGumiNow 566, calling for the arrest of a Northern Muslim religious leader who mediated between

Table 2.2 Focus of Hashtags Used in #PantamiMustGo Protest

Hashtag	Focus	Frequency	Total
#PantamiMustGo	Pro-resignation	17,230	29,316
#PantamiResignNow	Pro-resignation	9,081	
#PantamiResign	Pro-resignation	1,268	
#PantamiMustResign	Pro-resignation	1,156	
#PantamiIsATerrorist	Pro-resignation	581	
#PantamiMustStay	Anti-resignation	11,304	20,732
#IstandWithPantami	Anti-resignation	5,409	
#PantamiWillStay	Anti-resignation	3,604	
#PantamiWillNotResign	Anti-resignation	415	
#Pantami	Anti- and pro-resignation	598	
#BuhariMustGo	Other civic issue	3,521	9,389
#RevolutionNow	Other civic issue	2,392	
#ENDSARS	Other civic issue	2,171	
#impeachbuhari	Other civic issue	739	
#ArrestGumiNow	Other civic issue	566	
#BiafraExit	Secessionist	1,463	4,296
#SayNoToNigeria	Secessionist	1,345	
#BiafraNationNow	Secessionist	1,091	
#EndNigeriaNow	Secessionist	397	
#win	Unrelated	716	
Others	Sundry issues	16,805	
Total		81,852	

the Nigerian government and bandits who abducted students from several schools in northern Nigeria). Four other hashtags pursued secessionist causes (#BiafraExit 1,463, mobilizing for the breakaway of South-Eastern Nigeria to re-create the defunct Biafra state; #SayNoToNigeria 1,345, expressing the rejection of the continued existence of the Nigerian state; #BiafraNationNow 1,091, calling for the immediate breakaway of the South-East from Nigeria to re-create Biafra; and #EndNigeriaNow 397, calling for an immediate dissolution of Nigeria). In summary, pro-resignation hashtags constituted 45.1 per cent; anti-resignation 31.9 per cent; a hashtag which focused on both sides of the issue 0.9 per cent; those that pursued other civic causes 14.4 per cent; those that pursued secessionist causes 6.6 per cent; and those that were unrelated to the issue or any other civic cause, 1.1 per cent.

Issue consistency is a product of the unity among the diverse segments of the digital 'nation'. This in turn seems to wax or wane depending on the framing of the issue (see Benford and Snow 2000). The #ENDSARS case was framed as a problem of justice and human rights, and a national threat. For as long as it remained so, actors focused on the objective of the protest. This is not to suggest that #ENDSARS had no opposition: a pro-SARS protest also erupted in some northern cities. Although violent offline, the pro-SARS protest was barely visible on Twitter.

Manifestations of ethno-religious sentiments in tweets

We are interested in finding out whether ethno-religious fault lines impeded the expression of digital citizenship in the two cases. To ascertain this, we analysed keywords that are associated with ethno-religious divides in Nigeria and how they figured in tweets. Along the ethno-regional affinities, Nigeria is divided along the regional lines of North and South, and along the major ethnic lines of Hausa-Fulani, Igbo and Yoruba.

We found that these identities featured in few #ENDSARS tweets: regional identities (North 24 hits; South 27 hits) and ethnic identities (Fulani 4 hits; Hausa 20 hits; Igbo 17 hits; Yoruba 25 hits). However, in the Pantami tweets, the identities feature prominently: regional identities (North 2,143 hits; South 491 hits) and ethnic identities (Fulani 288 hits; Hausa 6 hits; Igbo 445 hits; Yoruba 467 hits). A similar finding is made in relation to the expression of religious identities in the two cases. While the keywords relating to religion feature only marginally in #ENDSARS tweets (religion 24 hits; Christian 5 hits; Muslim 7 hits), they feature prominently in Pantami tweets (religion 1,873 hits; Christian 94 hits; Islam 1,040; Muslim 198 hits).

Beyond the frequency of deployment of these polarizing identities in tweets, we also found that they were deployed in the two cases to achieve different ends. The following tweet exemplifies the use of these identities in #ENDSARS tweets:

> I have said it before and I will say it again #SoroSokeGeneration do not let anyone divide you guys with religion and ethnicity. We are strong when we believe in the spirit of diversity.
> Anonymous 1 (2020) Twitter post on 01/11/2020, accessed 01/11/ 2020

The tweet is a call to *avoid* pursuing ethnic or religious agendas within the #ENDSARS struggle and to block every attempt to introduce such agendas. It was believed that the government and its agents wanted to create divisions among the protesters. Conversely, in the Pantami tweets, the identities were deployed to a divisive end, as illustrated by the following tweet:

> This fight is just because Pantami is a Muslim and a religious type. Had it been Pantami cares not about his religion no one will accuse him. In conclusion, any Northerner against Pantami is ANNAMIMI [a mischief maker]
> Anonymous 2 Twitter post 23/04/2021, accessed 23/04/2021

The tweet clearly constructed the call to Pantami to resign as anti-Muslim and anti-North. Users from the South construe the anti-resignation stance as enabled by a misconception of Islam as pro-terrorism:

> If he's not a terrorist, and he represents Islam, what actually is Islam? Don't make nonsense of Islam because of one pronounced terrorist.
> Anonymous 3 (2021) Twitter post on 02/05/2021, accessed 02/05/2021

As we have shown already, Northerners who were against Pantami's resignation mobilized support for him on the grounds of religion and ethnicity and alleged that the Southerners who were calling for his resignation were anti-Islam and anti-North. The users who maintained this position diverted attention from the subject of the protest and pitched the two regions of the country against each other based on religion. The sensitivity of the Nigerian digital civic space to ethno-religious sentiments is well established in literature. The moment an event is successfully framed as 'we' versus 'them', it takes on a divisive nature that polarizes citizens and truncates their ability to collectively hold leaders accountable (Oladapo 2016; Oladapo 2017; Aina et al. 2019; Oriola 2021).

Actions in #ENDSARS and Pantami tweets

Existing literature documents diverse acts of citizenship expression. They include expressing rights such as security, freedom and good governance; denouncing and reporting all forms of violence, including police violence; and promoting and facilitating peaceful actions (Gaventa 2002; Yu and Oh 2018; Gaventa 2020). Citizenship expressions could also take the form of facilitating confrontational action/protest and inciting violent action. We examined Pantami and #ENDSARS tweets for the presence of tweets that fall into either category. The findings of that inquiry are presented next.

We found in the Pantami tweets views that promote divisive ethno-religious politics, as illustrated by this tweet:

The trends of #BuhariMustGo and #PantamiMustGo make me develop a mindset of voting only a Northerner/Muslim as a PRESIDENT no matter [who] he is or his political affiliation, such trends are borne [out] of hatred and dislike for Northerners and Islam.

Anonymous 4 (2021) Twitter post on 23/04/2021, accessed 23/04/2021

That user, like many others, thought that keeping a Northern Muslim in power was the only solution to what they perceived as an attack on the Northern Muslims. There are also tweets that called on Christians who held political office to resign in protest at the perceived support the current government gives to Islamists and Muslim fundamentalists:

Without being unreasonable, and very sincere, I think every Southern Christian that has a seat at the Federal Executive Council should resign. @ ProfOsinbajo should start the process. You can't be sitting down in a meeting with a Jihadist.

Anonymous 5 (2021) Twitter post on 23/04/2021, accessed 23/04/2021

The tweets in this category conceive of the issue as Muslims versus Christians, thus entrenching division along the religious line by calling on the vice-president to resign as an exemplar of Christians' dissociation from Jihadism. Another category of tweets calls into question cross-ethnic political alliance on the grounds of religion: 'If the Moslems amongst the Yoruba Nation still choose to align with the North, as Tinubu and co have shown, what then can be done?' Such tweets consider ethnic ties to be superior to political alliances, irrespective of religious affiliation. Some of the tweets promote loyalty to ethnic interest as superior to loyalty to national interest:

If you are an Igbo man who hates and speaks against Nnamdi Kanu, you are a bastard; If you are a Yoruba who hates and speaks against Sunday Igboho or Tinubu, it will not be better for you. Just imagine Hausa people defending Isa Pantami, a known and proven terrorist.

Anonymous 6 (2021) Twitter post on 23/04/2021, accessed 23/04/2021

To users who tweeted in this category, other ethnic groups have a lot to learn from how the Hausa defend one of them, despite the gravity of the allegations levelled against him. These tweets present ethnicity as the weakest point of the resilience of digital citizenship among Nigeria's Twitter users. Going by the sentiment they expressed, ethnic consideration is strong enough among them to truncate digital citizenship that is national in outlook, even when there are other unifying forces such as religion.

In the #EndSARS tweets, we found those that celebrate the spread of the protests across the Southern part of the country:

> The Wild West has woken, the tough tough East has come on. . . . It's appearing that the volatile South-South is about to . . .
>
> Anonymous 7 (2020) Twitter post on 19/11/2020, accessed 19/11/2020

'Wild Wild West' used in the tweet is a historical allusion to the riots that rocked South-West Nigeria between 1962 and 1966 and resulted in a widespread breakdown of law and order, which only ended after the country's first military coup. The tweet, like many others, prognosticates the descent of #ENDSARS protests into large-scale violence. Popular among #ENDSARS tweets are those that pursue rights:

> Whenever I think about #LekkiMassaccre I see mass freedom beyond #EndSARS protests. I don't know what this is to you but as for my personal self, I'll fight for my right until I'm gone!
>
> Anonymous 8 (2020) Twitter post on 25/10/2020, accessed 25/10/2020

The tweets in this category consider freedoms and rights as hallmarks of citizenship too fundamental to be sacrificed for anything, including personal safety. There were also numerous tweets reporting government persecution of #ENDSARS protesters and promising the return of protests to the streets:

> This demonic Buhari government is so desperate. They seized Moe's passport. Imagine if the #EndSARS movement had leaders, they would have just arrested the so-called leaders and throw them in jail. There would be another wave of protest and it will be massive.
>
> Anonymous 9 (2020) Twitter post on 03/11/2020, accessed 03/11/2020

Tweets such as the above maintain that oppressive treatment of protesters such as seizure of passport, a symbol of citizenship, will only invite more protests. A number of #ENDSARS tweets project a scathing assessment of the government, as illustrated by this tweet:

> The value of government is measured through how well it values its citizens. USA deployed military to rescue one citizen while Nigeria deployed military to kill her citizens. You can decode.
>
> > Anonymous 10 (2020) Twitter posted on 31/10/2020, accessed 31/10/2020.

The tweets question the value the Nigerian government places on Nigerians. They allege that the government treats Nigerians as subjects rather than as citizens who deserve the full complement of constitutionally guaranteed rights, importantly security and protection. Tweets that celebrate moves to sanction politicians implicated in the attacks against #ENDSARS protesters are also visible:

> We did it again guys!!! The UK GOVERNMENT voted to sanction Individuals in this useless government. Next we are going to the @IntlCrimCourt and @ UN. They will never have peace, whether they are dead or alive.
>
> > Anonymous 11 (2020) Twitter post on 24/11/2020, accessed 24/11/2020

Despite the dissimilarities found in the #ENDSARS and Pantami tweets, users in both cases appeared to have abstained from inciting people to violence. The closest we found in the #ENDSARS tweets is a wish for a natural force to strike and kill those responsible for the plight of the protesters:

> I wish thunder could strike and kill everyone involved in victimizing the innocent Nigerian youths fighting for a better governance and a better Nigeria.
>
> > Anonymous 12 (2020) Twitter post on 06/11/2020, accessed 06/11/2020

Another #ENDSARS tweet invites protesters to return to the streets, despite news of police shooting at protesters:

> I'm fuming right now and if you're not we both suffer in the end! Let's move back to this street, they CANNOT kill us all!
>
> > Anonymous 13 (2020) Twitter post on 18/11/2020, accessed 18/11/2020

The tweet invites protesters into an unavoidable confrontation with the police. Despite these few cases, we did not observe instances of tweets that promote, celebrate or invite others to violent actions. Mostly, what we found could be described as evaluative opinions, rather than calls to violence. The kind of violence we observed in the tweets was as expressed in this tweet:

Buharists and pro-regime people are pledging to counter our peaceful account closing protests by opening multiple new accounts with the bank. Let us show them we are the #SoroSokeGeneration. Tomorrow we move to #BoycottAccessBank.

> Anonymous 14 (2020) Twitter post on 15/11/2020, accessed 15/11/2020

The tweet alleges an attempt by those considered anti-#ENDSARS to neutralize their boycott of Access Bank, a bank reported to have placed a ban on accounts of #ENDSARS protesters.

Outcomes of #ENDSARS and anti-Pantami protests

While #ENDSARS and anti-Pantami protests were both forms of mass action by digital citizens, the two resulted in different outcomes. It is noteworthy that a kind of government–citizen synergy emerged from #ENDSARS, despite the initial confrontations and attacks. The government agreed to meet the demand of #ENDSARS protesters to disband SARS when it could no longer ignore the protests. It agreed to meet the five other demands issued by the protesters: immediate release of all arrested protesters; justice for all deceased victims of police brutality and appropriate compensation for their families; inauguration of an independent body to oversee the investigation and prosecution of all reports of police misconduct (with a ten-day timeline); in line with the new Police Act, psychological evaluation and retraining (to be confirmed by an independent body) of all disbanded SARS officers before they can be redeployed; and increase in police salary so that they are adequately compensated for protecting lives and property of citizens (The Cable 2020; Vanguard 2020).

In addition, the government promised to reform the police and created Special Weapon Tactical Team (SWAT) in place of SARS, ensuring that the personnel attached to the new unit would be well trained. The government also stipulated that affected states should convene a judicial panel of inquiry. Lagos inaugurated its panel on 19 October 2021 (Lagos State Government 2020), and some other affected states did so afterwards, all ensuring that youth representatives were included in the panel membership. Thus, #ENDSARS climaxed into a government–youth collective action towards ensuring that victims of police brutality would get justice.

However, the Pantami issue ended differently. The protest reached an anticlimax when the federal government issued a statement of support for the embattled minister. The statement circulated on social media platforms and blogs, thereby giving impetus to the #iStandWithPantami hashtag, which then co-trended with #PantamiMustResign. Although the government accepted that the minister's speeches and action were in support of terrorism, it dismissed them as having been informed by youthful exuberances some ten years earlier (Shehu 2021). With government support, the minister continued in office, the hashtags calling for his resignation stopped trending and the protest faded out.

Conclusion

How do Nigerians enact digital citizenship? Our analysis, on the surface, suggests the amorphousness of digital citizenship. In one instance, digital citizens are observed united and fully pressing for reforms against injustice and oppression; in another, they are at daggers drawn against each other. Three distinct forms of citizenship were found enacted in the Nigerian digital space: ethnic, religious and national citizenships. Expression of these digital citizenships in the Nigerian Twitter space is fluid, often responding to the nature of the issues and the attributes of the actors involved in them as exemplified by the two cases analysed. At one time it appeals to constitutionally guaranteed universal human rights, thereby attracting the solidarity of international community. At another time it is enacted much like the conventional citizenship, fractured by divisive considerations such as ethnicity and religion. In the latter case, many citizens, it seems, take a dispassionate look at issues and weigh them on a scale of importance that ranks ethnic, religious, national affiliation in a descending order. For these citizens, national interest is important only to the extent that it does not conflict, even remotely, with ethnic and religious loyalties. When issues do not have obvious ethnic and religious overtones, the resilience of digital citizens, borne out of their unity, is likely assured and the government may be wary of ignoring citizens' demands.

This raises the question of who should be left to frame issues. Digital activists should be firm and choosy in their framing of issues. One of the greatest limitations of the #PantamiMustGo protest was the framing of the minister as a sheikh or Islamic religious leader, rather than just a terrorist sympathizer. The religious label attached to him must have aroused a sympathetic response from

Muslim users, who quickly concluded that Islam, rather than terrorism, was under attack and felt it was their bounden duty to defend Islam by defending the sheikh. Framing is complicated; Mr Pantami is indeed a Muslim sheikh of the fundamentalist strain, and it would have been impossible to frame him as a terrorist sympathizer without that religious label. However, frames that ignored the line between Islam and Islamist terrorism were many among anti-Pantami users, and these were exploited by pro-Pantami users to discredit the protest.

The digital space is often thought of as a space free from the fault lines that bedevil and characterize the conventional space. Our analysis echoes the position of Musgrave (2015) on the similarities between the digital and the conventional. The same ethno-religious fault lines that have influenced Nigerians' interpretations of and responses to many national events continue to play similar roles among digital citizens. As apparent in the analysis, digital citizens are able to unite around a common goal when it does not offend their ethnic and religious sensibilities. When it does, they break into opposing factions, enacting in the digital space a form of citizenship that is fragmented along ethnic and religious lines.

Our analysis also shows that closing the civic space does not always have to involve the use of surveillance technologies, bots and site-blocking. Citizens taking sides with the government sometimes overwhelm and silence other citizens, as the case was in the #PantamiMustGo protest. Activists and researchers seeking to understand the nature of civic space have often focused on the technological efforts to close it or resist its closure (Hintz et al. 2017; Howard 2020). In the process, they have not paid significant attention to the active participation of some citizens in efforts to close the civic space. Citizens who promote ethnic and religious disinformation online, bots deployed to promote the same and external actors who exploit it could all be as actively involved in the closure of the digital civic space as an oppressive government that deploys restrictive laws, surveillance technology and other means to achieve the same goal.

Bibliography

Aina, T.A., M. Atela, A. Ojebode, P. Dayil, andF. Aremu (2019) *Beyond Tweets and Screams: Action for Empowerment and Accountability in Nigeria – The Case of the#*

BBOG Movement, IDS Working Paper 529, Brighton: Institute of Development Studies, accessed 18 October 2021.

Akinwotu, E. (2020) 'Nigeria Cracks Down on "End Sars" Protesters, Alleging Terrorism', *The Guardian*, 13 November, accessed 19 May 2021.

Alao, O. E. (2020) 'Ethno-Religious Mobilization, Militarization and the Rhetoric of Unity in Nigeria's Hundred Years of Nationhood (1914–2014)', *AIPGG Journal of Humanities and Peace Studies*, 1 (1): 21–47.

Ayitogo, N. (2020) '#EndSARS: Nigeria Dissolves Dreaded Police Unit, Announces Police Reforms', *Premium Times*, 11 October, accessed 18 October 2021.

Baker-Bracy, L. J. (2004) 'Political Participation in America: The Role of Race, Ethnicity, and Gender', MA dissertation, University of Arkansas, accessed 18 October 2021.

Balaton-Chrimes, S. (2016) *Ethnicity, Democracy and Citizenship in Africa: Political Marginalisation of Kenya's Nubians*, New York: Routledge.

Beattie, T., A. Zhang, and E. Thomas (2020) 'The Power Dynamics of Thailand's Digital Activism', *The Strategist, Australian Strategic Policy Institute blog*, 14 December, accessed 18 October 2021.

Benford, R. and D. A. Snow (2000) 'Framing Processes and Social Movements: An Overview and Assessment', *Annual Review of Sociology*, 26: 611–39.

Blewitt, J. and D. Tilbury (2014) *Searching for Resilience in Sustainable Development: Learning Journeys in Conservation*, Abingdon: Routledge.

Breindl, Y. (2010) 'Critique of the Democratic Potentialities of the Internet: A Review of Current Theory and Practice', *Triple C*, 8 (1): 43–59.

Brown, K. (2016) *Resilience, Development and Global Change*, Abingdon: Routledge.

Campbell. D. E. (2006) 'What Is Education's Impact on Civic and Social Engagement?' Paper presented at the Symposium on Social Outcomes of Learning, Danish University of Education (Copenhagen), 23–24 March.

Çancı, H. and O. A. Odukoya (2016) 'Ethnic and Religious Crises in Nigeria: A Specific Analysis upon Identities (1999–2013)', *African Journal on Conflict Resolution*, 16 (1): 87–100.

Carens, J. H. (2000) *Culture, Citizenship, and Community: A Contextual Exploration of Justice as Even Handedness*, Oxford: Oxford University Press on Demand.

Choi, H. H. and M. J. Kim (2018) 'Using the Digital Context to Overcome Design Fixation: A Strategy to Expand Students' Design Thinking', *Arch Net-IJAR: International Journal of Architectural Research*, 12 (1): 228–40.

Cohen, J. (1999) 'Changing Paradigms of Citizenship and the Exclusiveness of the Demos', *International Sociology*, 14 (3): 245–68.

Colpean, M. (2020) 'Muslim Women Against FEMEN: Asserting Agency in Online Spaces', *Journal of International and Intercultural Communication*, 13 (3): 274–90, accessed 18 October 2021.

Cortes, L. and M. J. Buchanan (2007) 'The Experience of Columbian Child Soldiers from a Resilience Perspective', *International Journal for the Advancement of Counselling*, 29 (1): 43–55.

Dagnino, E. (2005) *Meanings of Citizenship in Latin America*, IDS Working Paper 258, Brighton: Institute of Development Studies, accessed 18 October 2021.

Daka, T. (2020) '#EndSARS Protests Was Hijacked, Buhari Tells Former Leaders', *The Guardian*, 23 October, accessed 18 October 2021.

Egbunike, N. (2018) *Hashtags: Social Media, Politics and Ethnicity in Nigeria*, Lagos: Narrative Landscape Press.

Egwu, S. G. (2004) 'Ethnicity and Citizenship in Urban Nigeria: The Jos Case, 1960–2000', PhD thesis, University of Jos, Nigeria.

Ekeh, P. P. (1975) 'Colonialism and the Two Publics in Africa: A Theoretical Statement', *Comparative Studies in Society and History*, 17 (1): 91–112.

Ekeh, P. P. (1978) 'Colonialism and the Development of Citizenship in Africa: A Study of Ideologies of Legitimation', in Onigu Otite, *Themes in African Social and Political Thought*, Enugu: Fourth Dimension.

Gaventa, J. (2002) 'Introduction: Exploring Citizenship, Participation and Accountability', *IDS Bulletin*, 33 (2): 1–7, accessed 18 October 2021.

Gaventa, J. (2020) 'Seeing Like a Citizen': Re-claiming Citizenship in a Neoliberal World', in A. Fowler and C. Malunga (eds), *NGO Management: The Earthscan Companion*, 115–28, London: Routledge.

Hernandez, K. and T. Roberts (2018) *Leaving No One Behind in a Digital World. K4D Emerging Issues Report*, Brighton: Institute of Development Studies. https://assets .publishing.service.gov.uk/media/5c178371ed915d0b8a31a404/Emerging_Issues _LNOBDW_final.pdf.

Hicks, E. R. (2017) 'Digital Citizenship and Health Promotion Programs: The Power of Knowing', *Health Promotion Practice*, 18 (1): 8–10, accessed 18 October 2021.

Hintz, A., L. Dencik, and W. Wahl-Jorgensen (2017) 'Digital Citizenship and Surveillance Society', *International Journal of Communication*, 11: 731–9.

Hollandsworth, R., L. Dowdy, and J. Donovan (2011) 'Digital Citizenship in K-12: It Takes a Village', *Tech Trends*, 55 (4): 37–47.

Howard, P. N. (2020) *Lie Machines: How to Save Democracy from Troll Armies, Deceitful Robots, Junk News Operations, and Political Operatives*, New Haven: Yale University Press.

Hunter, E. (2016) *Citizenship, Belonging, and Political Community in Africa: Dialogues Between Past and Present*, Athens: Ohio University Press.

Kabeer, N. (2005) 'Introduction: The Search for Inclusive Citizenship: Meanings and Expressions in an Interconnected World', in N. Kabeer (ed.), *Inclusive Citizenship: Meanings and Expressions*, 5, London: Zed.

Kligler-Vilenchik, N. (2017) 'Alternative Citizenship Models: Contextualizing New Media and the New "Good Citizen"', *New Media & Society*, 19 (11): 1887–903, accessed 18 October 2021.

Krause, J. (2018) *Resilient Communities: Non-Violence and Civilian Agency in Communal War*, Cambridge: Cambridge University Press.

Kymlicka, W. (2000) 'Citizenship in Culturally Diverse Societies: Issues, Contexts, Concepts', in W. Kymlicka and W. Norman (eds), *Citizenship in Diverse Societies*, 1–41, Oxford: Oxford University Press.

Lagos State Government (2020) '#EndSARS: Sanwo-Olu Inaugurates Judicial Panel on Brutality, Human Rights Violations', *Lagos State Government Official Web Portal*, 19 October, accessed 18 October 2021.

Lee, T. (2018) 'The Thin Blue Line Between Protesters and Their Counter-Protesters', *Journal of Artificial Societies and Social Simulation*, 21 (2): 10, accessed 18 October 2021.

Lister, R. (2003) 'Investing in the Citizen-workers of the Future: Transformations in Citizenship and the State Under New Labour', *Social Policy & Administration*, 37 (5): 427–43.

Lokot, T. (2020) 'Articulating Networked Citizenship on the Russian Internet: A Case for Competing Affordances', *Social Media + Society*, 6 (4): 1–14.

Lonsdale, J. (2016) 'Rethinking Citizenship and Subjecthood in Southern Africa', in E. Hunter (ed.), *Citizenship, Belonging, and Political Community in Africa: Dialogues Between Past and Present*, 18–43, Athens: Ohio University Press.

Mamdani, M. (1996) *Citizen and Subject: Contemporary Africa and the Legacy of Late Colonialism*, Princeton: Princeton University Press.

Mamdani, M. (2001) 'Beyond Settler and Native as Political Identities: Overcoming the Political Legacy of Colonialism', *Comparative Studies in Society and History*, 43 (4): 651–64. http://www.jstor.org/stable/2696665.

McCarthy, S. (2000) 'Ethno-Religious Mobilisation and Citizenship Discourse in the People's Republic of China', *Asian Ethnicity*, 1 (2): 107–16.

Mehra, B., C. Merkel, and A. P. Bishop (2004) 'The Internet for Empowerment of Minority and Marginalized Users', *New Media & Society*, 6 (6): 781–802.

Mosavel, M., R. Ahmed, K. A. Ports, and C. Simon (2015) 'South African, Urban Youth Narratives: Resilience Within Community', *International Journal of Adolescence and Youth*, 20 (2), accessed 18 October 2021.

Mossberger, K. (2009) 'Toward Digital Citizenship: Addressing Inequality in the Information Age', in A. Chadwick and P. Howard (eds), *The Routledge Handbook of Internet Politics*, 173–86, London: Routledge.

Mossberger, K., C. Tolbert, and R. S. McNeal (2008) *Digital Citizenship: The Internet, Society, and Participation*, Cambridge, MA: MIT Press.

Musgrave, M. L. (2015) *Digital Citizenship in Twenty-First-Century Young Adult Literature: Imaginary Activism*, New York: Palgrave Macmillan.

National Bureau of Statistics (NBS) (2020) 'Telecoms Data: Active Voice and Internet per State, Porting and Tariff Information', accessed 18 October 2021.

Ndegwa, S. N. (1998) 'Citizenship amid Economic and Political Change in Kenya', *Africa Today*, 45 (3/4): 351–67.

Nyamnjoh, F. B. (2006) *Insiders & Outsiders: Citizenship and Xenophobia in Contemporary Southern Africa*, London and Dakar: Zed Books and CODESRIA Books.

Nyamnjoh, F. B. (2007) 'From Bounded to Flexible Citizenship: Lessons from Africa', *Citizenship Studies*, 11 (1): 73–82, accessed 18 October 2021.

Ojebuyi, B. R. and M. L. Lasisi (2019) 'Speaking Up or Staying Silent? Citizens' Engagement of Pro-Biafra Protests and Farmers-Herders Crises in the User-generated Content of Selected Nigerian Online Newspapers', *Ethiopian Journal of the Social Sciences and Humanities*, 15 (2): 25–51, accessed 18 October 2021.

Oladapo, O. A. (2016) 'Pro-Biafra Construction of *Nigerianness* in Twitter Protest Against Frivolous Petitions Bill 2015', *Journal of Communication and Language Arts*, 7 (1): 63–83. https://www.academia.edu/40864739/Pro_Biafra_Counterpublic_Identity_Construction_in_Twitter_Protest_against_the_Frivolous_Petitions_Bill.

Oladapo, O. A. (2017) 'Construction of the Political Other in Citizens' Comments on Politicians' Facebook Pages', *International Journal of E-Politics*, 8 (2): 17–29. https://www.igi-global.com/article/construction-of-the-political-other-in-citizens-comments-on-politicians-facebook-pages/180335.

Oladapo, O. and A. Ojebode (2021) 'Nigeria Digital Rights Landscape Report', in T. Roberts (ed.), *Digital Rights in Closing Civic Space: Lessons from Ten African Countries*, 145–66, Brighton: Institute of Development Studies, accessed 18 October 2021.

Olorunnisola, A. A. and B. L. Martin (2013) 'Influences of Media on Social Movements: Problematizing Hyperbolic Inferences About Impacts', *Telematics and Informatics*, 30 (3): 275–88.

Oosterom, M. A. (2016) 'Internal Displacement, the Camp and the Construction of Citizenship: Perspectives from Northern Uganda', *Journal of Refugee Studies*, 29 (3): 363–87.

Oosterom, M. A., J. Pan Maran, and S. Wilson (2019) '"Building Kachin". Youth and Everyday Action in One of Myanmar's Ethnic States', *Development and Change*, 50 (6): 1717–41, accessed 18 October 2021.

Oriola, T. B. (2021) 'Framing and Movement Outcomes: The #BringBackOurGirls Movement', *Third World Quarterly*, 42 (4): 641–60, accessed 18 October 2021.

Osaghae, E. E. (1990) 'The Problems of Citizenship in Nigeria', *Africa*, 45 (4): 593–611.

Osaghae, E. E. and R. T. Suberu (2005) *A History of Identities, Violence, and Stability in Nigeria*, CRISE Working Paper No. 6, Oxford: Centre for Research on Inequality, Human Security and Ethnicity, accessed 18 October 2021.

Otite, O. (1990) *Ethnic Pluralism and Ethnicity in Nigeria*, Ibadan: Shaneson C.I. Ltd.

Pontes, A. I., M. Henn, and M. D. Griffiths (2019) 'Youth Political (Dis)Engagement and the Need for Citizenship Education: Encouraging Young People's Civic and Political Participation Through the Curriculum', *Education, Citizenship and Social Justice*, 14 (1): 3–21.

Premium Times (2021) 'Editorial: Why Pantami Must Step Aside from Government', 4 May 2021, accessed 6 June 2021.

Punch (2020) 'Editorial: Looking Beyond #EndSARS: Youths and People Power', *19 October*, accessed 18 October 2021.

Roberts, T. (ed.) (2021) *Digital Rights in Closing Civic Space: Lessons from Ten African Countries*, Brighton: Institute of Development Studies, doi:10.19088/IDS.2021.003.

Roberts, T. and G. Marchais (2017) *Assessing the Role of Social Media and Digital Technology in Violence Reporting*, IDS Working Paper 492, Brighton: Institute of Development Studies, accessed 18 October 2021.

Samuel, O. (2020) *Livestreaming Lekki: Digital Evidence of #EndSARS Shooting in Nigeria Makes Impunity Much Harder*, accessed 11 August, https://theconversation .com/livestreaming-lekki-digital-evidence-of-endsars-shooting-in-nigeria-makes -impunity-much-harder-148696.

Shehu, O. (2021) 'Presidency Stands by Pantami Despite Pro-Terrorism Statements', *International Centre for Investigative Reporting*, 22 April, accessed 18 October 2021.

Sousa, C. A., M. M. Haj-Yahia, G. Feldman, and J. Lee (2013) 'Individual and Collective Dimensions of Resilience Within Political Violence', *Trauma, Violence, & Abuse*, 14 (3): 235–54.

The Cable (2020) 'FG Accepts 5-point Demand of #EndSARS Protesters', 13 October, accessed 19 May 2021.

The Guardian (2020) '#EndSARS Protests Gaining Global Attention', accessed 11 August 2022, https://guardian.ng/news/nigerians-endsars-protests-gaining -worldwide-attention/.

Turner, B. S. (2009) 'TH Marshall, Social Rights and English National Identity', *Citizenship Studies*, 13 (1): 65–73.

Udeagha, N. and G. Nwamah (2020) 'Ethno-Religious Sentiments and the Need for Restructuring in Nigeria', *Advances in Social Sciences Research Journal*, 7 (8): 17–34, accessed 18 October 2021.

Udwan, G., K. Leurs, and A. Alencar (2020) 'Digital Resilience Tactics of Syrian Refugees in the Netherlands: Social Media for Social Support, Health, and Identity', *Social Media and Society*, 6 (2), accessed 18 October 2021. https://journals.sagepub.com/doi/full/10.1177/2056305120915587.

Ukiwo, U. (2003) 'Politics, Ethno-Religious Conflicts and Democratic Consolidation in Nigeria', *The Journal of Modern African Studies*, 41 (1): 115–38.

Vanguard (2020) 'Five Demands From #EndSARS Protesters', 12 October, accessed 19 May 2021.

Vertigans, S. and N. Gibson (2020) 'Resilience and Social Cohesion Through the Lens of Residents in a Kenyan Informal Settlement', *Community Development Journal*, 55 (4): 624–44.

Waters, M. (1989) 'Citizenship and the Constitution of Structured Social Inequality', *International Journal of Comparative Sociology*, 30: 159–80.

Yu, R. P. and Y. W. Oh (2018) 'Social Media and Expressive Citizenship: Understanding the Relationships Between Social and Entertainment Expression on Facebook and Political Participation', *Telematics and Informatics*, 35 (8): 2299–311.

3

Digital crossroads

Continuity and change in Ethiopia's digital citizenship

Atnaf Brhane and Yohannes Eneyew

Introduction

Digital citizenship is a fluid concept. However, this chapter considers digital citizenship as the ability to participate in society online. When it comes to subjects of digital citizenship, we refer to digital citizens who are using the internet regularly and effectively (Mossberger, Tolbert and McNeal 2008). This chapter seeks to demonstrate how digital citizenship is framed in Ethiopia over a period of thirty years between 1991 and 2021. The scope of this chapter, however, is not simply limited to offering some analysis of digital citizenship in Ethiopia through a continuity and change approach; rather, it attempts to link it with ethnicity and to demonstrate how the web of ethnicity shapes digital citizenship in Ethiopia. Particularly, this chapter asks how Ethiopian digital citizenship has been shaped by its political history, ethnic divisions and legislative framework since 1991. This chapter draws on the work of Mamdani and Nyamnjoh, who argue that ethnicity is at least as important as nationality in African conceptions of (digital) citizenship.

Specifically, the chapter explores the evolving balance between state power and digital activism over the thirty-year period. It is structured along four critical epochs in the history of Ethiopia. The remainder of this chapter is organized into five sections. Consolidation of power by the EPRDF (1991–2005) section sketches the consolidation of power by the Ethiopian People's Revolutionary Democratic Front (EPRDF) from 1991 to 2005. The 2005 elections and the rise of digital authoritarianism (2005–15) section charts the ensuing digital authoritarianism in Ethiopia between 2005 and 2015 in the wake of the historic 2005 election. The Oromo/Amhara protests, mainly held between 2016 and 2018, will be examined in Oromo/Amhara protests and their repercussions (2015–18) section. Abiy's new experiment, between liberalization and control (2018–22) section interrogates how digital citizenship is conceived after the ascension of Abiy Ahmed in 2018, while Conclusion section summarizes the major findings and offers some recommendations on how to better protect the rights of digital citizens in Ethiopia.

Consolidation of power by the EPRDF (1991–2005)

Citizenship in general and digital citizenship in particular were given less emphasis during the early years of the EPRDF. The Ethiopian government, led by the EPRDF, introduced numerous pieces of legislation and policies that have shaped (digital) citizens' behaviour in the digital space and their participation in the country's affairs (Gagliardone 2014b).

The Ethiopian People's Revolutionary Democratic Front overthrew the Derg military regime in a guerrilla fight and popular revolution in 1991. Upon assuming power, the EPRDF ushered a series of positive reforms extending fundamental human rights and citizens' democratic participation in governance. However, the realization of these freedoms was marred by authoritarian measures taken in practice. The 1991 Charter of the Transitional Government of Ethiopia (TGE) was the harbinger for the introduction of human rights and democratic freedoms. The charter fully recognized human rights as contained in the United Nations' 1948 Universal Declaration of Human Rights (UDHR). Specifically, Article 1 of the charter sets out freedom of conscience, expression, association and peaceful assembly, as well as engaging in unrestricted political activity and political parties on the condition that such rights do not infringe the right of others. In this era, there was relative freedom for the press, which led to the blossoming of private press until repressive measures were put in place in subsequent years (Abebe 2020). For instance, the first private newspaper called *Iyyita* started publishing in January 1992. It was a weekly paper published and circulated on Wednesdays focusing on general issues such as economic, social and political affairs. Following *Iyyita*, more than 630 newspapers and 130 magazines had been granted a press licence, from which 401 newspapers and 130 magazines have been published and circulated in the period after the Press Proclamation up until February 2005. However, since the disputed election in 2005, the number of newspapers has been significantly reduced.

The transitional period has been regarded as an historic moment for press freedom in Ethiopia. This is mainly for three reasons. The first is that pre-publication censorship was officially outlawed by Article 3 of the 1992 Press Proclamation. As a result, the institutional procedure to get permission for publishing and circulating was cast-off and the institution executing such processes also ceased. Second, ownership of the press was permitted to private sector entities, unlike during the Derg regime, which had monopolized the country's press. The third reason is the rise of democratization in Africa, including Ethiopia (Huntington 1991). The transitional period was primarily aimed at writing up a new constitution and setting a foundation for Ethiopia.

In 1995, the EPRDF-led government adopted the constitution; one-third of its provisions found under chapter 3 are dedicated to human rights, including freedom of expression as well as the right of nation, nationalities and peoples (Federal Negarit Gazette 1995). While the constitution espoused a federal form of arrangement that favours Ethiopian people for self-government, others claim that the tribal-archetype of the federation is the 'original sin' responsible for the country's pandemonium, including the sprouting of divisive hate speech in the digital space (Fessha 2017). In this regard, Minasse Haile aptly articulated that 'the leaders of the Tigray People's Liberation Front (TPLF) (framers of the Constitution) applied the Soviet model of federation – based on ethnic self-determination to the nine tribal homelands they created' (Haile 2005). This would give rise to the over-politicization of ethnicity where ethnic groups tend to claim exclusive ownership of resources, privileges and entitlements in their respective regions. In this respect, Nyamnjoh (2006) argues that 'there is a hierarchy of citizenship fostered by political, economic, social and cultural inequalities, such that it makes some individuals and groups much more able to articulate their rights than others'.

In Ethiopia, some regional constitutions – like Article 2 of the Benishangul-Gumuz Constitution and Article 8 of the Harari Constitution – go as far as to incorporate clauses stating that some ethnic groups are 'native' while others are 'settler'. Mamdani (2020) famously argued that a 'native' versus 'settler' dichotomy is rooted in colonialism, where a white colonial elite were 'citizens' while the colonized Black majority were devalued as 'subjects' through creating a hierarchy of citizenship; it places some groups as permanent minorities via the politicization of identity. Inevitably, these divisions lead to violence (Mamdani 1996).

The 1995 Constitution of Ethiopia is founded on the recognition of ethnicity, favouring group rights over individual rights (Gebeye 2019). For instance, Article 8 of the constitution places the nations, nationalities and peoples instead of citizens as the ultimate sovereign powerholders and guardians of the country. More worryingly, defaming a nation, nationalities and peoples was a sedition crime under Article 10 of the 1992 Press Proclamation – which in turn resulted in a chilling effect on media freedom and individuals' free speech. Over the years, the EPRDF leadership, using various narratives, has successfully drowned out dissenting voices and labelled them as 'anti-peace', 'unitarists' and 'anti-constitution'.

When it comes to the rights of digital citizens, the first internet service was introduced in Ethiopia in 1997. Shortly after this, the internet became a space in which to discuss Ethiopian politics mainly for political elites, and the conversations through online blogs were rapidly captured by the polarized conversations that had characterized the press (Gagliardone 2014b). While the media landscape before the 2005 election was predominantly radio, television and newspaper-based, digital platforms such as Ethiopian Review, Nazret and Ethiomedia owned by Ethiopians in the diaspora hosted articles (and short blogs) that might as easily have appeared in the newspapers printed in Addis Ababa (Roberts 2019). Like mainstream media, the emerging digital platforms were largely captured by offline political discourses.

Within the context of a telecommunications monopoly, Ethiopia had launched its most ambitious projects in the history of digital citizenship, e-government and digitization in Africa through Woredanet and Schoolnet systems (Gagliardone 2014a). However, the Ethiopian government has been using Woredanet and Schoolnet projects to advance political ends and narrative control. Put simply, the Woredanet, for example, stands for 'network of district (*woreda*) administrations' and employs the same protocol that the internet is based on, but rather than allowing individuals to independently seek information and express their opinion, it enables government officials (and mainly ministers and cadres) in Addis Ababa to videoconference with the regional and district offices and instruct them in the modus operandi of governance through a top-down approach (Gagliardone and Golooba-Mutebi 2016). In its first roll-out, Woredanet was intended to link the federal government with the 11 regional and 550 district administrations. As such, using a 42-inch plasma TV screen installed in the Bureau of Capacity Building at the regional and *woreda* levels, local officials could receive training and instructions from other top-ranking ministers, including the prime minister, high-level civil servants and trainers in the capital (Gagliardone 2014a).

At the inception stage, Woredanet was initially designed to offer a variety of services on top of videoconferencing, such as enabling *woreda* officials to access the internet, to send and receive emails, and to use voice/video over internet protocols (IP) – the technology on which Skype is based – to communicate with each other. However, when the system started to be deployed and it became apparent that the bandwidth on the satellite was not enough to accommodate all these services, the government decided to switch off the channels allocated to all other services so as to free bandwidth to allow central and remote sites to be 'on screen'.

Since 2003, Schoolnet uses a comparable pattern to broadcast pre-recorded classes on a variety of subjects, from science to civics, to all secondary schools in the country while also offering political education to teachers and other government officials (Gagliardone 2014a). In the case of Schoolnet, 16,686 plasma TV screens were initially deployed to allow 775 secondary schools to receive broadcast lessons. Tellingly, Schoolnet was designed to reach targets in the peripheries in a more direct way. It mainly enables students living in rural areas to have access to the same quality of education as those in the major towns and cities, since students in remote areas no longer have to rely on poorly trained teachers for their education. Schoolnet was a powerful symbol of the EPRDF's commitment to guarantee (digital) citizens' equal opportunities; it was crucial in addressing the urban–rural education divide and was an overture for digitization in the country. Civic and ethical education was among the first subjects to be included in the Schoolnet programme. For instance, topics included human rights and democratic rights, digital citizenship, patriotism, industriousness and rule of law. However, both Woredanet and Schoolnet projects have been criticized for being a forum of narrative control tools and information-controlling channels (Gagliardone 2014a).

Between 1991 and 2005, the EPRDF-led government introduced ethnicity and ethnic federalism as governance frames and ideals whereby both Woredanet and Schoolnet programmes were implemented along these lines. The idea of ethnic federalism was formally introduced under the 1995 Constitution. The concept was conceived and championed by the TPLF during the guerrilla war waged against the Derg regime. At the heart of ethnic federalism, ethnicity was to be the basis of politics (Young 1996). While ethnic federalism empowered ethnic groups for self-administration, identities of previously dominant groups were silenced in the name of ethnic diversity and the idea of pan-Ethiopian identity and digital citizenship was de-emphasized (Abbink 2011). Importantly, what is missing in Ethiopia's ethnic federal experiment is common citizenship – a sense of citizenship-based nationalism (Abbink 2011). This is because of the TPLF/EPRDF's over-reliance on ethnic nationalism during the guerrilla war in the 1970s. As a result, ethnicity has become a prime basis of people's identity and permeates all public and private life in Ethiopia. For example, facts depend on ethnicity in that individuals interpret facts based on their respective ethnic point of view; ethnicity is a sine qua non for election; for identifying oneself during criminal investigation, ethnicity has become an informal defence before a court of law. Consequently, between 1991 and 2005, (digital) citizenship was not given the attention it deserves due to overly ethnic-based engagements in Ethiopia.

On the eve of the 2005 election, engaging in digital politics through joining the blogosphere was mushrooming in Ethiopia. Nevertheless, the online space was bifurcated between supporters of government and opposition. For instance, there was an exchange of allegations and barbs on a daily basis between pro-EPRDF websites such as Aiga Forum and opposition sites such as the Ethiopian Review (Lyons 2007). Digital platforms such as Weichegud, Ethiopundit and Dagmawi provided regular, sometimes satirical, and often highly partisan analysis while AddisFerengi and Seminawork covered field reports from Ethiopia. Blogging collectives like Enset were influential commentators from the diaspora, while others like Ethio-Zagol were contributing to the online debate from home (Hafkin 2006).

To sum up, between 1991 and 2005, the Ethiopian government consolidated its power through an ethnic form of governance by introducing opaque concepts like revolutionary democracy. This is because ethnicity is as important as (digital) citizenship (Mamdami 1996; Nyamnjoh 2006). Attempts to inform or otherwise shape digital citizens were made through continued efforts of Woredanet and Schoolnet projects. Importantly, the structures of ethnic federalism and media law established between 1991 and 2005 would have lasting repercussions that shaped digital citizenship in later periods. This is despite the fact that there was only minimal digital citizenship in Ethiopia prior to 2005 – a period in which levels of internet penetration in Ethiopia were extremely low and at a time before most social media companies had launched. From 2005 Ethiopia's unique Woredanet and Schoolnet are emblematic of centralized top-down imposed 'digital citizenship'.

The 2005 elections and the rise of digital authoritarianism (2005–15)

In the wake of the landmark 2005 election, digital citizenship was emerging and the digital space was the alternative venue for digital citizens to amplify their dissenting voices and claim their human rights. Specifically, Ethiopia had conducted two less competitive elections in 1995 and 2000 (Gudina 2011). However, such trends were reversed in 2005 when the EPRDF allowed the voting process to be free and fair. One of the most striking opportunities was the fact that opposition parties were given unprecedented access to state media and live broadcasting coverage, and numerous dissenting newspapers were able to circulate in Addis Ababa and throughout the country (Stremlau 2011).

Although internet penetration was limited (and less than 1 per cent), alternative and dissenting voices were heard through online platforms and offline media up until the EPRDF government blocked them. It should be noted that digital citizenship is an important tool for making rights claims, since Ethiopian activists in the diaspora and domestically have used the internet to call out rights abuses and hold the government accountable (Isin and Ruppert 2015).

The pursuit of information also led people to download and print news, commentaries and political manifestos, turning them into leaflets to be distributed to those without access to the internet. Most importantly, mobile phones, and especially SMS, were used to mobilize people in real time and to disseminate calls for action that had first emerged on other platforms. In the post-election days, when the EPRDF realized it had suffered greater losses than it was ready to accept and people started protesting over the delay in issuing the results, some of the channels used to mobilize protesters were shut down (Gagliardone 2014b). In the aftermath of the first wave of a series of demonstrations, on 6 June 2005, the SMS service was suspended and was only restored some two years later (US State Department 2006). Following the closure of the SMS messaging service, the Ethiopian government went on to shut down other communication channels to prevent protesters disseminating alternative information and narratives. In early November 2005, some of the most critical Ethiopian journalists who challenged the results of the election and called for more democracy were arrested and their newspapers forced to close. This marks the consolidation of digital authoritarianism in Ethiopia via internet shutdowns, blocking websites, arrests of bloggers, internet censorship, SMS shutdown, digital surveillance and so on. In May 2006, one year after the contested election, the government began to block and censor access to online spaces such as Nazret and Ethiomedia, as well as a number of individual blogs (Poetranto 2012).

Internet shutdown and SMS shutdown measures had received pushbacks from the international community (US State Department 2006). While the government sought to justify these actions as being necessary to control violence, no official justification was given for shutting down the SMS service and the censoring of the internet. Instead, these moves were presented simply as technical glitches, rather than deliberate measures undertaken to defend national security (Gagliardone 2014b).

After closing possible avenues of popular protests, the EPRDF government consolidated its power and continued to shrink the digital space and the media landscape through adopting draconian and repressive laws. These include the enactment of the 2008 Media and Access to Information Proclamation, the 2009 Anti-Terrorism Proclamation, the 2009 Civil Societies Proclamation and the 2012 Telecom Fraud Offences Proclamation. The post-2005 election crises were bristled with brutal repression by the then EPRDF-led regime. Laws that were introduced to control the media and civil-society organizations have debilitated the civic space for more than ten years, as well as squashed dissenting voices, both online and offline (Brechenmacher 2017). Media houses and political groups find themselves at a crossroads after the introduction of draconian laws. Months after the anti-terrorism law was ratified, the major printed newspaper *Addis Neger* was forced to close down and its founder fled for fear of prosecution (VoA News 2009). The crackdown on media continued in subsequent years. Another weekly newspaper,

Awramba Times, was forced to cease publication and its editor fled (Abdul 2011).

The rearrests of Birtukan Medekssa, the then chair of the major opposition party Unity for Democracy and Justice (UDJ), before the 2010 general election signalled that the regime would not tolerate criticism of any kind, taking strong measures against independent institutions, political leaders and activists (Rice 2010). The EPRDF won the 2010 general election by a landslide, with 99.6 per cent of the vote, but this did not stop the regime chasing dissenting voices in the country. The anti-terrorism law effectively started to gag critical voices. The arrest of renowned journalists such as Eskiner Nega and Reeyot Alemu under the terrorism law in 2011, who had been using the online space to reach readers, sent a clear message to individuals who wanted to express themselves freely online. The harsh sentence given to Andualem Aragae, a political party leader, created an environment where fear reigned (Gebeyehu 2016). Years of repression in civic spaces in Ethiopia have led citizens to find alternative spaces to voice their concerns. The coming of social media made it easy, fast and cheap to communicate and to network (Roberts 2019).

The narrow political space and the draconian laws forced activists and printing media outlets to migrate to social media. Activist groups and writers started finding unregulated spaces that the government could not quash easily. In May 2012, a group of activists and bloggers who were familiar with each other due to their online activities, including the co-author of this chapter, decided to meet in-person and go to visit political prisoners in Kality Federal Prison, where journalists and political leaders had been imprisoned, under harsh sentences. One of the journalists was Reeyot Alemu, winner of the Committee to Protect Journalists (CPJ) press freedom award in 2013. During that visit, Reeyot talked about prison conditions and how the prison superintendents separated prisoners from each other in eight different zones. The prison administration used these zones to separate prisoners based on the crimes they were accused of. Reeyot explained that prisoners inside Kality Federal Prison refer to the outside of the prison as 'Zone9', indicating that Ethiopia is a big prison and those of us who are not inside Kality are outside but with limited freedoms. After the visit, these activists and bloggers decided to form an informal group to act as an alternative voice in Ethiopia's socio-political sphere. They named the group Zone9 Activists and Blogging Collective (CPJ 2015). Later, Zone9 emerged as the first publicly known politically active group within the country. Zone9 bloggers used social media, mainly Facebook and Twitter, to campaign for the release of political prisoners, constitutionalism and freedom of expression with the hashtags: #RespectTheConstitution, #FreeAllPoliticalPrisoners, #FreedomOfAssembly and #FreedomOfExpression.

Zone9's approach was very moderate relative to the very polarized conversations in online spaces. Despite being reasoning voices, Zone9 members fell victim to Ethiopia's draconian anti-terrorism law before the 2015 general election, which the ruling party won 100 per cent. Six members of the collective were arrested and charged with terrorism (CPJ 2015). The arrest of Zone9 bloggers engulfed an online protest, with a hashtag #FreeZone9Bloggers trending in Ethiopia, where there was low internet penetration (BBC Trending 2014). Zone9 bloggers were accused of undermining the constitutional order, working with outlawed organization Ginbot 7 and conducting digital security training for journalists and activists inside Ethiopia. After spending eighteen months in prison, all Zone9 bloggers were acquitted and released. One of the ways digital citizens can confront authoritarian governments is through the use of hashtags. For example, hashtags play out an instrumental role in ethnic politics in Nigeria (Egbunike 2018).

The use of hashtags such as #DimitsachinYisema and #Ethiomuslims in Ethiopia was continued in 2012, when Ethiopian Muslim leaders detained in a crackdown by the Ethiopian government formed a new movement called Dimitsachin Yisema, which means Let Our Voices Be Heard, in the online space. The movement became one of the most peaceful movements in the country demanding the government stop meddling in religious affairs and Muslim institutions and condemning the arrest of their leaders (Omar 2020). The Muslim community and digital citizens have used social media, particularly Facebook, to call nationwide protests after Friday prayer. The movement was active until the majority of Muslim leaders who were given lengthy sentences on terrorism charges (of up to twenty-two years) were recently released from prison in a political decision made in 2018 (Omar 2020).

Between 2005 and 2015, the government used another form of digital authoritarianism, that is, digital surveillance as a strategy to quell political dissidents and target digital citizens participating in politics (Roberts and Bosch 2021). In a report entitled *They Know Everything We Do*, Human Rights Watch (HRW) documented how the Ethiopian government uses its control over the telecommunications system to restrict the right to privacy, freedom of expression, freedom of association and freedom of assembly (HRW 2014). These rights are entrenched under international law and in the Ethiopian Constitution but are routinely violated by the government. In practice, they are undercut by problematic national laws and practices by the authorities (e.g. warrantless interceptions and surveillance to counter-terrorism) that wholly disregard applicable human rights protections (Gebreegziabher 2018).

Overall, the shock of the 2005 election enabled the incumbent government to successfully eliminate formidable political foes, debilitate digital citizens, squeeze civic space and clamp down on the media (including online platforms). The government has introduced copious amounts of repressive legislation in the wake of the 2005 election in addition to the previously launched projects of Woredanet and Schoolnet. As a result of these measures, citizenship rights, including freedoms in the civic space, both offline and online, have been tightly squeezed. Remarkably, in this period, however, digital citizens were using hashtags to assert and amplify their rights, as observed in the case of Zone9 bloggers and the Muslim community's Let Our Voices Be Heard movement.

Oromo/Amhara protests and their repercussions (2015–18)

Between April 2014 and late 2015, a student protest erupted in Oromia region after the government announced a master plan to expand Addis Ababa to that neighbouring region. The protest, mainly by university students, started out of concern that the master plan would displace Oromo farmers surrounding the capital (Pinaud and Raleigh 2017). A large number of university students were arrested throughout Oromia region. According to an Amnesty International report, security forces were used to quash the protests, and a heavy security force presence was seen on university campuses. Amnesty International confirmed that more than sixty students were arrested by security forces to avoid further unrest (Amnesty International 2014). The Oromo University protests gave rise to a bigger popular movement, #OromoProtests.

In mid-November 2015, a second series of protests erupted across the Oromia region. The hashtag #OromoProtests was used to communicate the movement on social media. Oromo activists called these protests the Second Round of Protests opposing the 'Addis Ababa Integrated Development Plan (the Master Plan)'. The online space was used to call a protest and a labour strike in the Oromia region (Center for Advancement of Rights and Democracy (CARD) 2016). Activist Jawar Mohammed, then director of the Oromo Media Network (OMN) and with over a million Facebook followers, used his online platform and network to disseminate information about the Oromo protests (Chala 2017).

In August 2016, the protests expanded to the second most populous region, Amhara. Following the protests, security forces responded violently, leading to the deaths of many protesters in the regional capital, Bahir Dar (BBC News 2016). The spread of the protest to Ethiopia's second-largest ethnic group concerned the regime, which imposed a nationwide internet shutdown for two days to halt the protest spreading to other regions. The hashtags #AmahraPro tests/#AmharaResistance and #OromoProtests were used on social media to organize rallies, which subsequently forced the government to throttle (and slow down the speed of) the internet (Karanja, Xynou and Filastò 2016).

A stampede triggered by security forces using tear gas and discharging firearms among the large crowd at the Oromo Irreecha cultural festival on 2 October 2016 left hundreds of people dead (HRW 2017). Following the deadly protest, the government tightened its grip and imposed a state of emergency that restricted basic human rights. Mass arrests were conducted in Oromia, Amhara and Addis Ababa. According to the 2017 Human Rights Watch report *Fuel on the Fire*, 10,000 people were detained and sent to rehabilitation camps for 'reform' training. The directive that was introduced to implement the six-month-old state of emergency has articles that restrict freedom of expression and access to information. For example, writing or sharing content on the internet that may create misunderstanding among people was stated as a prohibited act. Accessing television channels of the Oromo Media Network and Ethiopian Satellite Television (ESAT) that are based abroad was also prohibited. Throughout the state of emergency, there were a series of internet shutdowns and other restrictions placed on mobile data (see Roberts and Anthonio, Chapter 4). The regime blamed social media for being a tool for 'anti-peace' elements (HRW 2016).

The Ethiopian government uses the anti-terror law, the media law and the civil-society proclamation to stifle citizens from expressing themselves online. Critics who use online space to express themselves become victims of the anti-terror law, and their social media posts are presented in court as evidence.

The case of activist Yonatan Tesfaye, who was a keen observer of Ethiopian politics at the time, is a clear example of how the Ethiopian government uses laws to silence critics (Freedom Now 2018). When protests flared across the country, the repression escalated and many activists were sent to prison. Yonatan Tesfaye was one of those activists who was charged under the terror law and found guilty over a Facebook post he wrote in 2015 (Public Prosecutor *v.* Yonatan Tesfaye case 2016).

Between 2016 and 2018, successive prime ministers in Ethiopia used internet shutdowns as a tool to muzzle freedom of expression (Ayalew 2019). Under the rule of the previous prime minister, Hailemariam, and particularly between 2016 and March 2018, the internet was shut down at least three times under the broader 'economic development narrative', to control cheating during exams, for national security and to quell civil disobedience (Ayalew 2019). Drawing on Mossberger et al.'s (2008) definition, which claims digital citizenship as the capacity to make daily use of the internet to seek information and to take action, the government should desist from using internet shutdowns as a strategy to undermine the rights of digital citizens.

Abiy's new experiment, between liberalization and control (2018–22)

Protests across the Oromia and Amhara regions between 2016 and 2018 forced the ruling party to reform itself. The resignation of Prime Minister Hailemariam Desalegn in 2018 led the country into a new era. In March 2018, the ruling party coalition EPRDF elected a new chairperson of the party, Abiy Ahmed Ali, who was sworn in as prime minister in April 2018 (Mohamed 2018). Prime Minister Abiy has moved away from dogmatic tenets of revolutionary democracy and started his political ideology of *Medemer* (synergy) as a political frame for post-2018 Ethiopia. Following this, the government created optimal conditions for enabling digital citizenship. As a result, restrictions on access to the internet were lifted and more than 200 websites (mainly opposition outlets, critics of the government and personal blogs) that had been blocked were unblocked (Taye 2018).

The government launched its national Digital Strategy (2020–25), which seeks to catalyse Ethiopia's digital transformation by the year 2025. In terms of continuity, the Woredanet project will continue to be implemented in the years to come. Accordingly, the Digital Strategy seeks to modernize and overhaul the Woredanet system via creating a fibre network backbone able to provide high-speed connectivity to public offices and institutions. This is to be conducted under the supervision of the Ministry of Innovation and Technology (Digital Strategy 2020).

One of the reforms introduced during the early reign of Abiy's leadership was amending the laws that were used to narrow the civic space for the past ten years. The new administration formed a Legal and Justice Affairs Advisory Council to work on laws to help widen the political space (Ibrahim and Idris 2020). A legal reform working team – a combination of independent experts and lawyers – drafted a new anti-terror law, civil-society law and media law, which were later ratified by the Ethiopian Parliament. Abiy has been praised for initiating law reforms that aim to widen the political sphere (HRW 2019). While the practical enforcement of digital rights is far from perfect, these laws have helped digital citizens to enjoy their civil and political rights.

Citizens' internet access has grown exponentially over the past decade, from 1.1 per cent in 2011 to 21.1 per cent in 2022. As per the Ethio Telecom report in 2022, there are around 25.6 million internet subscribers in Ethiopia, comprising 21.1 per cent of the total population. This increasing internet penetration in Ethiopia has not been without challenges, however. Since Abiy Ahmed took office, digital citizens have found themselves in polarized camps. Ethnic-based media such as the Oromo Media Network, Tigray Media House (TMH) and Amhara-affiliated media outlet called 'Asrat' (but defunct since June 2020) have led to filter bubbles, eco chambers and the polarization of conversations on social media. Prominent activists and political leaders have used inflammatory and derogatory terms online, contributing to violence offline (Skjerdal and Moges 2021). In October 2019, a protest erupted in Oromia region after the prominent activist and politician Jawar Mohammed wrote on his personal Facebook page that he was surrounded by security forces. Following his post, youth from the Oromia region marched to his house in the capital to protect him (Negari and Paravicini 2019). This ethnic cleavage has been intensified and fuelled by hate speech, both online and offline, through creating 'us' and 'them' narratives, resulting in social fissure and resentment in the country (Ayalew 2021).

As a response to the growing amount of disinformation and usage of inflammatory terms, the government introduced a law that regulates online media. In 2020, it passed the Hate Speech and Disinformation Prevention and Suppression Proclamation No.1185/2020. This law aimed to counter hate speech in Ethiopia, including ethnic vilification both offline and online. However, the law fails to define the main ingredient of hate speech, that is, 'hatred', which in turn impinges on the legality requirement under Ethiopian and international human rights law (Ayalew 2021).

When a conflict erupted between the Ethiopian National Defense Force (ENDF) and the TPLF in November 2020 after the TPLF attacked the ENDF's Northern Command, supporters of both parties used the online space to misinform and set contradictory narratives. Distorted images with false contexts were shared online (Mwai 2020). Since that time, the ongoing conflict has had a total communication blackout which involves shutdown of internet and telephone services in Tigray region and partial blackouts in the Afar and Amhara regions (Access Now 2021).

Although there was a supportive environment for online space in the early stages of Abiy's administration, the government has since imposed multiple internet shutdowns across the country, and shutdown is the government's response to any violence that is happening in the country. In June 2019, when high-level army and Amhara regional officials were assassinated, the government imposed a week-long total internet shutdown that left millions of people with no access to information (Meseret 2019). In June 2020, following the assassination of Oromo artist Hachalu Hundessa, a country-wide internet shutdown was imposed to control the violence that left hundreds killed in Oromia region (Bearak 2020; Feldstein 2021).

Thus, viewed from Mossberger et al.'s (2008) conception of digital citizenship as the capacity to make daily use of the internet to seek information and take action, internet shutdowns violate citizens' digital rights and prevent them from exercising digital citizenship in Ethiopia.

Conclusion

While successive governments seek to consolidate power and have tampered with the rights of digital citizens, the major legal and political reforms started in 2018 have helped Ethiopia traverse the roads of digital authoritarianism. This means that digital citizenship is at a crossroads in Ethiopia. This chapter has demonstrated how successive governments have consolidated their powers through using techniques of digital authoritarianism to control the behaviour of digital citizens. It has charted how the Ethiopian government has implemented authoritarian techniques to trammel digital citizens' right to freedom of expression and other civil rights in the past thirty years. When it comes to continuity of digitization programmes, Woredanet (for example) – a project launched by the EPRDF to tame the behaviour of digital citizens – continues to be applied by the governing Prosperity Party.

Whereas the period from 1991 to 2018 had arguably been sensitive and required a careful engagement, Prime Minister Abiy's experiment through *Medemer* represents a new governing framework in the post-2018 period. It was initially characterized by greater relative freedoms for digital citizens' despite such efforts are being marred by recurrent internet shutdowns and other forms of digital authoritarianism.

In the pre-2018 period, the EPRDF-led government implemented ethnic federalism and ethnicity as governing frames whereby various laws, policies and strategies were funnelled through these concepts. As a result, there were conflict-sensitive and repression of freedom of expression in online and social media conversation. Those who speak truth to power have easily been targeted by the government. Digital citizens who use the internet, including human rights activists, journalists and political leaders, have been targeted because they used the online space to express themselves and communicate with their supporters. This chapter has discussed how digital citizenship has played an instrumental role for diaspora activists to organize a movement that demanded greater freedoms for citizens and the release of political prisoners in 2018. It should be noted that draconian laws and policies have been reformed since 2018. While legal reform is a step in the right direction, this should, however, be reflected in practice, through building robust independent institutions. Overall, the government's digital authoritarianism in the form of internet shutdowns and digital surveillance, as well as polarized social media engagement, means that digital citizens are at a crossroads when it comes to exercising their rights in the digital age in Ethiopia. Future research on digital citizenship in the country should focus on tackling the challenges that are yet to be addressed, including ethnification of the media, spread of disinformation, politicization of content moderation and radicalization of groups online. In addition, the affirmative roles of digital citizenship and internet access have not received enough attention. As such, there should be more research into the contributions of (for example) the Let Our Voices Be Heard (the online movement of Muslims in Ethiopia), the Zone9 bloggers' digital struggle and Amhara/Oromo protests, as these help us to understand the positive roles of digital citizenship and digital rights in Ethiopia or beyond.

In conclusion, Ethiopia's political history and ethnic federalism experiment in the past thirty years had a mixed bag of results on digital citizenship. On the one hand, the opening of civic space helped digital citizens exercise their civil and political rights, off and online. On the other hand, government's authoritarian practices such as internet shutdown and digital surveillance continue to shackle citizens' rights in the digital ecosystem despite such practices having drawn fire from civil societies and the international community. As such, the government must take the human rights of digital citizens seriously. This requires establishing robust independent institutions and granting courts an active role in interpreting digital human rights. Ultimately, we argue that the government must initiate a constitutional amendment process to whittle down the impacts of negative ethnicity that was entrenched in public and private lives and expressly recognize the fundamental rights of (digital) citizens.

Bibliography

Abbink, J. (2011) 'Ethnic-Based Federalism and Ethnicity in Ethiopia: Reassessing the Experiment After 20 Years', *Journal of Eastern African Studies*, 5 (4): 596–618.

Abdul, H. (2011) 'Awramba Times Is Latest Ethiopian Paper to Vanish', *Committee to Protect Journalists*, 9 December, accessed 12 August 2021.

Abebe, M. M. (2020) 'The Historical Development of Media in Unconquered Africa', *Media History*, 26 (4): 373–90.

Access Now (2021) 'What's Happening in Tigray? Internet Shutdowns Avert Accountability', 29 July, accessed 12 August 2021.

Amnesty International (2014) *'Because I Am Oromo': Sweeping Repression in the Oromia Region of Ethiopia*, London: Amnesty International, accessed 12 August 2021.

Ayalew, Y. E. (2019) 'The Internet Shutdown Muzzle(s) Freedom of Expression in Ethiopia: Competing Narratives', *Information & Communications Technology Law*, 28 (2): 208–24.

Ayalew, Y. E. (2021) 'Why Ethiopia's One-Year-Old Hate Speech Law Is Off the Mark', *The Conversation*, 15 February, accessed 12 August 2021.

BBC News (2016) 'Ethiopia Protests: "Nearly 100 Killed" in Oromia and Amhara', 8 August, accessed 12 August 2021.

BBC Trending (2014) '#BBCtrending: Jailed Bloggers Spark Ethiopia Trend', 30 April, accessed 12 August 2021.

Bearak, M. (2020) 'Ethiopia Protests Spark Internet Shutdown and Fears of High Death Toll After Popular Singer Killed', *Washington Post*, 1 July, accessed 12 August 2021.

Brechenmacher, S. (2017) *Civil Society Under Assault: Repressions and Responses in Russia, Egypt, and Ethiopia*, Washington, DC: Carnegie Endowment for International Peace, accessed 18 October 2021.

Center for Advancement of Rights and Democracy (CARD) (2016) *#OromoProtests: 100 Days of Public Protests*, accessed 12 August 2021.

Chala, E. (2017) 'Residents of Ethiopia's Oromia Region Strike to Demand Release of Political Prisoners', *Global Voices*, 25 August, accessed 12 August 2021.

Committee to Protect Journalists (2015), In Ethiopia, drawn out Zone 9 trial serves to further punish bloggers, Committee to Protect Journalists webite. https://cpj.org/2015/10/in-ethiopia-drawn-out-zone-9-trial-serves-to-furth/.

Constitution of the Federal Democratic Republic of Ethiopia (1995) *Federal Negarit Gazette*, 21 August,1st Year No.1 Addis Ababa, articles 13–44.

Digital Strategy (202) 'Digital Ethiopia Strategy 202–2025, Ethiopian Government Ministry of Innovation and Technology', Addis Ababa. https://mint.gov.et/docs/digital-ethiopia-2025-strategy-english-version/?lang=en

Egbunike, N. (2018) *Hashtags: Social Media, Politics and Ethnicity in Nigeria*, Lagos: Narrative Landscape Press.

Ethio telecom (2021/2) Annual Business Performance Summary Report (28 July 2022), accessed 20 August 2022.

Federal Negarit Gazette (1995) 'Constitution of Ethiopia, Federal Negarit Gazeta of the Federal Democratic Government of Ethiopia', Addis Ababa. https://ethiopianembassy.be/wp-content/uploads/Constitution-of-the-FDRE.pdf

Feldstein, S. (2021) *The Rise of Digital Repression*,177–211, Oxford: Oxford University Press.

Fessha, Y. T. (2017) 'The Original Sin of Ethiopian Federalism', *Ethnopolitics*, 16 (3): 232–45.

Freedom Now (2018) 'Cases: Yonatan Tesfaye'. https://www.freedom-now.org/cases/yonatan-tesfaye/.

Gagliardone, I. (2014a) '"A Country in Order": Technopolitics, Nation Building, and the Development of ICT in Ethiopia', *Information Technologies & International Development*, 10 (1). https://itidjournal.org/index.php/itid/article/view/1162.html.

Gagliardone, I. (2014b) 'New Media and the Developmental State in Ethiopia', *African Affairs*, 113 (451): 279–99, accessed 19 October 2021.

Gagliardone, I. and Golooba-Mutebi, F. (2016) 'The Evolution of the Internet in Ethiopia and Rwanda: Towards a "Developmental" Model?' *Stability: International Journal of Security & Development*, 5 (1): 8, 1–24. doi: http://dx.doi.org/10.5334/sta.344.

Gebeye, B. A. (2019) 'Citizenship and Human Rights in the Ethiopian Federal Republic', *Ethiopian Constitutional and Public Law Series*, 10: 9–44.

Gebeyehu, H. A. (2016) 'Freedom of Expression and the Ethiopian Anti-Terrorism Proclamation: A Comparative Analysis', *Haramaya Law Review*, 5: 10.

Gebreegziabher, H. W. (2018) 'The Right to Privacy in the Age of Surveillance to Counter Terrorism in Ethiopia', *African Human Rights Law Journal*, 18: 392–412.

Gudina, M. (2011) 'Elections and Democratization in Ethiopia, 1991–2010', *Journal of Eastern African Studies*, 5: 669.

Hafkin, N. J. (2006) '"Whatsupoch" on the Net: The Role of Information and Communication Technology in the Shaping of Transnational Ethiopian Identity', *Diaspora: A Journal of Transnational Studies*, 15 (2–3): 221–45, accessed 19 October 2021.

Haile, M. (2005) 'Comparing Human Rights in Two Ethiopian Constitutions: The Emperor's and the Republic's Cucullus Non Facit Monachum', *Cardozo Journal of International and Comparative Law*, 13: 1–60.

Human Rights Watch (2013) *Ethiopia: Muslim Protesters Face Unfair Trial*, New York: Human Rights Watch, 2 April, accessed 12 August 2021.

Human Rights Watch (2014) *"They Know Everything We Do": Telecom and Internet Surveillance in Ethiopia*, New York: Human Rights Watch, accessed 6 August 2021.

Human Rights Watch (2016) *Legal Analysis of Ethiopia's State of Emergency*, New York: Human Rights Watch, 30 October, accessed 12 August 2021.

Human Rights Watch (2017) *Fuel on the Fire: Security Force Response to the 2016 Irreecha Cultural Festival*, New York: Human Rights Watch, accessed 12 August 2021.

Human Rights Watch (2019) *Abiy's First Year as Prime Minister, Review of Freedom of Association*, New York: Human Rights Watch, accessed 12 August 2021.

Huntington, S. (1991) 'Democracy's Third Wave', *Journal of Democracy*, 2 (2): 12–34.

Ibrahim, A. M. and A. K. Idris (2020) 'The Silent Fighters: The Volunteers Behind Ethiopia's Democratic Reforms', *Addis Standard*, 27 February, accessed 12 August 2021.

Isin, E. and E. Ruppert (2015) *Being Digital Citizens*, London: Rowman & Littlefield.

Karanja, M., M. Xynou, and A. Filastò (2016) 'Internet Shutdown Amidst Recent Protests?' *Open Observatory of Network Interference (OONI)*, accessed 12 August 2021.

Lyons, T. (2007) 'Conflict-Generated Diasporas and Transnational Politics in Ethiopia', *Conflict, Security & Development*, 7 (4): 529–49.

Mamdani, M. (1996) *Citizen and Subject: Contemporary Africa and the Legacy of Late Colonialism*, Princeton: Princeton University Press.

Mamdani, M. (2020) *Neither Settler Nor Native – The Making and Unmaking of Permanent Minorities*, Cambridge, MA: Harvard University Press.

Meseret, E. (2019) 'Internet Restored in Ethiopia 10 Days After Assassinations', *ABC News*, 2 July, accessed 12 August 2021.

Mohamed, H. (2018) 'Ex-Political Prisoners Revel in New-found Freedom', *Aljazeera*, 4 July, accessed 12 August 2021.

Mossberger, K., C. J. Tolbert, and R. S. McNeal (2008) *Digital Citizenship: The Internet, Society, and Participation*, Cambridge, MA: MIT Press.

Mwai, P. (2020) 'Ethiopia's Tigray Conflict Sparks Spread of Misinformation', *BBC News*, 11 November, accessed 12 August 2021.

Negari, T. and G. Paravicini (2019) 'Protests Spread After Stand-off at Ethiopian Activist's Home', *Reuters*, 23 October, accessed 12 August 2021.

Nyamnjoh, F. (2006) *Insiders & Outsiders: Citizenship and Xenophobia in Contemporary Southern Africa*, London: Zed Books.

Omar, A. (2020) 'The Ethiopian Muslims Protest in the Era of Social Media Activism', MA thesis, Uppsala University.

Pinaud, M. and C. Raleigh (2017) *Data Analysis: The Roots of Popular Mobilization in Ethiopia*, Global Observatory, accessed 12 August 2021.

Poetranto, I. (2012) 'Update on Information Controls in Ethiopia', *OpenNet Initiative*, 1 November, accessed 6 August 2021.

Public Prosecutor v. Yonatan Tesfaye, Federal High Court of Ethiopia, Lideta District (Judgment) No. F/P/P 414/08, May 2016 (The case on author's file).

Rice, X. (2010) 'Jailed But Not Forgotten: Birtukan Mideksa, Ethiopia's Famous Prisoner', *The Guardian*, 9 January, accessed 12 August 2021.

Roberts, T. (2019) *Closing Civic Space and Inclusive Development in Ethiopia*, IDS Working Paper 527, Brighton: IDS.

Roberts, T. and T. Bosch (2021) 'Case Study: Digital Citizenship or Digital Authoritarianism?' in *OECD, Development Co-operation Report 2021: Shaping a Just Digital Transformation*, Paris: OECD Publishing, https://doi.org/10.1787/ce08832f-en.

Skjerdal, T. and M. A. Moges (2021) *The Ethnification of the Ethiopian Media: A Research Report*, Addis Ababa: Fojo Media Institute and International Media Support, accessed 19 October 2021.

Stremlau, N. (2011) 'The Press and the Political Restructuring of Ethiopia', *Journal of Eastern African Studies*, 5 (4): 716–32, accessed 19 October 2021.

Taye, B. (2018) 'Verifying the Unblocking of Websites', *Access Now*, 3 July, accessed 12 August 2021.

US Department of State (2006) *Country Report on Human Rights Practices 2005*, Ethiopia: US Department of State, Bureau of Democracy, Human Rights, and Labor, accessed 6 August 2021.

VoA News (2009) 'Ethiopian Newspaper Shutdown, Editors Flee', 6 December, accessed 19 October 2021.

Young, J. (1996) 'Ethnicity and Power in Ethiopia', *Review of African Political Economy*, 23 (70): 531–42.

4

Internet shutdowns and digital citizenship

Felicia Anthonio and Tony Roberts

Introduction

An internet shutdown is an intentional disruption of connectivity that prevents the free flow of information and communication. Ordered by governments and implemented by mobile and internet companies, internet shutdowns are a violation of fundamental human rights, including the freedom of expression, communication and association. As social, economic and political life is increasingly conducted online, the costs of connectivity disruption to businesses, families and democracies can be devastating, yet the use of internet shutdowns is becoming more frequent; they are lasting longer and are evolving to take on new forms. Access Now and the #KeepItOn coalition have documented at least 935 incidents of shutdowns in 60 countries globally from January 2016 to December 2021 (Guest 2022). Around 34 African countries accounted for 120 incidents of the shutdowns recorded during this period. This will be discussed in detail in the next section.

The chapter begins with a review of concepts of citizenship and digital citizenship and explores what particular action possibilities or 'affordances' digital technologies provide for citizenship. Having established this conceptual framing, the chapter then documents the different types of internet shutdowns that have been evolving in African countries over the past six years, from nationwide shutdowns of all internet traffic and mobile communications to more targeted geographical shutdowns or shutting down of a single social media platform. The chapter will also provide a brief historical overview of how authorities in Egypt, Guinea and other parts of the world resorted to shutdowns to silence dissent. Case studies from Ethiopia, Nigeria and Uganda provide context and allow us to analyse the causes and effects of internet shutdowns on digital citizenship. We then document the range of methods and strategies that citizens and civil-society organizations use to evade, mitigate and end internet shutdowns. The chapter concludes with recommendations arising from our analysis for how to end internet shutdowns and thereby increase the space for digital citizenship.

How internet shutdowns constrain digital citizenship

The ability to use mobile phones, internet communications and social media platforms has enhanced the speed, scale and scope of citizens' ability to organize and aggregate their voice to claim rights and otherwise participate in policy debates (DW 2018). For those able to access mobile and internet technologies, it has become possible to access and share information across borders, in some cases making it possible to bring global attention to a local rights issue. In their study of the impact of technology on citizen participation in local governance, Erete and Burrell (2017) point to the capacity to use digital technologies to heighten the visibility of citizens' concerns, to create novel spaces for participation in governance and to provide new mechanisms to call governments to account. However, they also point out that while communities may make effective use of digital technologies to raise issues, this does not necessarily increase their political power to have those issues resolved. Having a greater voice does not necessarily mean having greater power.

As in other parts of the world, governments across Africa are increasingly resorting to internet shutdowns as a means of control (Access Now 2021a). The Shutdown Tracker Optimization Project (STOP) run by the non-governmental organization (NGO) Access Now has documented more than 935 cases of intentional internet shutdowns in 60 countries globally from January 2016 to December 2021. Access Now documented a total of 118 internet shutdowns in 36 African countries between January 2016 and December 2021 (see Table 4.1). Ethiopia has shut down the internet twenty-two times, twice as many times as the next highest country (Algeria and Sudan, with eleven and ten shutdowns respectively), followed by Chad with seven and the Democratic Republic of Congo (DRC) with six shutdowns. During the same period, Benin, Burkina Faso, Burundi, Cameroon, Egypt, Eswatini (formerly Swaziland), Guinea,

Table 4.1 Incidence of Internet Shutdowns in Africa, January 2016 to December 2021

Number of shutdowns	Countries
22	Ethiopia
11	Algeria
10	Sudan
7	Chad
6	Democratic Republic of Congo
5	Cameroon, Egypt, Mali, Togo, Uganda
3	Nigeria, Gabon
2	Benin, Equatorial Guinea, Eswatini, Guinea, Kenya, Zimbabwe, Morocco,
1	Burkina Faso, Burundi, Côte d'Ivoire, Eritrea, The Gambia, Liberia, Libya, Malawi, Mauritania, Niger, Rep. of Congo, Senegal, Sierra Leone, South Sudan, Somalia, Tanzania, Zambia
118	**Total**

Source: Adapted from Access Now (2021) STOP Database. https://docs.google.com/spreadsheets/d/19uWafg_nDavtX_KpQAuTWp762s3yC6KeilkfLV5ZQeI/edit#gid=0

Liberia, Niger, Liberia, Republic of Congo, Mali, Togo and Uganda had also imposed internet shutdowns or social media blackouts. Although a majority of the shutdowns documented in Africa were ordered or perpetrated by state actors, it is important to note that shutdowns reported in countries such as Côte d'Ivoire (Reuters Staff 2018) and Kenya (Goldman, 2020; The Star 2020) were as a result of third-party attacks or actors.

Over the past years, authorities in Africa have shut down the internet and digital communication platforms during key national events, including elections, referendums, protests and conflict or communal violence, visits by government officials and inauguration ceremonies (Taye 2021). Countries such as Cameroon, Chad and Ethiopia have also imposed shutdowns lasting several months (and on occasion for more than a year). Elsewhere, internet shutdowns have been weaponized against minority groups or vulnerable communities, including refugees and displaced persons (Taye 2019). In the past, African governments tended to use nationwide shutdowns that affected all citizens and businesses, but by 2019, 20 per cent of Africa's internet shutdowns were sub-national and targeted specific districts or regions (Access Now 2021b).

Given the increasing centrality of digital communications to social, economic and political life, cutting off the internet comes at an enormous cost, to the economy, to personal lives and to human rights. Internet shutdowns prevent citizens from actively participating and contributing to social, economic and political life online. In this chapter, we show how internet shutdowns violate citizens' fundamental human rights to freely access information and exercise their freedom of association and speech. This builds on the work of Anthonio and Cheng (2021) and Mare (2020) who have highlight how internet shutdowns in Tanzania, Uganda and Zimbabwe have stripped citizens of their right to engage in the electoral process.

Conceptual framing

Citizenship is often understood in a narrow sense to refer to the legal status bestowed by the state on individuals. This legalistic conception of citizenship is certified with a national identity (ID) card or passport that confers rights and responsibilities. Understood in a broader sense, citizenship can describe a person's active engagement in social and political life, perhaps as a member of a school governance board, running a climate group or participating in elections. In a classic definition of citizenship, Marshall (1950: 14) describes citizenship as 'a status bestowed on those who are full members of a community'. This frames citizens as relatively passive recipients of a status by those with power to grant that status. Gaventa (2002) is among those who argue that to be meaningful, any conception of citizenship carries with it a conception of rights and entitlements. However, Nyamu-Musembi (2005) has pointed out that citizenship rights are rarely 'bestowed' upon excluded groups without active struggle for suffrage or equality. Her understanding of citizenship is 'based on the recognition that rights are shaped through actual struggles informed by peoples' own understandings of what they are entitled to'. This agency-based conception of citizenship as the active engagement of individuals in the political, economic and social life of their community (regardless of their legal status) is the one that we use in this chapter.

Building on this definition, *digital citizenship* is the process of active engagement in the civic life of a community using digital tools or online spaces. This may or may not involve participation in formal politics; however, not all online activity can be considered citizenship (take online gambling, for instance). Determining exactly what does and does not constitute digital citizenship is contested. At the most basic level, Mossberger, Tolbert and

McNeal (2008) define digital citizenship as the ability to participate (daily) in civic life online and to use mobile and internet tools in economic activity. Unlike citizenship, digital citizenship is not a status bestowed upon individuals; anyone with digital devices, connectivity and literacies can engage in civic life online. This may, for example, be by engaging with online communities, debates, petitions or hashtag campaigns. The case studies discussed in this chapter include examples of digital citizenship such as the #ENDSARS protest in Nigeria, claiming the right to freedom from police violence, and the #KeepItOn campaign against internet shutdowns, claiming the rights to online expression and communication. From this perspective, digital citizenship is understood not as a status but as an agency-based process of civic engagement and rights-claiming (Isin and Ruppert 2015: Hintz, Dencik and Wahl-Jorgensen 2019).

The concept of affordances is useful for understanding what it is about a particular technology that 'affords' a specific possibility for action. In this case, what is it about social media that affords us the possibility for viral campaigning or what is it about the internet 'kill switch' that affords a president the action possibility of a shutdown? Norman (1988) used the term 'affordances' to refer to the specific features of a technology that invite, facilitate or enable particular actionable possibilities. Hutchby (2001: 5) argues that affordances 'frame, while not determining, the possibilities for action in relation to an object' and provide us with a means for empirically analysing the 'effects' and 'constraints' associated with particular technologies. We will use the concept of affordances to understand the effects and constraints of the emerging range of new 'shutdown technologies' as well as the technologies of digital citizenship, including hashtags and virtual private networks (VPNs). First, we address some definitional issues before presenting a typology of different forms of internet shutdowns.

Defining internet shutdowns

The two most often quoted definitions of internet shutdowns are provided by Access Now (2021a):

> An internet shutdown happens when someone – usually a government – intentionally disrupts the internet or mobile apps to control what people say or do. Shutdowns are also sometimes called 'blackouts' or 'kill switches'.

And the more technical definition:

> An internet shutdown is an intentional disruption of internet or electronic communications, rendering them inaccessible or effectively unusable, for a specific population or within a location, often to exert control over the flow of information.[1]

Typology of internet shutdowns

An internet shutdown can be a complete shutdown of all internet traffic nationwide. This was the original form of internet shutdown and remains the most common form. However, it can also take the form of a partial shutdown of a single website or of a specific district (Malik 2020). The recent Twitter ban in Nigeria is an example of only shutting down a specific social media platform. The internet shutdown in the Ethiopian region of Tigray at the time of writing is another example of a shutdown in a specific geography. The technology enabling more targeted shutdowns is becoming more sophisticated. States are now buying surveillance software that uses artificial intelligence with automated keyword search that can be used to target specific websites for shutdowns. Given the economic and political costs of nationwide shutdowns, we predict internet shutdowns will become more targeted over time.

Another way that governments repress digital dissent is by imposing mobile shutdowns, as recently reported in Niger, when authorities shut down mobile internet connection for ten days in response to post-election protests in the country (AFP 2021a). The impact of this form of internet shutdown is most effective in developing countries, where the vast majority of internet access is via mobile phones.

In 2019, 93 per cent of the sub-Saharan region was covered by a mobile phone signal, of which 75% included 3G and 50% included 4G mobile internet (Wyrzykowski 2020). In such cases, instructing the mobile phone companies to shut down removes internet connections from everyone except the small

---

[1] Access Now (2021) #KeepItOn FAQs.

percentage privileged to have domestic broadband connections. Mobile internet connectivity also affords the state the 'action possibility' of disrupting communications in ways that fall short of a shutdown. The technique of 'throttling', for example, enables states to slow internet speeds sufficiently to make digital citizenship on social media practically impossible, without completely shutting off the internet. This can be achieved by reducing the mobile connection from the fourth-generation service (4G) that allows us to use Twitter and TikTok on our phones back to the 2G service that only allows voice and SMS. By such means, governments can control the flow of information and silence dissenting voices. This is not only a violation of citizens' constitutional and human rights to freedom of expression and freedom of information, but intentional internet shutdowns and disruption close down the space for digital citizenship. This is always illegal in international law:

> Filtering of content on the Internet, using communications 'kill switches' (i.e. shutting down entire parts of communications systems) and the physical takeover of broadcasting stations are measures which can never be justified under human rights law.
>
> Joint Declaration on Freedom of Expression and responses to conflict situations, 4c.
>
> (OHCHR 2015)

Governments resort to different tactics to shut down the internet. In most countries, private companies are responsible for implementing internet shutdowns that have been ordered by the state. The switch is operated by telecommunication service providers (telcos) and internet service providers (ISPs). These orders could be to shut down all services nationwide, to cut off a particular region, a particular social media platform, or to throttle services to make them practically useless.

For instance, in August 2019, authorities in India ordered ISPs to shut down the internet and all communications in the disputed region of Jammu and Kashmir (Masih, Irfan and Slater 2019). Access to landlines and 2G mobile phone calls were restored two months later but the 4G internet remained blocked, throttling internet speeds until full access was restored in February 2021 (Tiwary, Sharma and Iqbal 2021). The people of Jammu and Kashmir continue to experience intermittent internet shutdowns, with the most recent being ordered on 2 September 2021 following the death of the Kashmiri separatist leader Syed Ali Shah Geelani. India is the world's most frequent perpetrator of shutdowns, most often using targeted sub-national shutdowns that coincide with civic protest and digital citizenship (Mukhtar and Aafaq 2021).

An alternative to a full internet shutdown is to block particular websites or social media platforms, which is achieved when ISP companies block certain website addresses to make them inaccessible (Minges 2007). Governments are finding innovative ways to automate the implementation of these partial internet shutdowns through the use of artificial intelligence. The Israeli company Allot sells Deep Packet Inspection (DPI) technology, which can be used to intercept and block any content deemed 'harmful', and 'record detailed web activity logs' and control 'dangerous' traffic (Woodhams and O'Donnell 2021). Allot has provided the Tanzanian government with such internet filtering equipment that was used to intentionally disrupt access to Twitter, WhatsApp and Telegram before the election in October 2020 (Woodhams and O'Donnell 2021). These instances show not only that internet shutdowns are increasing but that governments are increasing spending on actions to disrupt citizens' right to information and communication during elections and popular protest (Tackett, Krapiva and Anthonio 2020). The increasing sophistication of more narrowly targeted shutdowns aids the ability of states to limit the violation of rights to smaller demographics. The examples also show that the ability of the state to violate human rights depends on the cooperation of private companies, both those that supply the surveillance and shutdown technologies and the telcos and ISPs that operate the kill switch.

Why and when do internet shutdowns happen?

Having explored the range of shutdown types, this section discusses when and why they happen: both in terms of justifications offered by governments and those suggested by critics.

Lewis (2021) argues that the internet and digital technologies are transforming society, business and politics as people respond to new opportunities online and change their behaviour accordingly. The internet and new media platforms such as Facebook, Twitter, WhatsApp and Signal have provided citizens with new means to effectively mobilize and participate in democratic discourse. Nabatchi and Mergel (2010) refer to this as Participation 2.0 and argue that internet and social media technologies have become essential tools allowing citizen engagement in governance at both national and local levels. They further intimate that in addition to the other benefits these platforms provide, they serve as a channel to facilitate 'open and transparent government, increase citizen trust and political efficacy, and improve the responsiveness of government to citizen needs and concerns'. Writing about the popular uprising across North Africa in 2011, Chatora (2012) shows how the use of the microblogging site Twitter, social networking site Facebook and mobile telephony played a key role in facilitating active political expression during the so-called Arab Spring that resulted in the ousting of Presidents Ben Ali (in Tunisia) and Mubarak (in Egypt). In her book *Twitter and Tear Gas*, Tufekci (2017) writes that Mubarak's government did not initially grasp the powerful affordances of social media that enabled the instant interactive nationwide communication used to mobilize and inform the popular uprising against continued rights violations by the state.

When Mubarak realized that digital citizenship threatened his hold on power, he implemented a full-scale internet shutdown drawing international condemnation and attention to the use of such repressive tactics to weaken digital citizenship. The Egyptian government intentionally cut off voice, SMS and social media functionality in an attempt to quell protests that were being coordinated partly by using digital tools (Marchant and Stremlau 2020). The first internet shutdown in Africa occurred in Zambia in 1996, and in both Guinea and Ethiopia in 2007, but it was the internet shutdown in Egypt during the 2011 Arab Spring that created global awareness of the phenomenon (Okunola 2018). These first internet shutdowns were also seminal acts of 'digital authoritarianism', in which the affordances of digital technologies are used by those in power to restrict citizens' freedoms and rights. Prior to the shutdown in Egypt, countries such as Iran had imposed internet shutdowns while authorities in Tunisia tightened its control online by censoring websites in response to protests (Jigsaw 2021). Since that time, internet shutdowns have become weaponized as a technological means to dampen dissent and to silence the public acts of rights-claiming that characterize digital citizenship (Ritzen 2021).

When states implement internet shutdowns, they do not say their intention is to violate the freedom of communication of political opposition or to disrupt the coordination of peaceful protest. In seeking to justify the use of internet shutdowns, governments cite diverse reasons, including the need to ensure 'national security and restore public order or for precautionary measures', to 'prevent the spread of misinformation or hate speech or illegal content' or 'to prevent cheating during school exams' (Internet Society 2019). In other instances, authorities do not provide any explanation as to why a shutdown is happening. However, shutdowns are frequently timed to coincide with elections or protests and have the effect of silencing digital citizenship and peaceful opposition. Taye (2021) has also shown the correlation between internet shutdowns and human rights violations carried out by the state. Her research cites incidents when shutdowns coincide with police and military operations against opposition groups. Shutdowns also make it difficult for journalists and activists to effectively document political activity and publish on time during important events (Rozen 2017).

Internet shutdowns can suppress the truth about human rights abuses committed by the state. Amnesty International's (2020) analysis of the five-day Iranian internet shutdown in November 2019 shows that more than 300 men, women and children were killed during the protests. The internet shutdown made it difficult for people to share information about what was happening, thereby obstructing research into the reported incidents of human rights violations. Human Rights Watch (2019) documented that during the month-long internet shutdown in Sudan imposed in response to peaceful protests in June 2019, state security forces killed at least 100 civilians. Rozen (2017) shows how internet shutdowns make it difficult for journalists to document and draw attention to human rights violations perpetrated by the state.

Some governments, including Bangladesh, India, Myanmar and Indonesia, have imposed internet shutdowns in order to silence voices of specific populations, such as members of oppressed or marginalized minority groups, refugees and others whose human rights are at risk (Taye 2019). In 2019, the authorities in Bangladesh shut down 3G and 4G mobile internet services in the Cox's Bazar refugee camps and its surroundings, which housed millions of Rohingyas who had fled Myanmar to avoid persecution and also made it illegal for refugees to get access to SIM cards (Human Rights Watch 2019). Similarly, in neighbouring Myanmar, the Ministry of Transport and Communication ordered all telecom service providers to shut down the internet in nine townships in Rakhine and Chin states in June 2019, amid violence and conflict (ARTICLE 19 2019).

India shut down the internet for 175 days in Jammu and Kashmir in response to protests following the government's introduction of legislation aimed at changing its political structure. The government also banned public gatherings, arrested local leaders and deployed thousands of troops to enforce the order. There were reports of heinous human rights violations reported in Kashmir perpetrated by government forces including arbitrary arrests and physical assaults against Kashmiris including children as young as nine years (Ghoshal et al.).

It is sometimes argued that internet shutdowns and state violence go hand in hand. Gohdes (2015) analysed the daily record of documented state killings during the Syrian civil war and noted that internet shutdowns correlate with 'significantly higher levels of state repression, most notably in areas where government forces are actively fighting violent opposition groups'. She adds that communication blackouts are a tactic of war designed to decrease opposition groups' capabilities to successfully coordinate and implement attacks against the state, giving regime forces time to strengthen their position. Gohdes's research shows that internet shutdowns are used to weaken opposition groups' capabilities to coordinate and mobilize online. This highlights both the affordances of digital technologies for enabling civic mobilization and the affordances of state shutdowns for repression.

Analysis across these examples shows that internet shutdowns do not happen in isolation. Before a shutdown is imposed, there is usually a trigger such as street demonstrations or online protests, upcoming elections or 'security operations'. In authoritarian settings, digital citizenship can be perceived as a threat to the interests of powerholders who sometimes use internet shutdowns to extinguish its threat. Internet shutdowns are often either a reaction to government opposition or a proactive step to pre-empt opposition. Repressive states often impose internet shutdowns when they fear that digital citizenship is a threat to their interests and hold on power. Put most succinctly, internet shutdowns are designed to constrain digital citizenship.

Internet shutdowns violate human rights

The legal basis for the right to unrestricted internet communication could not be clearer. Article 19 of the Universal Declaration of Human Rights

(United Nations Office of the High Commissioner for Human Rights 1966) states that 'Everyone has the right to freedom of opinion and expression; this right includes freedom to hold opinions without interference and to seek, receive and impart information and ideas through any media and regardless of frontiers'. This fundamental human right is guaranteed to all citizens and was given legal force by the International Covenant on Civil and Political Rights in 1976 (United Nations 1967). In 2012, the UN Human Rights Council (UNHRC) unanimously passed a resolution on the promotion, protection and enjoyment of human rights on the internet, which 'Affirms that the same rights that people have offline must also be protected online, in particular freedom of expression, which is applicable regardless of frontiers and through any media of one's choice, in accordance with articles 19 of the Universal Declaration of Human Rights and the International Covenant on Civil and Political Rights' (UNHRC 2012). As part of the formal decolonisation process at the point of political independence, most African nations explicitly wrote freedom of information and communication into their new constitutions and subsequently codified those rights into domestic law (Roberts and Mohamed Ali 2021). Despite these strong legal foundations, the number of internet shutdowns violating citizens' rights continues to increase.

The justifications that states provide for internet shutdowns often are not credible in law. International law makes it clear that it is only possible for a state to violate fundamental human rights in instances that are 'legal, necessary and proportionate'. A state can pass a law that prescribes limited circumstances in which an individual's right can be violated in order to prevent a greater evil. International law requires that the 'legitimate aims' of rights violations must be stipulated in law, and must be necessary and proportionate in scope to the harm being averted. The United Nations asserts that any restrictions to online expression must be strictly necessary and proportionate to achieve a legitimate function, stating that any 'restrictive measures must . . . be the least intrusive instrument amongst those which might achieve their protective function; they must be proportionate to the interest to be protected' (UNHRC 1999).

Internet shutdowns are never proportionate. They violate the human rights of all citizens, not only those suspected of committing the most serious crimes. The UN Special Rapporteur has denounced internet shutdowns as a violation of international human rights law, which cannot be justified under any circumstances (UN General Assembly, Human Rights Council 2021). The Special Rapporteur on the rights to freedom of peaceful assembly and association reaffirmed his concern, expressed in 2019, that 'network disruptions amid peaceful assemblies' have 'become a dangerous global trend'. The report stated that 'shutdowns are lasting longer, becoming harder to detect and targeting particular social media and messaging applications and specific localities and communities' (UN General Assembly, Human Rights Council 2021).

As explained earlier, although internet shutdowns are ordered by the state, they are carried out by private companies, internet service providers (ISPs) and mobile phone companies. This makes private companies complicit in human rights violations. Companies have clear obligations with regard to human rights violations. The United Nations Guiding Principles on Business and Human Rights (OHCHR 2011) and the OECD (2011) Guidelines for Multinational Enterprises clearly state the obligation of companies to respect human rights, prevent or mitigate potential harms and provide remedy for harms they cause or contribute to. Where civil society finds it impossible to put pressure on governments to end internet shutdowns, they may have more leverage putting pressure on the companies that operate the kill switch by demanding that they fulfil their obligations to protect human rights.

Given the increased use of internet shutdowns around the world, a number of regional and international efforts have been undertaken by diverse actors to bring an end to this increasing threat to democratic values and principles. In its thirty-second session, the United Nations Human Rights Council recognized the centrality of access to the internet to citizenship and called on all nations to promote and protect the enjoyment of human rights, including the right to freedom of opinion and expression, on the internet and using other information and communication technologies (ICTs), noting that the 'Internet can be an important tool for fostering citizen and civil-society participation, for the realisation of development in every community and for exercising human rights'. The United Nations expressed deep concern about measures aiming to or that intentionally prevent or disrupt access to or dissemination of information online, in violation of international human rights law' (UN 2016: 4). Similarly, the African Commission on Human and Peoples' Rights (2016) passed a resolution condemning the use of internet shutdowns by state parties during elections and protests. The Freedom Online Coalition (FOC), which was set up in 2017 and constitutes thirty governments, continues to declare its commitment to fighting internet shutdowns through periodic statements.

The next sections examine case studies from Ethiopia, Nigeria and Uganda to provide greater empirical depth to our analysis of internet shutdowns and digital citizenship.

Ethiopia

Ethiopia has implemented more internet shutdowns than any other country in Africa. Since 2016, authorities have imposed a series of shutdowns at national and sub-national scale, in order to quash protests or in response to communal violence or conflict. Seven national internet shutdowns were imposed while the remaining fifteen affected one or more regions during the monitoring period. At the time of writing (August 2022), the most recent shutdown which started on 4 November 2020 in the Tigray region and later affected the Afar and Amhara regions following the spread of the conflict had been ongoing for nearly two years. This case study highlights how authorities in Ethiopia use internet shutdowns to repress freedom of speech and to cover up violence perpetrated during peaceful protests and episodes of conflict.

In Ethiopia's north-west region of Tigray, conflict broke out between the federal government and the Tigray People's Liberation Front (TPLF) in 2020. An internet shutdown has effectively cut off the region from the rest of the world, disrupting reporting on human rights abuses being perpetrated against the civilian population. Both warring parties claim the other side is responsible for the communication blackout. In a statement issued by the state-owned Ethio Telecom, accusations were levelled against the TPLF, accusing them of intentionally destroying the phone and internet communication infrastructure in Tigray (Addis Fortune 2020). There have been reports of egregious human rights violations being carried out against Tigrayan civilians, including mass rape, mass murder and violent abuse of refugees by forces from Ethiopia and Eritrea (Debotch 2021). Testimonies collected show how the ongoing internet shutdown is making it difficult for families in and outside the region to stay connected and sustain their livelihoods (Access Now 2021a). Anna (2021) reports that the communication blackout has made it extremely difficult for journalists to cover what is taking place, while humanitarian aid workers are unable to access parts of the Tigray region and provide support for displaced persons and refugees (Parker 2021). Shutting down complete access to the internet and telecommunications during armed conflict contributes to further harm and endangers more lives. The current shutdown in Tigray is making it difficult for people fleeing the region to find safe havens (Dewaal 2021).

This is not the first time the internet has been shut off in parts of Ethiopia during armed conflict. In January 2020, the authorities disconnected telecommunications and internet services in several parts of western Oromia (Corey-Boulet 2020). The shutdowns happened amid reports of government military operations against the armed wing of the Oromo Liberation Front (OLF), which was once banned in the country (Aljazeera 2018). Corey-Boulet (2020) reported widescale human rights violations, including murder and mass detentions by government security forces, which were documented at the time. Again, in June 2020, authorities imposed a nationwide internet blackout that lasted over two weeks in response to protests following the murder of Oromo musician and social activist Hachalu Hundessa, who was shot dead in the capital, Addis Ababa (Access Now 2020).

Nigeria

Nigerian citizens are making increasing use of the mobile internet and social media applications (apps) to make demands on the government and to claim their rights. The number of social media users in Nigeria was estimated to be twenty-eight million in 2020 (Statista.com 2021). Social media apps have been used to enhance citizens' voice on issues that were not given prominence in traditional media outlets. Ajisafe, Ojo and Monyani (2021) argue that social media has reduced dependency on establishment media and has given people the opportunity to obtain and share information through unmediated communication channels. Nigeria experienced a surge in social media usage in recent years (Statista.com 2021), which has benefited social movements and expanded the space for digital citizenship.

The rise of the #ENDSARS movement in 2020 (explored in more detail in the Nigeria chapters) is a case in point. The off and online campaign called for the country's Special Anti-Robbery Squad (SARS) to be disbanded. The notorious police unit stands accused of systematic human rights violations.

The online campaign went viral internationally, amplified by Nigerians in the diaspora. Obia (2020) argues that the way in which the #ENDSARS protests were coordinated provides insights into how Twitter serves as a coordinating platform for oppositional discourse and activism in Nigeria. Kazeem (2020) also highlights how youth in Nigeria leveraged Twitter to organize online and off.

On 4 June 2021, authorities in Nigeria banned Twitter, making it inaccessible across the country without specialist circumvention tools. The immediate trigger for the ban was the company's deletion of a tweet posted by Nigeria's president Muhammadu Buhari. However, activists believe that the president's motives included silencing the online dissent of millions who rely on Twitter as a platform for their digital citizenship (Asadu 2021). Despite threats by the government to prosecute anyone who attempted to violate the ban, many Nigerians circumvented it by using VPNs to access the censored platform. Several civil-society organizations inside and outside of the country also challenged the legality of the ban in local and regional courts. A number of lawsuits were lodged against Nigeria's Twitter ban in the ECOWAS Court, the Community Court of Justice for the Economic Community of West African States. These lawsuits have since been merged into a single filing and are pending adjudication (Silas 2021).

Uganda

A few days before elections scheduled for 14 January 2021, authorities tightened control of Uganda's off and online civic space. Amid reports of a crackdown on dissidents and opposition politicians, the Uganda Communications Commission (UCC) ordered the country's ISPs to implement a partial shutdown by blocking access to specific social media apps, including Facebook, Twitter, WhatsApp, Instagram and Google Play Store (Kafeero 2021). The authorities also blocked access to several VPNs in an attempt to prevent circumvention of the shutdowns. On the eve of elections, the government ordered a complete internet blackout, leaving millions of people in digital darkness. The shutdown made it impossible for Ugandans to access information about the election process, to freely express themselves or to stay in touch with their families (Anthonio 2021). Ugandans were unable to engage in online commerce in the absence of essential services such as mobile payment services and internet banking, with unquantified costs to local businesses. The government justified the four-day internet shutdown as a 'national security' measure (AFP 2021b). However, Facebook remained blocked almost a year later. General Museveni, who captured power in 1986, said in a televised state broadcast that he had blocked Facebook in response to the company's suspension of pro-government accounts for their 'coordinated inauthentic behaviour' – a term used to refer to the activity of actors designed to covertly manipulate online debate (Facebook 2021).

This was not the first internet shutdown during elections in Uganda. On 18 February 2016, authorities shut down social media platforms and mobile transaction services during the presidential elections. Internet users could not access platforms such as Facebook, Twitter, WhatsApp and other communication tools unless they had circumvention tools. The Associated Press (Muhumuza and Curtis 2016) reported that according to the UCC, the shutdown was imposed following orders from the Electoral Commission for 'security reasons'. At that time, President Museveni admitted to the media that he had ordered the shutdown because 'steps must be taken for security to stop so many [social media users] from getting in trouble; it is temporary because some people use those pathways for telling lies'. The shutdown lasted four days. In May of the same year, during President Museveni's inauguration ceremony, authorities ordered ISPs to shut down social media platforms for 'national security reasons' (Nanfuka 2016). Prior to the social media shutdown, authorities banned live media coverage of opposition-led activities as they protested against what they considered as yet another rigged election. During the same period, journalists and artists had decried the deteriorating state of freedom of expression in the country (Kalemera 2016).

In November 2016, Unwanted Witness Uganda, a civil-society organization, filed two lawsuits in Uganda's High Court and Constitutional Court against the government and ISPs who implemented the social media blackouts. They argued that the internet shutdowns violated fundamental human rights and contravened national, regional and international legal frameworks. The case, which had been delayed for several years, is back on the agenda of the courts but is still awaiting a judgement. After the January 2021 shutdown, Unwanted Witness (2021) again filed a court petition urging the court to prevent the government and ISPs from imposing future arbitrary and unjustified internet shutdowns in violation of human rights.

How are citizens acting to recover their digital citizenship?

As noted in the aforementioned case studies, citizens are not passive in the face of the human rights violations that internet shutdowns present. They are using a range of tactics to reassert digital citizenship by circumventing or challenging internet shutdowns. This includes technical, legal and political tactics. Technical circumvention tools such as VPNs anonymized web browsers like Tor or messaging apps like Signal, and mesh networks enable citizens to technically bypass surveillance and internet shutdowns. Also, monitoring and advocacy campaigns like the #KeepItOn campaign[2] fight internet shutdowns globally. The following sections discuss the various ways governments shut down the internet – and highlight main tools available to counter the different types of internet shutdowns currently experienced.

Technical tools to overcome shutdowns

Partial shutdowns: When shutdowns affect specific platforms, circumvention tools like VPNs are useful to enable citizens to continue accessing the blocked applications. VPNs allow individuals to redirect their internet connection through a remote server in another country to bypass the internet shutdown in their own country. By this means, Ugandans can pretend to be logging on from Kenya and circumvent a partial shutdown in Uganda. In most cases, VPNs also add a layer of security and privacy to protect against surveillance. Although the use of VPNs has increased exponentially, some countries like Tanzania, Uganda and the regional government in Jammu and Kashmir in India have cracked down on the use of VPNs and other tools for security, anonymity and

[2] A global campaign that unites over 240 organizations around the world using a wide range of approaches to challenge internet shutdowns, including grassroots advocacy, direct policymaker engagement, technical support, corporate accountability and legal intervention. https://www.accessnow.org/keepiton/

circumvention, such as those from the Tor Project. The government of Belarus has blocked VPN providers and the Tor site since 2015.

Throttling: This term refers to the intentional slowing down of internet speeds or bandwidth to make it difficult to upload or download content (Surfshark 2020). Throttling is an artificial restriction, but not entirely stopping, of the flow of data through a communications network. This means that internet access may seem available but not usable due to the interference (Björksten 2022). This type of shutdown is often difficult to identify or detect as it can be attributed to a poor internet connection. However, users can accurately detect throttling by running online speed tests and installing VPNs or proxies to encrypt their location and reroute their connection. To run an effective speed test, it is important to first run the test without a VPN and then with a VPN installed. This allows users to compare and analyse local internet speeds.

Complete internet shutdown: Also known as a 'blackout' or 'kill switch', this occurs when internet access drops to near-zero. The technical impact of a complete shutdown can extend beyond borders and threaten the global internet infrastructure. Circumventing complete internet shutdowns remains a challenge for both technical and non-technical actors. A number of tactics are currently employed, as described here:

Use of satellite dishes: Independent satellite connections can be used to circumvent ISP connections and provide an alternative means of accessing information during a complete shutdown. For instance, Iranians in the diaspora launched Toosheh, or 'Knapsack', a satellite file-casting app that aggregates uncensored digital content, like news articles, YouTube videos and podcasts, and makes them available via satellite TV to locations otherwise disconnected due to remote geography, internet shutdowns or high costs (Net Freedom Pioneers 2016). This technology is currently in use in Iran and the Middle East. It is advisable for users to download the app ahead of time to allow the satellite transfers to circumvent the internet shutdown entirely.

Mesh networks: Mesh networks allow users to tap into radio frequencies to access connectivity during full internet shutdowns. Mesh network services mostly rely on Bluetooth, allowing users to communicate through a network of devices that are linked locally, rather than over an internet connection. The FireChat mesh network, which uses wireless mesh networking to enable smartphones to connect via Bluetooth or WiFi without an internet connection, was also used during Hong Kong's democracy protests in 2014 (Sruthijith 2014). More recently, the Bridgefy app and software development kit have been introduced, which allow for offline text messages to be sent via Bluetooth when there is no access to the internet, making it possible to keep lines of communication open during complete shutdowns. In response to a potential shutdown threat during the 2019 pro-democracy demonstrations in Hong Kong, protesters began downloading mesh networks, and Bridgefy soared in popularity during the aftermath of the 2021 coup in Myanmar (Jigsaw 2021).

Use of international SIM cards with roaming services: Another way to circumvent internet shutdowns is the use of foreign mobile SIM cards or travel to neighbouring countries or regions in order to access the internet. The use of SIM cards from neighbouring countries was a common tactic among activists in Sudan during the 2019 internet shutdown (Hamad 2020). Sudanese citizens resorted to using SIM cards from India, Saudi Arabia, Egypt and the United Arab Emirates. When authorities became aware of this tactic, they disabled the roaming feature on cellular data networks.

Although use of satellites is expensive and the use of foreign SIM cards is insecure, they are the most common tools currently used in African countries to bypass complete internet shutdowns. There is a need for further research and investment in public awareness by civil-society actors and the media to enable people to freely and safely bypass complete internet shutdowns and restore their right to free speech and association.

Non-technical means of advocating against internet shutdowns

It is vital that civil society can continue monitoring, documenting, analysing and raising awareness about internet shutdowns through global coordinated efforts such as the #KeepItOn campaign. Advocacy work to disseminate information about technical circumvention is critical to enable people to exercise digital citizenship. Creating global awareness about state abuse of human rights is also vital to dissuade future internet shutdowns. This section looks at how civil-society groups and individuals have used strategic litigation to challenge and bring an end to internet shutdowns in both regional and national courts in Africa:

Strategic litigation

Citizens and activists around the world are increasingly resorting to courts to challenge internet shutdowns (Micek and Libbey 2019). A recent ruling by the Zambian High Court, for example, ordered President Edgar Lungu's government to restore internet services that had been blocked on 12 August, which was election day (New Zimbabwe 2021). The lawsuit was filed by a civil-society activist against the government. Most African nations have strong legal protections for unrestricted private communications, making this a potentially fruitful avenue of resistance in some countries (Roberts and Mohamed Ali 2021).

For the second time within two years, the Community Court of Justice of the Economic Community for West African States (ECOWAS Court) has declared internet shutdowns to be unlawful and in violation of fundamental rights. After several months of civil-society organisations both locally and internationally fighting the Nigerian government in court for shutting down microblogging application, Twitter for over seven months, the ECOWAS Court on July 14, 2022 ruled that the Twitter ban in Nigeria was unlawful and ordered the government to pay litigation fees of plaintiffs. The ECOWAS Court also held that the shutdown contravened both the African Charter on Human and Peoples' Rights and the United Nations Charter, and ordered the Nigerian government to take appropriate legislative steps to guarantee the rights of the plaintiffs (Media Rights Agenda 2022).

Similarly, the ECOWAS Court passed a landmark judgement in June 2020 upholding the right of freedom of expression in Togo and other African states in a lawsuit filed by local civil-society groups, with support from other regional and international NGOs. The ruling, which was in response to the Togolese government's decision to shut down the internet during anti-government protests in 2017, indicated that the shutdown was illegal, and the court cautioned the government not to repeat its action (Hughes 2020). The Court ruled that the shutdowns were imposed were in violation of fundamental human rights and that the government's justification for disrupting the internet in response to 'national security' arguments was unpersuasive, and insufficient under local or international law.

Over the years, activists and individuals in Sudan have leveraged national courts in response to the uptick in the use of internet shutdowns imposed by Sudanese authorities. There have been at least four court decisions against shutdowns in Sudan since 2019. Most recently, the Sudanese Consumer Protection Organization sued the Telecommunication and Post Regulatory Authority (TPRA) for shutting down the internet in October 2021. The presiding judge subsequently ordered access to be restored on November 11, 2021 (Reuters 2021). The TPRA argued against the restoration on the grounds of 'national security' and a 'state of emergency', arguments the court dismissed. The judge took an unprecedented step of issuing an arrest warrant for the chief executive officers of the telecom companies due to their failure to restore internet access. That is when access was finally restored. In an unrelated case, a Sudanese court in 2019 ordered mobile operator Zain Sudan to restore internet services after access was cut off to quell protests in the country. The case was filed by an individual lawyer, Abdel-Adheem Hassan, who filed his case against Zain Sudan over the military-ordered blackout. Internet access was subsequently restored across the country following the ruling. (Abdelaziz et al. 2019)

In Zimbabwe, civil-society activists successfully sued the state for shutting down the internet in 2019 during planned protests (Associated Press 2019). In a landmark decision, the court ruled that the Minister of State in the President's Office Responsible for National Security 'does not have the authority to issue any directives in terms of the Interception of Communications Act', making the order that led to the Zimbabwean internet shutdown illegal and without effect. (MISA-Zimbabwe 2019)

Although the use of litigation has not brought a complete end to the fight against internet shutdowns, it has contributed significantly to holding governments accountable and in setting precedents to deter others from normalizing the use of internet shutdowns. It is important for civil-society actors to remain resilient in the fight against shutdown legally at national, regional and even international levels.

Conclusion

This chapter has shown that digital citizenship can stimulate repressive governments to impose internet shutdowns and that internet blackouts can close down the space for digital citizenship. Internet shutdowns are a reflection both of the strength of authoritarian governments and of their fragility. That presidents fear online activity sufficiently to shut down the infrastructure of social, economic and political life is a testament to the growing strength of digital citizenship. Citizens have used online spaces creatively to exercise digital citizenship and are now innovating workarounds to internet shutdowns so that they continue to do so.

The cases presented in this chapter highlight concerns raised by civil-society groups around the world. The frequency of shutdowns is increasing, and they are lasting longer. The technologies of shutdowns are becoming more sophisticated, more targeted, harder to detect and as such may become extremely difficult to end the practice of internet shutdowns completely or draw less criticism to the issue. However, this in no way reduces the impact on those citizens whose rights are violated. Internet shutdowns cut off citizens and businesses, constraining livelihoods, education, family relationships and people's ability to take part in social, economic and political life. All individuals have a right to take part in open debate and decision-making on issues that affect their lives or call attention to human rights abuses being carried out by the state.

Internet shutdowns are evidence of the growing power of digital citizenship. Repressive governments are evidently threatened by the enhanced power and voice that use of digital technologies gives citizens. Regimes pay a political and economic cost when they shut down the internet, and they must expect to face domestic and international criticism and reduction in support. For this reason, internet shutdowns are perhaps easier to sustain in African countries where a relatively small percentage of the economy is online and political opposition is relatively weak. If this holds true, then, as economies increasingly move online and the economic costs of internet shutdowns grow, we should expect increased use of more narrowly targeted shutdowns and platform-specific measures like Nigeria's recent seven-month-long Twitter ban which was imposed by authorities on 4 June 2021.

To end the rights violations that internet shutdowns represent, it is necessary to bring irresistible pressure on states and on private mobile and internet service providers to end the practice. While the use of VPNs, satellite connectivity and mesh networks are valuable tactical responses that relieve the symptoms of this problem, the solution must be to make it politically untenable to impose shutdowns in the first place, through adoption of rights-respecting legislation, strategic litigation, electoral politics and advocacy – including by means of digital citizenship.

All internet shutdowns are a violation of human rights. The use of internet shutdowns is one weapon in the wider arsenal of digital authoritarianism. This chapter has shown how citizens experience internet shutdowns as a violation of human rights, as a silencing of their freedom of expression and as a curtailment of their ability to exercise, defend and claim fundamental human rights. Addressing these attacks on fundamental freedoms requires urgent action by all relevant actors, including national and foreign governments, private corporations, regional and international blocks, media outlets and civil-society groups.

Arising from the analysis in this chapter, we propose the following recommendations for policy, practice and further research.

Recommendations

The fight to end internet shutdowns to enable citizens to enjoy the full benefits of the internet and digital applications requires collective action by all parties. Here, we present a number of recommendations directed at regional and international organizations, governments, the private sector and civil society on how to strengthen the fight against internet shutdowns.

National governments should adopt human rights–centric legislation that refrains them from imposing internet shutdowns during important national events.

The international community should denounce the use of shutdowns increasingly and promptly as a violation of fundamental human rights and caution authorities to stop imposing them at all times. Additionally, international cooperation and aid institutions that seek to expand connectivity must include explicit references to preventing shutdowns in their licensing agreements. Companies and businesses must push back against internet shutdowns and undertake human rights due diligence with regard to potential adverse impacts from network shutdowns when entering or renegotiating licence agreements with governments at all levels. Finally, civil-society actors, academia and individuals must continue to work together through global initiatives like the #KeepItOn campaign to monitor, document and respond to shutdown threats around the world.

Bibliography

Abdelaziz, K (2019) 'Sudan Court Orders Company to End Military-Ordered Internet Blackout: Lawyer', Reuters website. https://www.reuters.com/article/us -sudan-politics-internet-idUSKCN1TO0FV.

Abrougui, A. (2021) 'Internet Shutdowns and Election Handbook', *Access Now*, 31 March, accessed 17 October 2021.

Access Now (2016) 'No More Internet Shutdowns! Let's #KeepItOn', accessed September 2021.

Access Now (2020) 'Back in the Dark: Ethiopia Shuts Down Internet Once Again', 16 July, accessed October 2021.

Access Now (2021a) 'Voices from Tigray: Ongoing Internet Shutdown Tearing Families, Communities, Businesses Apart', 13 September, accessed 17 October 2021.

Access Now (2021b) 'What's Happening in Tigray? Internet Shutdowns Avert Accountability', 29 July, accessed 17 October 2021.

Addis Fortune (2020) 'Ethio Telecom Claims Regional Operations in Meqelle Tampered With', 10 December, accessed 17 October 2021.

AFP (2021b) 'Uganda Eases Internet Shutdown Imposed over Election', *France 24*, 18 January, accessed September 2021.

African Commission on Human and Peoples' Rights (2016) '362 Resolution on the Right to Freedom of Information and Expression on the Internet in Africa', accessed 17 October 2021.

African School on Internet Governance (2016) 'Statement on Intentional Internet Shutdowns', accessed 17 October 2021.

Agence France Presse (AFP) (2021a) 'Internet Back in Niger After Post-Election Blackout', *The Guardian Nigeria*, 6 March, accessed 17 October 2021.

Ajisafe, D., A. Ojo, and M. Monyani (2021) 'The Impacts of Social Media on the #EndSARS# Youth Protests in Nigeria', in *Proceedings of the International Conference of Information Communication Technologies Enhanced Social Sciences and Humanities (ICTeSSH) 2021 Conference*, accessed 17 October 2021.

Aljazeera (2018) 'Thousands of Ethiopians Hail Return of Once-Banned Oromo Group', 15 September, accessed 17 October 2021.

Amnesty International (2020) 'A Web of Impunity. The Killings Iran's Internet Shutdown Hid', accessed 17 October 2021.

Anna, C. (2021) '"We'll Be Left Without Families": Fear in Ethiopia's Tigray', *AP News*, 11 February, accessed 17 October 2021.

Anthonio, F. (2021) '"No Matter What They Do, The World Is Watching": Some Ugandans Are Back Online After Internet Shutdown During Presidential Election', *Access Now*, 20 January, accessed 17 October 2021.

Anthonio, F. and S. Cheng (2021) 'Cutting Internet Access When People Need It the Most: Stories from Uganda', *Access Now*, 9 February, accessed 17 October 2021.

Asadu, C. (2021) 'Nigeria's Twitter Blackout: What's Really Behind Buhari's Social Media Ban?', *Nigeria, The Africa Report*, 7 June, accessed 17 October 2021.

Associated Press (2019) 'Zim High Court Rules Internet Shutdown Illegal, Orders Govt to Restore Full Internet to the Country', *Harare, News24*, 21 January, accessed 17 October 2021.

Best, M. and A. Meng (2015) 'Twitter Democracy: Policy Versus Identity Politics in Three Emerging African Democracies', in *Proceedings of the Seventh International Conference on Information and Communication Technologies and Development*, accessed October 2021.

Björksten, G. (2022) 'A Taxonomy of Internet Shutdown: The Technologies Behind Network Interference', *Access Now*, 1 June, accessed 14 August 2022.

Bridgefy (2020) 'How Does the Bridgefy App Work?', accessed 17 October 2021.

Chatora, A. (2012) *Encouraging Political Participation in Africa: The Potential of Social Media Platforms*, Pretoria: Institute for Security Studies, accessed 17 October 2021.

Corey-Boulet, R. (2020) 'Ethiopia's Abiy Faces Outcry over Crackdown on Rebels', *AFP*, 29 February, accessed August 2021.

Debotch, R. (2021) 'Vicious Mass Rape of Women Has Become a Weapon Against the Tigray in Ethiopian War', *Global Voices*, 5 July, accessed 17 October 2021.

Dewaal, A. (2021) 'Switch Tigray's Internet Back On, World Peace Foundation', 21 April, accessed September 2021.

DW (2018) 'How the Internet Changes Political Debate', *DW*, 29 June, accessed August 24, 2022.

ECOWAS Community Court of Justice (2020) 'Economic Community for West African States (ECOWAS) Community Court of Justice Ruling', 25 June, accessed 17 October 2021.

Erete, S. and J. Burrell (2017) 'Empowered Participation: How Citizens Use Technology in Local Governance', in *Proceedings of the 2017 CHI Conference on Human Factors in Computing Systems*.

Facebook (2021) 'What Does Coordinated Inauthentic Behaviour Mean?', 6 December, accessed 17 October 2021.

Flores, W. and R. Benmayor (1997) *Latino Cultural Citizenship: Claiming Identity, Space and Rights*, Boston: Beacon Press.

Freedom Online Coalition (2017) 'Joint Statement on State Sponsored Network Disruptions', accessed July 2021.

Freedom Online Coalition (2021) 'FOC Issues Joint Statement on COVID-19 and Internet Freedom', 27 May, accessed 17 October 2021.

Gaventa, J. (2002) 'Exploring Citizenship, Participation and Accountability', *IDS Bulletin*, 33 (2): 1–14, accessed 17 October 2021.

Gohdes, A. (2015) 'Pulling the Plug: Network Disruptions and Violence in Civil Conflict', *Journal of Peace Research*, 52 (3): 352–67, accessed July 2021.

Goldman, D. (2020) 'Agent Saboteurs Within Somalia Army Jam Kenya's Safaricom BTS-Mast in Mandera Frontier', *Strategic Intelligence*, 2 March, accessed 24 August 2022.

Guest, P. (2022) 'In the Dark: The Internet Sparked a Revolution, Then It Was Turned Off', *Rest of World*, 22 April, accessed 14 August 2022.

Hamad, K. (2020) 'Internet Shutdowns in Sudan: The Story Behind the Numbers and Statistics', *Global Voices*, 8 June, accessed 17 October 2021.

Hintz, A., L. Dencik, and K. Wahl-Jorgensen (2019) *Digital Citizenship in a Datafied Society*, Cambridge: Polity Press.

Hughes, P. (2020) 'Landmark Judgment: ECOWAS Court Finds Togo Violated FoE with Internet Shutdown', *Media Defence*, 25 June, accessed 17 October 2021.

Human Rights Watch (2019) 'Sudan: End Network Shutdown Immediately', 12 June, accessed 17 October 2021.

Hutchby, I. (2001) 'Technologies, Texts and Affordances', *Sociology*, 35 (2): 441–56.

Internet Society (2019) 'Policy Brief: Internet Shutdowns', accessed August 2021.

Isin, E. and E. Ruppert (2015) *Being Digital Citizens*, London: Rowman & Littlefield.

Isin, E. and P. Wood (1999) *Citizenship and Identity, Politics and Culture Series*, London: Sage Publications.

Jigsaw (2021) 'The Internet Shutdowns Issue', *The Current*, accessed 17 October 2021.

Jones, E. and J. Gaventa (2002) *Concepts of Citizenship: A Review*, Brighton: Institute of Development Studies, accessed 17 October 2021.

Kabeer, N. (2005) *Inclusive Citizenship: Meanings and Expressions*, London: Zed Books.

Kafeero, S. (2021) 'Uganda Has Shut Down All Social Media Two Days Ahead of a Tense Election', *Quartz Africa*, 12 January, accessed 17 October 2021.

Kalemera, A. (2016) 'Ugandan Artists, Journalists Decry Declining Freedom of Expression', *CIPESA*, 5 May, accessed 17 October 2021.

Kazeem, Y. (2020) 'How a Youth-Led Digital Movement Is Driving Nigeria's Largest Protests in a Decade', *Quartz Africa*, 13 October, accessed 17 October 2021.

Lewis, J. (2021) 'A Short Discussion of the Internet's Effect on Politics', *Centre for Strategic and International Studies*, 29 January, accessed 14 August 2022.

Lister, R. (2003) *Citizenship: Feminist Perspectives*, London: Palgrave Macmillan.

Malik, I. (2020) 'A Year Without High-Speed Internet Has Been a Nightmare for J&K's Entrepreneurs', *The Wire*, 2 August, accessed 17 October 2021.

Marchant, E. and N. Stremlau (2020) 'The Changing Landscape of Internet Shutdowns in Africa', *International Journal of Communication*, 14 (1): 4216, accessed September 2021.

Mare, A. (2020) 'Internet Shutdowns in Africa| State-Ordered Internet Shutdowns and Digital Authoritarianism in Zimbabwe', *International Journal of Communications*, accessed September 2021.

Marshall, T. (1950) *Citizenship and Social Class*, Cambridge: Cambridge University Press.

Masih, N., S. Irfan, and J. Slater (2019) 'India's Internet Shutdown in Kashmir Is the Longest Ever in a Democracy', *Washington Post*, 16 December, accessed 17 October 2021.

Media Rights Agenda (2022) 'Media Rights Agenda, Others Win Suit over Twitter Ban as ECOWAS Court Rules Nigerian Government's Action Unlawful', Media Rights Agenda website. https://mediarightsagenda.org/media-rights-agenda-others-win-suit-over-twitter-ban-as-ecowas-court-rules-nigerian-governments-action-unlawful/.

Micek, P. and M. Libbey (2019) 'Judges Raise the Gavel to #KeepItOn Around the World', *Access Now*, 23 September, accessed 17 October 2021.

Minges, M. (2007) *Mobile Internet for Developing Countries*, Geneva: International Telecommunication Union.

MISA Zimbabwe (2019) 'High Court Sets Aside Internet Shutdown Directives', Media Institute for Southern Africa website. https://zimbabwe.misa.org/2019/01/21/high-court-sets-aside-internet-shut-down-directives/.

Mossberger, K., C. J. Tolbert, and R. S. McNeal (2008) *Digital Citizenship: The Internet, Society, and Participation*, Cambridge, MA: MIT Press.

Muhumuza, R. and B. Curtis (2016) 'Voting in Uganda Plagued by Delays; Social Media Shut Down', *Global News*, 18 February, accessed September 2021.

Mukhtar, U. and Z. Aafaq (2021) '"It Is Humiliation for Us": Internet Shutdown Blocks News in Kashmir', *The Wire*, 2 September, accessed 17 October 2021.

Nabatchi, T. and I. Mergel (2010) *Participation 2.0: Using Internet and Social Media Technologies to Promote Distributed Democracy and Create Digital Neighborhoods*, accessed August 2021.

Nanfuka, J. (2016) 'Uganda Again Blocks Social Media to Stifle Anti-Museveni Protests', 12 May, accessed September 2021.

Net Freedom Pioneers (2016) 'Empowering Offline Communities Anywhere Information Can Transform Lives', accessed September 2021.

New Zimbabwe (2021) 'High Court Orders Restoration of Internet Services, Zambia', *All Africa*, 15 August, accessed 17 October 2021.

Norman, D. (1988) *The Design of Everyday Things*, New York: Basic Books.

Nyamu-Musembi, C. (2005) 'Towards an Actor-Oriented Perspective on Human Rights', in N. Kabeer (ed.), *Inclusive Citizenship: Meanings and Expressions*, London: Zed Books, accessed August 2021.

Obia, V. A. (2020) '#EndSARS, A Unique Twittersphere and Social Media Regulation in Nigeria', *LSE Blog*, 11 November, accessed 17 October 2021.

OECD (2011) *OECD Guidelines for Multinational Enterprises*, Paris: OECD Publishing, accessed 17 October 2021.

OHCHR (1966) *Universal Declaration of Human Rights*, accessed 17 October 2021.

OHCHR (UN Office of the High Commissioner for Human Rights) (2011) *United Nations Guiding Principles on Business and Human Rights*, Geneva: United Nations, accessed 17 October 2021.

OHCHR (2015) *Joint Declaration on Freedom of Expression and Responses to Conflict Situations*, accessed 17 October 2021.

OHCHR (2019) 'Sudan: UN Experts Denounce Internet Shutdown, Call for Immediate Restoration', 8 July, accessed 17 October 2021.

Okunola, A. (2018) A Timeline of Internet Blockages in Africa, Tech Cabal. https://techcabal.com/2018/05/03/a-timeline-of-internet-blockages-in-africa/#:~:text=Guinea%20(February%202007),protests%20calling%20for%20his%20resignation.

Parker, B. (2021) 'Relief for Tigray Stalled as Ethiopian Government Curbs Access', *The New Humanitarian*, 11 February, accessed 17 October 2021.

Repucci, S. and A. Slipowitz (2021) *Democracy Under Siege*, Washington, DC: Freedom House, accessed 17 October 2021.

Reuters Staff (2018) 'UPDATE 2-Orange Official Calls Ivory Coast Telecoms Fire Act of "Sabotage"', *Reuters*, 15 May, accessed 24 August 2022.

Reuters Staff (2019) 'Some Internet Service Restored in Sudan After Court Ruling', *Reuters*, 9 July, accessed 17 October 2021.

Reuters Staff (2021) 'Sudan Court Orders Restoral of Internet, But No Sign of Services Returning', *Reuters*, 9 November, accessed October 2021.

Ritzen, Y. (2021) 'Rising Internet Shutdowns Aimed at Silencing Dissent', *Al-Jazeera*, accessed 26 October 2021.

Roberts, T. and A. Mohamed Ali (2021) 'Opening and Closing Online Civic Space in Africa: An Introduction to the Ten Digital Rights Landscape Reports', in T.

Roberts (ed.), *Digital Rights in Closing Civic Space: Lessons from Ten African Countries*, Brighton: Institute of Development Studies, accessed September 2021.

Rozen, J. (2017) 'Journalists Under Duress: Internet Shutdowns in Africa Are Stifling Press Freedom', *Africa Portal*, 17 August, accessed 17 October 2021.

Shoker, S. and R. Shoker (2020) 'Using Artificial Intelligence to Predict Internet Shutdowns', accessed 17 October 2021.

Silas, D. (2021) 'Twitter Ban: ECOWAS Court Merges 4 Suits Against Nigerian Government', *Daily Post*, 9 July, accessed 17 October 2021.

Sruthijith, K. K. (2014) 'Firechat Was Sparking Interest in India, Even Before It Became a Mainstay of the Hong Kong Protests', *Quartz*, 1 October, accessed 17 October 2021.

Statista.com (2021) 'Number of Social Network Users in Nigeria from 2017 to 2026'.

Surfshark (2020) 'How to Do a VPN Speed Test and How to Read the Results', accessed 17 October 2021.

Tackett, C., N. Krapiva, and F. Anthonio (2020) 'As Conflict Escalates, Azerbaijan's Internet Shutdown Puts Lives Further at Risk', *Access Now*, 15 October, accessed 17 October 2021.

Taye, B. (2019) *Targeted, Cut Off, and Left in the Dark. The #KeepItOn Report on Internet Shutdowns in 2019*, accessed 17 October 2021.

Taye, B. (2021) 'Shattered Dreams and Lost Opportunities: A Year in the Fight to# KeepItOn', *Access Now*, accessed 17 October 2021.

The Star (2020) '*Al Shabaab Destroys Safaricom Mast in Mandera*', 18 December, accessed 24 August 2022.

Tiwary, D., A. Sharma, and N. Iqbal (2021) '18 Months After Split, Downgrade, 4G Mobile Internet Back in J&K', *The Indian Express*, 6 February, accessed 17 October 2021.

Tufekci, Z. (2017) *Twitter and Tear Gas: The Power and Fragility of Networked Protest*, New Haven: Yale University Press.

UN Human Rights Committee (2011) *General Comment No. 34: Article 19: Freedoms of Opinion and Expression*, Geneva: United Nations, accessed August 2021.

UN General Assembly, Human Rights Council 2021 (2021) *Ending Internet Shutdowns: A Path Forward, Report of the Special Rapporteur on the Rights to Freedom of Peaceful Assembly and of Association*, Geneva: Human Rights Council, accessed 17 October 2021.

UNHRC (1999) 'General Comment 27, Freedom of Movement (Art.12)', *UN Human Rights Committee*, accessed 17 October 2021.

UNHRC (2012) *The Promotion, Protection and Enjoyment of Human Rights on the Internet A/HRC/32/L.20*, Geneva: United Nations Human Rights Council.

United Nations (1967) 'International Covenant on Civil and Political Rights', accessed October 2021.

United Nations Human Rights Council (UNHRC) (2016) *Report of the Special Rapporteur on the Promotion and Protection of the Right to Freedom of Opinion and Expression*, New York: United Nations General Assembly.

Unwanted Witness (2021) 'News Brief: High Court in Uganda Sets Hearing Date for Internet Shutdown Lawsuit', *Unwanted Witness*, 30 March, accessed 17 October 2021.

Vertemati, L. (2021) 'Ethiopia's Internet Shutdowns: Contributing to Humanitarian Catastrophe in the Tigray', *Security Distillery*, 16 April, accessed 17 October 2021.

Woodhams, S. and C. O'Donnell (2021) 'The Tech Companies Behind Internet Shutdowns: Allot Ltd', *Top10VPN*, 29 June, accessed 17 October 2021.

Wyrzykowski, R. (2020) 'Mobile Connectivity in Sub-Saharan Africa: 4G and 3G Connections Overtake 2G for the First Time', GSMA website. https://www.gsma.com/mobilefordevelopment/blog/mobile-connectivity-in-sub-saharan-africa-4g-and-3g-connections-overtake-2g-for-the-first-time/.

Yural-Davis, N. and P. Werbner (eds) (1999) *Women, Citizenship and Difference*, London: Zed Books.

5

Feminist digital citizenship in Nigeria

Sandra Ajaja

Introduction

This chapter examines the dynamics of feminist digital citizenship in Nigeria. It addresses the problem of closing offline civic space in Nigeria by examining two recent cases in which digital citizenship was used to open new online civic space: the Bring Back Our Girls campaign (#BBOG) for the release of the kidnapped schoolgirls from Chibok and the anti-police violence campaign #ENDSARS both of which went viral globally. The two campaigns are used as emblematic case studies illustrative of a wider increase in feminist digital citizenship in Nigeria. Acknowledging the gendered inequality of digital access and use, the two cases are analysed using a framework that combines cyberfeminism with the five 'A's of technology access.

Nigeria is a country characterized by political tensions, insecurities, riots, violent protests and police responses (Human Rights Watch 2021). It has become increasingly difficult for citizens to safely exercise their rights to free speech, freedom of expression and opinion (CIVICUS 2019; Freedom House 2019). Persons criticizing the president or taking part in street demonstrations regularly experience police violence, arrest and/or incarceration (Oladapo and Ojebode 2021). Denied the space for peaceful civic engagement offline, Nigerians increasingly use social media to engage in digital citizenship online. As the use of digital tools increases in the country, digital space has become a site for civic engagement, allowing people to speak up against injustice (Uwalaka and Watkins 2018). Campaigners sought the release of kidnapped girls, the arrest of activists, justice for those affected and wider systemic change within government and law enforcement in Nigeria (Vanguard 2020).

Both the #BBOG and #ENDSARS protests involved heavy use of social media by tech-savvy young people, and women played a key leadership role in both campaigns (Olugbemi 2011). Women's contribution to the civic movement for change in Nigeria has often not been credited and is thus largely invisible. Women have been under-represented in political, cultural or traditional leadership roles due to cultural and social norms. Although their stories are under-represented in written history, Nigeria has a history of female leadership in the liberation struggle and civil-society organizations (Afolabi 2019). This chapter foregrounds their leading role in recent digital citizenship.

Recent years have witnessed a new wave of feminist action and collectivization of women to fight against oppression globally (Molyneux et al. 2021). This comes in response to the gendered nature of exclusions and barriers to active civic participation in Nigeria. Women are increasingly using online spaces including social media to organize, donate, fundraise and finance protests, revealing a shift in civic engagement in Nigeria, with women becoming more active participants (Olaoluwa 2020). This chapter foregrounds the increase in female activism and participation in recent episodes of political contestation through feminist digital citizenship in Nigeria.

There is a relative lack of empirical literature documenting and analysing Nigerian women's digital citizenship. Much of the existing literature on digital citizenship is situated in the Global North (Khazraee and Novak 2018; Roberts and Mohamed Ali 2021). This chapter adds to the existing literature by focusing on the under-researched context of women's digital citizenship in Nigeria and seeks to understand why and how Nigerian women have used digital spaces to make their voices heard through online activism and protest.

The specific question that this chapter seeks to address is what factors restrict *feminist digital citizenship in Nigeria*. The existing literature on digital citizenship in Africa and Nigeria largely focuses on the technological and social inequalities that hinder online civic engagement and participation, at the expense of investigating the experience and practice of citizens as they navigate the use of digital tools for civic participation. This gap in the literature is especially pronounced in Nigerian women's practices of digital citizenship. Highlighting and understanding the actual experiences of different kinds of citizens, based on their different social and economic contexts, gender, race or class, is essential to uncover the shades of social inequality that exist in digital spaces (Oladapo and Ojebode 2021).

I begin by establishing the gendered inequities in access to digital technologies in Nigeria. Not all Nigerian women have access to digital technologies and therefore to digital citizenship. I argue that women's increased access to digital technology, awareness of their rights and higher levels of feminist consciousness and agency are factors contributing to increased digital citizenship. The digital space affords unprecedented opportunities for women's collective action and, to some extent, enables them to transcend existential divides like gender, ethnicity and geographic and socio-economic differences. Feminist digital citizenship can exploit the global virality of internet communication and, in the two case studies featured, compel the government to acknowledge the issues raised – police brutality, nationwide attacks and violence targeted at women and girls – and create systems that tackle the root causes of these issues. Tackling issues of gendered digital exclusions has never been more pertinent and, as online spaces become the new sites for citizen engagement, activism and female organizing, it is essential to understand the issues, gaps, power relations and dynamics to advance women's rights-claiming in Nigeria (Earl and Kimport 2011).

Digital citizenship

A theoretical analysis of citizenship is required for a foundation for the evolution of the concept of digital citizenship and feminist digital citizenship. Roberts (2004) defines citizenship as a substantive ethical and sociological statement, which comprises notions of community, duty and civility. This understanding is grounded in the attainment of rights, from civil, political, economic, social and cultural rights to the right to participation itself. Gaventa (2002) builds on this understanding to argue that citizenship is about the 'right to have rights' and the right to participate in struggles for the creation of new rights. Lister (1997) argues that to be a citizen in the legal and sociological sense means to enjoy the rights of citizenship necessary for agency and social and political participation. Lister (2003) reflects on the need for a feminist understanding of citizenship asserting the need for 'a feminist citizenship project thus encourages an approach to theory and practice that gives due accord to women's agency rather than simply seeing us as victims of discrimination and oppressive male-dominated political, economic and social institutions' (Lister

2003: 6). The literature on African and feminist citizenship has often been concerned both with who is excluded from citizenship and with hybrid and flexible forms of citizenship where ethnicity, gender or religious identities may be central to conceptions of citizenship (Agbalajobi 2010; Madunagu 2008).

Despite debates about definitions and theories of citizenship, there is a broad consensus that citizenship is a concept that involves rights. These rights can be categorized as legal rights, political rights, social rights and participation rights. Therefore, in this chapter, I define citizenship as a process of actively engaging in the civic life of a community or state involving making rights claims (Lister 1998, 2003; Gaventa 2002; Roberts 2004).

The early digital citizenship literature focuses primarily on the technological and social inequalities that hinder civic engagement and participation, rather than the investigation of the experiences of citizens as they navigate the use of digital tools for civic participation. These experiences of citizen agency are typically shaped by societal constraints that structure layers of marginalization and (dis)advantage influenced by the identity of users. Further research is needed on people's experience of digital citizenship to address this gap in the digital citizenship literature. Highlighting and understanding the actual experiences of different kinds of citizens, based on their different social and economic contexts, gender, race, class, will uncover the different layers and shades of social inequalities that exist in digital spaces.

According to Lister (1998), to be a citizen in the legal and sociological sense means to enjoy the rights of citizenship that are necessary for agency and social and political participation. Digital spaces afford a mode of communication that allows the boundaries of the collective to be fluid, flexible and inclusive, and by creating avenues for direct participation and engagement (Kavada 2015). Therefore, digital spaces continue to be useful in collective organizing as they make mass mobilization within social movements (Polletta and Jasper 2001). In support of these spaces, Oyedemi (2015) argues that the concept of human rights, based on fairness, equality and justice, is relevant for the theorization of digital citizenship. By this, he introduces the concept of internet access as a fundamental citizen's right in the literature of digital citizenship.

Not all citizens have access to digital tools and connectivity. Access to technology is uneven between and within countries including along gendered lines in Nigeria. An empirical analysis of patterns of access in any population is necessary to understand how unequal access is structured (Roberts and

Hernandez 2019). Roberts and Hernandez argue that citizens' unequal access to digital technology is enabled or restricted by the five 'A's: availability, affordability, awareness, abilities and agency. These five 'A's are a useful analytic tool for understanding structural barriers to citizens' technology access. The framework allows for reflecting on the issue of technology access through the lens of five key elements:

Availability – to whom is technology connectivity available in this population?

Affordability – who can afford to make use of digital technologies?

Awareness – who is aware of the existence of specific technologies?

Abilities – what digital skills and capabilities exist to enable effective use?

Agency – who has self-efficacy and power within to utilize digital technologies?

The five 'A's are used in this chapter to analyse the disparities that exist in Nigerian women's access to digital technologies for civic participation and feminist action (Figure 5.1).

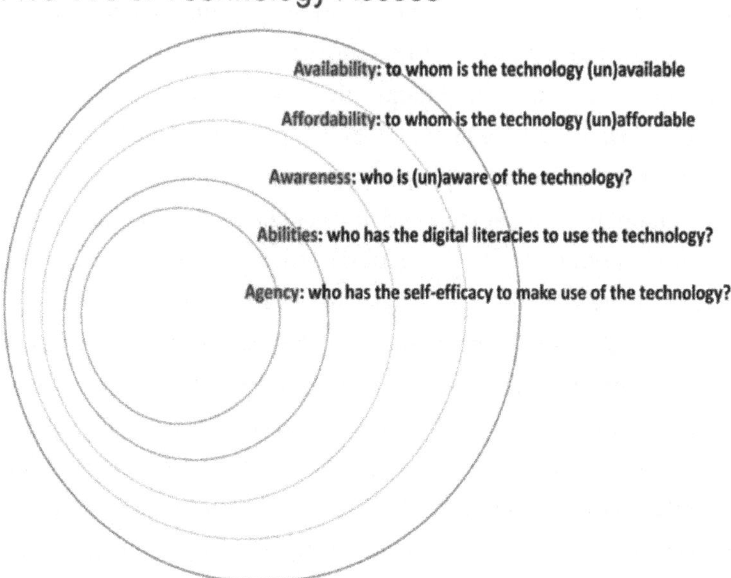

Figure 5.1 The five 'A's of technology access. *Source*: Roberts and Hernandez 2019.

Feminist digital citizenship

In this chapter, feminist digital citizenship is defined using cyber-feminist theories. Lister (2003) reflects on the need for a feminist understanding of citizenship, asserting that 'a feminist citizenship project thus encourages an approach to theory and practice that gives due accord to women's agency rather than simply seeing women as victims of discrimination and oppressive male-dominated political, economic, and social institutions' (Lister 2003: 6).

Cyberfeminism is a concept that began in the twentieth century, gathering feminists in the digital space to complement the work being done by feminists in the physical space calling for gender equality (Hall 1996). In the early 1990s, feminists started to organize online under cyberfeminism, bringing more women into a male-dominated space (Pollock and Sutton 1999). In *A Manifesto for Cyborgs*, Donna Haraway (1991) pioneers the idea of cyberfeminism – an alliance between women, machinery and new technology. In her view, cyberfeminism represents the future of feminism, which is the blurring of the boundaries between humans and machines that will eventually make the problematic and binary categories of female and male obsolete.

The foundation of cyberfeminism is the notion that futuristic technology will free its users from the limitations of the physical world, and by this, Haraway means the burden of being forced into identities that mirror social dichotomies of male/female and heterosexual/homosexual. This postmodernist ideology of the computer as a 'liberating utopia' that does not recognize gender, race, or sexuality is what Hall (1996) calls 'liberal cyberfeminism'. This contrasting perspective is grounded in a reality of the computer and new technologies as male-dominant, patriarchal tools and tools of female domination. Hall (1996) introduces the notion of radical cyberfeminism as a movement where women organize to create women-only spaces where participants can collaboratively construct an oppositional gender. Braidotti (2003) explains cyberfeminism as a movement created mainly by postmodern feminists, believing that knowledge is power, and aims to create a collective voice to challenge socially constructed gender norms. They seek to challenge gender norms by redefining gender roles in the digital space through this collective voice. Cyberfeminists use hashtags (#) to organize, raise awareness of gender inequality and mobilize resources to create transitional justice for all who face inequality (Flores et al. 2018).

Digital technologies have affordances that allow feminists to connect across local and transnational networks and build intersectional connections between diverse groups of feminists – essentially de-individualizing the ethos of neoliberalism and allowing new forms of communal organizing (McLean 2018). In this light, Baer (2016) argues that the digital facilitates the co-mingling of individual stories and collective modalities across national and transnational borders, rendering gender oppression visible on a global scale and connecting various feminist movements (Baer 2016: 18). Operating within the hegemony of neoliberalism, Baer asks if digital feminist activism can exist without co-option as a tool of neoliberal political action. Baer is concerned that the potentially toxic nature of the online space can divide as well as enable feminist solidarity (Baer 2016: 18). Boothroyd et al. (2017) are concerned that digital will also be a flourishing ground for counter-feminist ideas and the contradictory possibilities of feminist action pursued, either in part or entirely, in digital spaces.

More recent ideas on feminism in digital spaces contribute to the literature by reiterating that an open digital space is crucial to the production and promotion of dissenting feminist thoughts and action (Mapes 2016; Richardson 2000; Henry et al. 2021). Feminist scholars argue the lack of intersectionality and diversity existing within digital spaces creates versions of feminism that are not representing feminist diversity (Crenshaw 1989; Renfrow 2016). Digital spaces are sites where hosts of complex, nuanced feminist conversations occur. With uneven and unequal access to these sites, the more privileged have access to digital spaces (Van Dijk 2006) and therefore greater authority in debates. Hence, feminism discursively produced online is predominantly representative of these privileged groups that shape feminism more broadly (hooks 2000).

Drawing on the earlier conceptions of agency-based citizenship, rights-claiming digital citizenship and cyberfeminism, in this chapter, to analyse women's digital citizenship in the #BBOG and #ENDSARS campaigns I will use a conceptual framework based on women's agency, digital rights-claiming and cyber-feminist action.

The political context

On 1 October 1960, Nigeria became independent from its former colonist, the UK. The volatile nature of the civic space in Nigeria is rooted in colonization.

Britain's formal decolonisation of Nigeria, which lasted from 1960 to 1963, resulted in the partitioning of the country into three regions (north, west and east), creating division in access to public resources and favouring one region at the expense of the other as the northern region had a slightly higher population than the other two regions combined (Ibezim-Ohaeri 2017). During the period of transition from military rule to democracy, in 1960, political unrest, tensions and violent conflict characterized Nigeria's civic and public space. The period between 1993 and 1999 was characterized by arrest, imprisonment, murder and disappearances of those who spoke against the inhumanity of military rule in the country (Ojebode 2011). The final transition from military to civilian rule took place on 29 May 1999.

At the core of Nigeria's systemic problems is the crisis of governance, which manifests in the declining capacity of the state to cope with a range of internal political and social upheavals. Political elites consistently violate fundamental principles associated with liberal democratic systems – such as competitive elections, the rule of law and political freedom, often exploiting poverty and illiteracy to mobilize voters (Okoi and Iwara 2021). This suggests that Nigeria's political culture rewards incompetent leaders over reform-minded leaders who demonstrate the intellectualism and problem-solving capabilities needed to adequately address systemic issues of poverty and inequality (Elaigwu 2005).

Women's place within the public space

The Nigerian citizenship landscape can hardly be described as gender-inclusive (Agbalajobi 2010, Agbaje 2019). Globally, Nigeria ranks 185 out of 189 countries on the UN Women 'Women in Parliament' index, with 3.34 per cent representation in the lower or single house (2020), putting it among the lowest ten countries for the proportion of women in national parliaments globally (Inter-Parliamentary Union (IPU) 2020). In the 2019 general elections, women made up only 3.4 per cent of the elected officials in the House of Representatives as well as 7 per cent in the House of Senate post-2019 elections (IPU 2020). The Nigerian Senate's rejection of the Gender and Equal Opportunities Bill (2016) was a setback to the campaign for gender equality in the country (UN Women 2019) Despite these barriers, women have been active contributors to social and economic progress in Nigeria. Courtesy of digital technologies and voiceless sections of Nigerian society, including women and minority groups, have become empowered to the extent that they can adopt the technologies to amplify their voices. The #BBOG and #ENDSARS protests are women-led online protests that exemplify this increased digital citizenship among women in Nigeria (Feminist Coalition 2020).

The digital civic space in Nigeria

Since the introduction of the internet to Nigeria in 1996, its platform makes for a richer public/civic sphere and for opportunities to construct counter-publics and counter-discourses that shape the national political landscape (Nip 2004; Adomi 2005). In 2022, Nigeria had 105 million internet users. With Nigeria's population being over 261.7 million (World Bank 2022), internet penetration amounted to 51 per cent in 2020 and is set to reach 65.2 per cent in 2025. Several online campaigns against repressive government laws and activities have taken place on these platforms. One example is the #OccupyNigeria hashtag, which trended on Twitter and Facebook in 2012 to mobilize the public against an increase in fuel prices by the government. This chapter focuses on two other examples #BBOG and #ENDSARS (Egbunike 2018). The #NoToSocialMediaBill also trended in 2019 to protest the passing of legislation that sought to criminalize social media use for critical political commentary within the country (Oladapo and Ojebuyi 2017).

In 2019, CIVICUS downgraded the state of Nigeria's civic space from obstructed to repressed – a situation that is uncharacteristic for a democratic administration (CIVICUS 2019). As digital use increases across Nigeria, contestations within these spaces are also increasing. The Nigerian government allegedly uses surveillance technology to track and monitor citizens (Freedom House 2019; Ibezim-Ohaeri 2021; Roberts et al. 2021). On several occasions, the government has shut down access to internet services in multiple places and times (Jacob and Akpan 2015), claiming that these actions are to protect national security (Oladapo and Ojebode 2021). Digital rights in Nigeria are uncertain, as the president is yet to approve the Digital Rights Bill (2019) already passed by the National Assembly (Oladapo and Ojebode 2021) On 5 June 2021 the government implemented a nationwide shutdown of the social media platform Twitter after the platform deleted threatening tweets made by Nigeria's president Muhammadu Buhari. According to the Minister of Communications, the government's action was based on the 'litany of issues of misinformation and fake news caused by the social media platform in Nigeria' (BBC 2021).

The Bring Back Our Girls protests (#BBOG)

The #BBOG movement erupted in April 2014 following the abduction of 276 schoolgirls from Chibok Secondary School, north-east Nigeria, by the Boko Haram Islamist insurgency group. The organization opposes the Westernization of Nigerian society, which it claims is the cause of corruption and demands the formation of an Islamic state in Nigeria as the panacea (Akinola and Tell 2013). The kidnap of the 276 Chibok girls while in school was a statement of the group's grievances against Western education for women (Oriola 2017).

The objective of #BBOG was to put pressure on the government to rescue the abductees and prosecute the responsible group. Infuriated by the government's slow response to this gendered security challenge, the group organized a public protest on 30 April 2014 in Nigeria's capital, Abuja. Led by former minister Oby Ezekwesili, protests were held on the streets, on social media and even spread around the world, calling on the Nigerian government to take the necessary actions to secure the girls' release. The hashtags #BringBackOurGirls and #BBOG were used as a form of online activism and went viral on Twitter trending globally by May (BBC News 2014). Oby Ezekwesili and Aisha Yesufu have been described as co-founders and leaders of the movement (Uwazuruike 2021). The movement has yielded the return of more than 100 girls and extended its concern to include demands for good governance and advocacy for security concerns and kidnapping in Nigeria (Ojebode and Oladapo 2018). The movement, being women-led, represents a remarkable event in Nigeria, legitimizing women's active role in civic matters.

The #ENDSARS protests

#ENDSARS was a series of mass protests against police brutality in Nigeria. The protest takes its name from the hashtag started in 2017 as a Twitter campaign to demand the disbanding of the Special Anti-Robbery Squad (SARS) unit of the Nigerian Police Force (Ojedokun et al. 2021). SARS was a branch that came under the State Criminal Investigation and Intelligence Department (SCIID) established in late 1992 to detain, investigate and prosecute people involved in cybercrimes, armed robbery, fraud and kidnapping (Armed Conflict Location and Event Data Project 2021). The squad had been accused of several human rights violations, illegal 'stop and searches', illegal arrests and detentions, extrajudicial killings, sexual harassment of women, and brutalizing of young male Nigerians (Aluko 2021). In 2017, Nigerian youth took to the streets in a peaceful protest to spread awareness of SARS brutality, demanding that the unit be disbanded. The protests also moved to social media using the hashtag #ENDSARS (Ekoh and George 2021).

On 20 October 2020, video evidence emerged on social media showing the Nigerian police and army opening fire on unarmed protesters at Lekki Tollgate. It was alleged that the Nigerian army was sent by the government to repress the peaceful protest, which resulted in the death of twelve civilians (Olaoluwa 2020). The Nigerian government was also accused of arresting protesters, freezing the bank accounts of those identified as leaders of the protest and fining news agencies that reported the alleged shooting (Amnesty International 2020). #ENDSARS protests were staged internationally across Europe, the United States and major cities in Africa. Women also played a key role in these protests, such as Aisha Yesufu, the co-convener of the Bring Back Our Girls movement. A picture of Aisha protesting (wearing a hijab) soon became the iconic symbol for the movement (BBC 2020).

Barriers to technology access in Nigeria

If digital citizenship is understood as civic engagement via digital tools and in digital spaces, then understanding people's ability to access and use those digital tools and spaces is pertinent. Technology access or exclusion is central to understanding the factors that explain women's level of digital citizenship in Nigeria in the case of #ENDSARS and #BBOG. This chapter adopts Roberts and Hernandez's (2019) framework, the five 'A's of technology access – availability, affordability, awareness, abilities and agency – to understand

Nigerian women's ability to engage in digital citizenship. Four of the five categories were found to be particularly relevant to the study context.

Availability

Mobile and internet connectivity is not available in many rural areas of the country, acting as a substantial barrier to digital citizenship for millions of Nigerians. Access to internet connectivity remains unevenly distributed. Digital connectivity is unavailable in most rural communities of Borno, Jigawa Zamfara and Yobe in north-east Nigeria, where millions of citizens do not have electricity, cellular coverage or internet connection. These availability challenges often reflect and accentuate existing patterns of socio-economic (dis)advantage. Broadband internet connections and the fastest cellular connections are mainly found in relatively prosperous metropolitan areas such as Lagos, Abuja, Port Harcourt and Kano. Women, especially rural women, are often the least connected (Adomi 2005; Carboni et al. 2021).

Availability is unpredictable and intermittent, fluctuating as the power supply cuts in and out or as cellular coverage fluctuates. In my opinion, even when a citizen lives in an area where the internet is normally available, questions of reliability and quality remain. Consequently, this broadens the divide as it creates inequitable implications for civic participation as only certain sectors and classes of society have access to this privilege. Ahiakwo (2001) identified the main barriers to internet connectivity in Nigeria as a lack of adequate telecommunication infrastructure and poverty levels. However, in recent years, private sector investment has increased internet access and availability. Although some parts of the country still lack access and availability, increasing numbers of citizens are now able to access digital platforms.

Affordability

Even in areas where connectivity is available, many people cannot afford to access the internet. This is due to the high cost of the internet, lack of infrastructure like electricity and internet cafes are expensive to use. Broadband affordability in Nigeria has improved over time as a result of competition between service providers (Nigerian National Broadband Plan 2020). Nigeria ranks twenty-eighth (out of ninety-nine countries surveyed) on the 2019

Affordability Drivers Index (ADI). High-income disparity, persistent inflation and high unemployment make mobile internet connectivity unaffordable for most Nigerians. The situation is worse for women, who typically have less disposable income due to prevailing gender inequalities, which particularly affect women in rural areas (Adeosun and Owolabi 2021).

Abilities

The lack of digital skills can limit a person's ability to translate digital connectivity into active digital citizenship even when issues of availability, affordability and awareness have been addressed. There is a large gender gap in digital literacy in Nigeria (Carboni et al. 2021). As gender norms lead to the under-representation of women and girls in science, technology, engineering and mathematics (STEM), gender-inclusive programming may need to pay particular attention to the training needs of women and girls (UN 2011). Over recent years, there has been increased digital literacy training for girls in Nigeria by civil-society organizations. However, these initiatives are concentrated in urban areas (especially Lagos) where digital technologies are more readily available. As a result, women who have access to these initiatives tend to be those with a certain level of education, social status and class, while rural women remain excluded from these opportunities. Not all women are equally (dis)advantaged. However, women who do gain digital skills become empowered as a result, using those skills to access knowledge and information for civic participation (Adomi 2005).

Agency

Even when digital technologies are available and affordable, and women have the necessary awareness and abilities to make effective use of them, a lack of agency can still prevent women from engaging in digital citizenship (Archibong et al. 2021). With the presence of patriarchal social norms and cultures, gender discriminatory laws and policies, which persist in Nigerian society, women's agency is often limited. A large part of Nigerian tradition has subjugated women to the role of the caregiver (Oluyemi 2015). Even today, for many communities and individuals, a woman's 'place' is considered to be at home. All their lives, women are told they do not belong in civic spaces and that their voices do not matter. The continuous perpetuation of women in this light has reinforced a position of inferiority. The effect of this marginalization has led women to internalize feelings of inferiority and low self-esteem (Chuku 2009). However, emerging women-led activism and large-scale protests against injustice in the digital space are proof that this trend is changing. Feminist ideologies have progressed in Nigeria (Zukas 2009) and even more with digital. And as more women have access to education, knowledge and information, this leads to increased empowerment, opportunities and agency.

#BBOG protest – A claim for citizenship rights

Active citizenship is described as the claiming of rights and participation in civil, political, economic, social and cultural aspects of society (Lister 1998, Jones and Gaventa 2004, Roberts 2004). The determinants of access to as well as the nature and quality of participation within the public and civic spheres are often important definers of the experiences and citizenship participation of marginalized groups (McLean 2019). For the #BBOG protest, the rights claim was simple: a demand for the safe return of the abducted girls to their families. The protesters were advocating for their right to safety and justice for the girls' families. Having been denied justice for the loss and kidnap of their daughters when complaining in traditional civic spaces, the #BBOG protesters began expressing their citizenship on social media, most notably on Twitter. The interest of the Chibok girls and their families was not sufficiently prioritized by the government. The historical inability of Nigeria's government to provide basic security or effective services triggered anger and distrust that the government would do anything about the Chibok kidnap (Ragozzino 2021). The participants displayed an awareness of their basic rights as citizens and used their agency to hold the government accountable, making rights claims that meet the definition of citizenship as rights-claiming and agency-based (Lister 1998; Gaventa 2002). It also reveals an awareness of the capability of digital media and technologies for virality, to force the government to pay attention to their needs. The use of social media amplified the reach of the campaigners and enabled them to secure solidarity from millions of Nigerians and supporters from around the world.

Through the protests, the aggrieved families and their allies exerted their digital citizenship to claim rights in a situation where some felt powerless to influence domestic politics, drawing international attention to a situation that reflected patriarchal innuendos in the civic space, which was male-dominated and not in favour of the women in question proven by the government's slow response to the situation and their inability to successfully negotiate the release of the Chibok girls. A space has been predominantly male-dominated, and women have no voice or agency to make their demands heard until digital tools enable them to mobilize millions of supporters around the world.

#ENDSARS

In the case of #ENDSARS, we see the same trend of marginalization and defiance of the rights of a section of society manifested by the lackadaisical and nonchalant point that the government was non-responsive to citizens in both cases (until they used digital tools to grow their support and lend weight to their rights-claiming). In this case, the aggrieved group was young people who were victims of police brutalization by SARS and who decided to hold protests to fight for a better Nigeria. Nigeria's high inflation rates, security challenges, rising unemployment rates, ineffective governance and government distrust, combined with the large youth population, triggered the protests, with those involved claiming their rights to security and freedom of movement. Phrases like 'Stop Killing Us' were consistently posted on social media.

The pent-up rage of many of the country's youth and women over unfair profiling and harassment by SARS found an outlet in these protests, which started with no defined or central leadership. The protesters' demands at the beginning were for the government to abolish SARS, provide justice to victims of police brutality and reform the police. However, their demands widened, premised on the pervasive failure of the government to deliver equitable economic prosperity for citizens, which enraged youth in particular.

The protests evolved from a single focus on the abuses perpetrated by the SARS unit to claiming rights to employment opportunities, political participation for youth and women, economic development and good governance. The slogan of the protest became Soro Soke, which in Yoruba means 'Speak Up'. Soon, the message of the #ENDSARS protest became that young Nigerians wanted to speak up against inequality, corrupt practices by elite government officials that perpetually act against citizens' interests, to take back their country from the entrenched political order that they believe has not served their interests. Against this background, the #ENDSARS protests have become a symbol of broader resentment and opened the path for marginalized Nigerian youths to vent pent-up grievances against the government, starting with the excesses of SARS, which the government has failed to address after several promises of reform. This is a valid display of citizenship, in line with our framing of the term as agency-based actions for the claiming and recognition of human rights (Lister 1998; Gaventa 2002).

Alternative safe space for women

Women's contributions to Nigeria's history have been written out of history. Nigerian women have always played a major role in all social and economic activities (Adeosun and Owolabi 2021). There is evidence of the political influence of women dating back to the precolonial era. From the Borno women, who occupied important administrative positions in the royal family in the precolonial era, to Queen Bakwa Turk, who founded the Modern Zaria, the contributions of women in Nigeria's political history can also be found in the Aba women's riot of 1929 against colonial repression (Zukas 2009) during which at least fifty women were killed. Even though some narratives maintain that these women were violent and unlawful, they were merely fighting against the oppression imposed on them by colonialism (Adeosun and Owolabi 2021).

Young women in Nigeria represent a group that is even more marginalized in their access to top political leadership and participation based on their gender and age. The patriarchal nature of the Nigerian political arena is dominated by middle-aged and old men, predominantly from the northern parts of the country (Abah and Okwori 2009: 27).

Reflecting on the messaging of both #ENDSARS and #BBOG is useful in analysing women's agency and power in these situations. The most frequent theme comes from the grievances relating to the denial of rights and freedoms. The lack of rights to security and safety in the Nigerian public space limits citizens' ability to engage in democratic processes, which the presence of safe public spaces fosters. This shrinking of civic space offline created the need to create civic space online (Roberts and Mohamed Ali 2021). By moving online, activists created a safer realm of expression for women, which explains women increased civic participation in the digital space. This notion is in line with the framing of cyberfeminism as a creation of alternative safe spaces for women in cyberspace where they can collectively advocate for the issues that concern them (Haraway 1991).

Increased feminist consciousness

Over the last fifty years, there has been increased feminist consciousness among women in Nigeria. This is evidenced by the evolution of the feminist community and feminist organizations in Nigeria. The oldest and largest women's movement in Nigeria is the National Council of Women's Societies (NCWS), founded in early 1958 (Madunagu 2008). According to Basu's (1995) statement of the NCWS:

> an unarmed movement, that is non-confrontational. It is a movement for the progressive upliftment of women for motherhood, nationhood, and development. This movement is 'at home' with the protection of our culture and tradition as well as with the supremacy of men. It will not rock the boat. (Madunagu 2008)

This reveals that the feminist movement in Nigeria evolved from being complacent to becoming more radical, consistent and organized, with clear objectives and ideology as we can see in recent times. The first national feminist movement was inaugurated in 1982, at a national conference held at Ahmadu Bello University. It came into being with the inauguration, in 1983, of the organization Women in Nigeria (WIN) following the 1982 national conference on the same theme (Madunagu 2008). The papers presented at this event indicate a growing awareness by Nigeria's university-educated women that the place of women in society required a concerted effort and a place on the national agenda: the public perception (Madunagu 2008). WIN achieved many successes and established the groundwork for feminist activism in Nigeria. Nigerian feminists along with various institutions have been at the forefront of influencing the state to annul policies that are against the interest of women. The increased female education and political participation of women, abolishment of female genital mutilation and reproductive healthcare for women were the successes of the feminist movement in Nigeria. Over the years, more women-centred NGOs have taken up women's issues.

In the #BBOG and #ENDSARS campaigns, one of the main themes is the notion of agency and feminist consciousness – that women are in charge of their destiny and have to believe this as a precondition for any change in their situation. However, it is difficult to say that these protests themselves sparked increased feminist consciousness, as most of those who joined in the protests were women and people who had personal stakes in the outcomes: including victims' families, an abductee's relative, owner of a threatened roadside business or residents of a neighbourhood marked for demolition (Ojebode 2018). Through the #ENDSARS protest being predominantly led by women, we see the female participants comfortable with protesting online and offline, regardless of security issues.

Mass mobilization for collective action

The #ENDSARS movement mobilized one of the world's largest Black youth populations to protest against government oppression. The Feminist Coalition – a women-led NGO campaigning for gender equality in Nigeria – played an instrumental role in sustaining the protest, and over the course of the protest, they raised over eighty million naira through crowdfunding towards supporting the protest with food, legal and medical aid (Okunola 2021). Even after the protests ended, they continued to cover legal and health costs. Women of the Nigerian feminist coalition were at the forefront of the negotiations with the government, and media postings of the protest published comprehensive documentation of how the donations were spent (Feminist Coalition 2021). Their level of organization, accountability and the urgency with which they delivered real-time security updates for participants are evidence of the impact of mass collectivization, leadership and action, which took the form of multiple councils, meetings and contributions towards making a difference based on feminist values and ideologies.

Reflecting on the above and the entire movement reveals that in Nigeria, with its history and root problems of gender discrimination and ethno-religious divides, the #ENDSARS movement proved women's willingness to exercise agency and citizenship rights, and this time leveraging the power of social media and digital tools to collectivize in an organized united front and successfully garnering global attention. This reveals the expression of the thirst for active citizenship engagements by a group that had been marginalized by egocentric and incompetent leadership, revealing a working nation and, more importantly, the change that young people in Nigeria are demanding.

Conclusion

This chapter set out to analyse women's access to digital technologies in Nigeria and how they have used it for feminist action and citizenship rights. I explored the issues restricting women's digital citizenship using case studies #BBOG to #ENDSARS through a unique conceptual framework combining elements of the five 'A's, digital citizenship and cyberfeminism. The research showed that factors explaining women's increased digital citizenship included increased access to technology, increased rights violations and the safety of online spaces enabling more visible, feminist agency. The digital space afforded the power to voices that were unable to secure government action in the offline public sphere. The opening up of digital spaces allowed Nigerian feminists to use social networks, including sites like Facebook and Twitter to organize impactful protests and campaigns against injustices.

The five 'A's proved to be useful analytically in showing how increased (but uneven) access to digital technologies advantaged some groups but left others behind. The digital citizenship lens proved useful analytically to show how these spaces were used for agency-based rights-claiming to demand responsive government and social justice. Finally, the cyberfeminism lens improved the analysis by showing how the safety of online spaces compared to male-dominant offline spaces enabled a new brand of digital feminist agency to emerge as experienced in the leadership of the #BBOG and #ENDSARS campaigns. These campaigns were qualitatively different from and significantly more successful than the offline patriarchal demonstrations that preceded them and failed to secure government action. I argue that none of these analytical elements alone could have produced this analysis in isolation and that it was only by combining all three that a comprehensive analysis was possible.

Agency is a recurrent theme across the analysis of the case studies foregrounded by the analytical framework of technology access, digital citizenship and cyberfeminism. There exists a sense of growing sense of citizen agency, which leads to positive collective action to claim rights and change people's social circumstances. This growing practice of citizenship and digital citizenship takes the form of offline and online protests that avoid the ethnic and gender divisions that weaken other social movements.

Arising from this analysis, the following recommendations for policy, practice and further research emerge. The government of Nigeria needs to ensure that all citizens have equal and unrestricted access to civic space and are free to air their grievances without the need to resort to violence. More specifically, women's issues need to be recognized and women's voices should be heard. Moving forward, access to and participation in digital citizenship should be recognized as part of the broader issues of civil rights and gender equality in society, and this should be reflected in policymaking processes across all levels of government.

Much research has explored the shrinking of civic space in contested settings like Nigeria (Roberts 2021). However, we can see that even as the civic space is shrinking, citizens make creative use of digital tools and spaces to claim rights and express citizenship. Civic space is not just shrinking but dynamically changing. Further research is needed to document and analyse the changing dynamics of digital civic spaces and what that means for people who have less and less access to digital technologies. Gender access gaps must be bridged to ensure that all citizens have unrestricted access to digital citizenship.

Bibliography

ActionAid (2013) *Making Care Visible: Women's Unpaid Care Work in Nepal, Nigeria, Uganda and Kenya*, Johannesburg: ActionAid International, accessed 12 July 2021.

Adaji, S. (2017) 'Women and Non-Passage of the 35% Affirmative Action Bill', *Nigeria Parliamentarians, Lawyers Alert*, accessed 15 December 2020.

Adeosun, O. T. and K. E. Owolabi (2021) 'Gender Inequality: Determinants and Outcomes in Nigeria', *Journal of Business and Socio-Economic Development*. https://doi.org/10.1108/JBSED-01-2021-0007.

Adeoye, A. (2019) *Bring Back Our Girls Activist Oby Ezekwesili Withdraws from Nigeria's Presidential Race.* https://www.cnn.com/2019/01/24/africa/oby-ezekwesili -quits-nigeria-elections.

Adomi, E. E. (2005) 'Internet Development and Connectivity in Nigeria', *Program*, 39 (3): 257–68. http://doi.org/10.1108/00330330510610591.

Afolabi CY (2019) 'The Invisibility of Women's Organizations in Decision Making Process and Governance in Nigeria', *Frontiers in Sociology*, 3: 40. doi:10.3389/ fsoc.2018.00040.

Agbaje, F. I. (2019) 'Colonialism and Gender in Africa: A Critical History', in *The Palgrave Handbook of African Women's Studies*, 1275–94, London: Palgrave MacMillan.

Agbalajobi, T. (2010) 'Women's Participation and the Political Process in Nigeria: Problems and Prospects', *African Journal of Political Science and International Relations*, 4 (2): 75–82.

Ajayi, K. (2005) 'Women in Politics', Presented at the Symposium on the Role of Women in Politics, University of Ado Ekiti, Nigeria.

Akinola, A. O. and O. Tella (2013) 'Boko Haram Terrorism and Nigeria's Security Dilemma: Rethinking the State's Capacity', *International Journal of Innovative Social Sciences and Humanities Research*, 1 (2): 70–8.

Aluko, O. A. (2021) 'Leadership and Governance Crisis in Nigeria: The Case of the #Endsars Protest', *Journal of Public Administration and Governance*, 11 (2): 246–57. http://doi.org/10.5296/jpag.v11i2.18733.

Amnesty International (2020) 'Nigeria: The Lekki Toll Gate Massacre – New Investigative Timeline', Amnesty International website. https://www.amnesty.org /en/latest/news/2020/10/nigeria-the-lekki-toll-gate-massacre-new-investigative -timeline/.

Archibong, B. and N. Obikili (2021) 'When Women March: The 1929 Aba Women's Tax Revolt, and Gender Gaps in Political Participation in Nigeria'. Presented at the Harvard University Seminar in Economic Development, jointly sponsored with the Massachusetts Institute of Technology, 15 April.

Armed Conflict Location & Event Data Project (2021) *Lessons From the #EndSARS Movement in Nigeria*, Armed Conflict Location & Event Data Project, accessed 15 October 2021.

Ash, J., R. Kitchin, and A. Leszczynski (2016) 'Digital Turn, Digital Geographies?' *Progress in Human Geography*, 42 (1): 25–43. https://doi.org/10.1177 /0309132516664800.

Ashiakwo, C. (2001) 'The Role of Internet Connectivity in Nigeria', *African Journal of Science and Technology*, 2 (1): 164–6.

Ashraf, D. and I. Farah (2007) 'Education and Women's Empowerment: Re-examining the Relationship', *Education, Gender and Empowerment: Perspectives From South Asia*, 15–31.

Baer, H. (2016) 'Redoing Feminism: Digital Activism, Body Politics, and Neoliberalism', *Feminist Media Studies*, 16 (1): 17–34. doi:10.1080/14680777.2015.1093070.

Basu, A. (ed.) (1995) *The Challenge of Local Feminisms: Women's Movements in Global Perspective*, Boulder: Westview Press.

BBC (2014) 'Abducted Nigerian Girls: Mothers Hold Demonstration in Abuja', BBC News website. https://www.bbc.co.uk/news/av/world-africa-27228994.

BBC (2020) 'Nigeria: Aisha Yesufu on the End SARS Protests', BBC Focus on Africa website. https://www.bbc.co.uk/programmes/p08ynt32.

BBC (2021) 'Nigeria's Twitter Ban: Government Orders Prosecution of Violators', BBC News website. https://www.bbc.co.uk/news/world-africa-57368535.

Bellah, R., R. Madsen, W. M. Sullivan, A. Swidler, and S. M. Tiptonet (1985) *Habits of the Heart: Individualism and Commitment in American Life*, California: University of California Press.

Bennett, W. L. and A. Segerberg (2011) 'Digital Media and the Personalization of Collective Action', *Information, Communication & Society*, 14: 770–99. doi:10.1080/1369118X.2011.579141.

Berlin, I. (1958) *Two Concepts of Liberty*, Oxford: Clarendon Press.

Boothroyd, S. et al. (2017) '(Re)producing Feminine Bodies: Emergent Spaces Through Contestation in the Women's March on Washington', *Gender, Place & Culture*, 24 (5): 711–21. https://doi.org/10.1080/0966369X.2017.1339673.

Boyd, D. (2011) 'Social Network Sites as Networked Publics: Affordances, Dynamics, and Implications', in Z. Papacharissi (ed.), *A Networked Self: Identity, Community, and Culture on Social Network Sites*, 39–58, New York: Routledge.

Braidotti, R. (2003) 'Cyberfeminism with a Difference', in M. Peters, M. Olssen, and C. Lankshear (eds), *Futures of Critical Theory: Dreams of Difference*, 239–61, Washington, DC: Rowman & Littlefield.

British Council Nigeria (2012) *Gender in Nigeria Report 2012: Improving the Lives of Girls and Women in Nigeria*, accessed 13 October 2021.

Buyse, A. (2018) 'Squeezing Civic Space: Restrictions on Civil Society Organizations and the Linkages with Human Rights', *The International Journal of Human Rights*, 22 (8): 966–88, doi:10.1080/13642987.201.1492916.

Carboni, I., N. Jeffrie, D. Lindsey, M. Shanahan, and C. Sibthorpe (2021) *GSMA Connected Women: The Mobile Gender Gap Report 2021*, London: GSMA, accessed 12 October 2021.

Chuku, G. (2009) 'Igbo Women and Political Participation in Nigeria, 1800s–2005'. *The International Journal of African Historical Studies*, 42 (1): 81–103.

CIVICUS (2019) 'Nigeria Downgraded in New CIVICUS Monitor Report After an Increase in Restrictions on Civic Space', *CIVICUS Press Release*, 4 December, accessed 13 October 2021.

Crenshaw, K. (1989). 'Demarginalising the Intersection of Race and Sex: A Black Feminist Critique of Antidiscrimination Doctrine and Antiracist Politics', *University of Chicago Legal Forum*, 1989: 139–67.

Earl, J. and K. Kimport (2011) *Digitally Enabled Social Change: Activism in the Internet Age*, Cambridge, MA: MIT Press.

Egbunike, N. (2018) *Hashtags: Social Media, Politics and Ethnicity in Nigeria*, Lagos: Narrative Landscape Press.

Ekine, S. (ed.) (2010) *SMS Uprising: Mobile Activism in Africa*, Cape Town: Pambazuka Press.

Ekoh, P. C. and E. O. George (2021) 'The Role of Digital Technology in the EndSars Protest in Nigeria During COVID-19 Pandemic', *Journal of Human Rights and Social Work*, 6: 161–2. http://doi.org/10.1007/s41134-021-00161-5.

Elaigwu, J. I. (2005) *The Politics of Federalism in Nigeria*. Jos: Aha Publishing House.

Falola, O. (2007) 'The Role of Nigerian Women', *Encyclopaedia Britannica*, accessed 22 December 2020.

Feminist Coalition (2020) 'In Our Own Words: The Feminist Coalition', *Medium*, December 17, accessed May 2021, https://feministcoalition.medium.com/in-our -own-words-the-feminist-coalition-61bc658446dd.

Feminist Coalition (2020) https://feministcoalition2020.com/.

Flores, P., N. R. Gómez, A. F. Roa, and R. Whitson (2018) 'Reviving Feminism Through Social Media: From the Classroom to Online and Offline Public Spaces', *Gender and Education*, 32 (6): 751–66. https://doi.org/10.1080/09540253.2018 .1513454.

Freedom House (2019) *Freedom in the World*, accessed 2 May 2021.

Gaventa, J. (2002) 'Exploring Citizenship, Participation and Accountability', *IDS Bulletin*, 33 (2): 1–14. https://opendocs.ids.ac.uk/opendocs/handle/20.500.12413 /8655.

Hall, K. (1996) 'Cyberfeminism', in S. C. Herring (ed.), *Computer-Mediated Communication: Linguistic, Social, and Cross-Cultural Perspectives*, 147–70, Amsterdam: John Benjamins Publishing Co.

Haraway, D. (1991) *Simians, Cyborgs, and Women – The Reinvention of Nature*, London: Routledge.

Henry, N. et al. (2021) 'Digital Citizenship in a Global Society: A Feminist Approach', *Feminist Media Studies*. https://www-tandfonline-com.ezproxy.uct.ac.za/doi/full /10.1080/14680777.2021.1937269.

Hermes, J. (2006) 'Citizenship in the Age of the Internet', *European Journal of Communication*, 21 (3): 295–309.

Hernandez, K. and T. Roberts (2018) *Leaving No One Behind in a Digital World*, K4D Emerging Issues Report, Brighton: Institute of Development Studies, accessed 13 October 2021.

hooks, b. (2000) *Feminism Is for Everybody: Passionate Politics*, Cambridge, MA: South End Books.

Human Rights Watch (2021) 'Nigeria: A Year On, No Justice for #EndSARS Crackdown', Human Rights Watch website. https://www.hrw.org/news/2021/10/19 /nigeria-year-no-justice-endsars-crackdown.

Ibezim-Ohaeri, V. (2017) 'Confronting Closing Civic Spaces in Nigeria', *SUR International Journal on Human Rights*, 14 (26): 129–40. https://ssrn.com/abstract =3396581.

Ibezim-Ohaeri, V., J. Olufemi, L. Nwodo, O. Olufemi, N. Juba-Nwosu, TIER (2021) *Security Playbook of Digital Authoritarianism in Nigeria*, Lagos: Action Group on Free Civic Space.

Inter-Parliamentary Union (IPU) (2020) 'Women in Politics 2020: Situation on 2 January 2020', accessed 12 July 2021.

Irazábal, C. (2008) *Ordinary Places, Extraordinary Events: Citizenship, Democracy, and Public Space in Latin America*, Abingdon: Routledge.

Jacob, J. and I. Akpan (2015) 'Silencing Boko Haram: Mobile Phone Blackout and Counterinsurgency in Nigeria's Northeast Region', *Stability: International Journal of Security & Development*, 4 (1): art. 8. http://dx.doi.org/10.5334/ sta.ey.

Janoski, T. (1998) *Citizenship and Civil Society: A Framework of Rights and Obligations in Liberal, Traditional, and Social Democratic Regimes*, New York: Cambridge University Press.

Jones, E. and J. Gaventa (2004) *Concepts of Citizenship: A Review*, Brighton: Institute of Development Studies, accessed 13 October 2021.

Jupp, V. (2006) *The SAGE Dictionary of Social Research Methods*, London: SAGE Publications Ltd. doi:10.4135/9780857020116.

Kabeer, N. (2002) 'Citizenship, Affiliation, and Exclusion: Perspectives From the South', *IDS Bulletin*, 33 (2): 1–15, accessed 13 October 2021.

Kabeer, N. (2005) *Inclusive Citizenship: Meanings and Expressions*, London: Zed Books.

Kavada, A. (2015) 'Creating the Collective: Social Media, the Occupy Movement, and Its Constitution as a Collective Actor', *Information, Communication & Society*, 18: 872–86. doi:10.1080/1369118X.2015.1043318

Khazraee, E. and Novak, A. N. (2018) 'Digitally Mediated Protest: Social Media Affordances for Collective Identity Construction', *Social Media + Society*, 4 (1). doi:10.1177/2056305118765740

Kolawole, O. (2020) 'Nigerians May Have a Hard Time Meeting New SIM Registration Requirements in 2020', *Techpoint Africa*, 11 February, accessed 13 October 2021.

Kolawole, T.; K. Adeigbe, A. A. Adebayo, and M. B. Abubakar (2013) 'Women Participation in the Political Process in Nigeria', *Centrepoint Journal (Humanities Edition)*, 2: 15.

Lister, R. (1997) 'Citizenship: Towards a Feminist Synthesis', *Feminist Review*, 57 (1): 28–48.

Lister, R. (2003) *Citizenship: Feminist Perspectives*, London: Palgrave Macmillan.

Lister, R. (2012) 'Citizenship and Gender', in E. Amenta, K. Nash and A. Scott (eds), *The Wiley-Blackwell Companion to Political Sociology*, New Jersey: Blackwall Publishing. doi:10.1002/9781444355093.

Loza, S. (2014) 'Hashtag Feminism, #SolidarityIsForWhiteWomen, and the Other #FemFuture', *Ada: A Journal of Gender, New Media, & Technology*, 5. doi:10.7264/N337770V.

Madunagu, B. E. (2008) 'The Nigerian Feminist Movement: Lessons From "Women in Nigeria", WIN', *Review of African Political Economy*, 35 (118): 666–72. www.jstor.org/stable/20406565.

Mamdani, M. (1996) *Citizen and Subjects: Contemporary Africa and the Legacy of Late Colonialism*, Princeton: Princeton University Press.

Mamdani, M. (ed.) (2000) *Beyond Rights Talk and Culture Talk: Comparative Essays on the Politics of Rights and Culture*, Cape Town: David Philip Publishers.

Mansell, R. (2002) 'From Digital Divides to Digital Entitlements in Knowledge Societies', *Current Sociology*, 50: 407–26.

Mapes, M. (2016) 'Globalized Backlash: Women Against Feminism's New Media Matrix of (Anti) Feminist Testimony', PhD thesis, Southern Illinois University, accessed 14 October 2021.

Marshall, T. H. (1950) *Citizenship and Social Class*, Cambridge: Cambridge University Press.

Marshall, T. H. (2009) 'Citizenship and Social Class', in J. Manza and M. Sauder (eds), *Inequality and Society: Social Science Perspectives on Social Stratification*, 148–54, New York: W.W. Norton and Co.

McGee, R., D. Edwards, H. Hudson, C. Anderson, and F. Feruglio (2018) *Appropriating Technology for Accountability: Messages from Making All Voices Count*, Brighton: Institute of Development Studies.

McLean, J. (2019) 'Feminist Digital Spaces', chapter in McLean, J. (2020) *Changing Digital Geographies*, Cambridge: Palgrave Macmillan. https://doi.org/10.1007/978 -3-030-28307-0_9.

McLean, N. (2018) 'Rethinking Publics and Participation in a Digital Era: A Case Study of HOLAA! and African Queer Women's Digital Interactions', *Empowering Women for Gender Equity*, 32 (2): 70–5. https://www.tandfonline.com/doi/abs/10 .1080/10130950.2018.1445345.

Molyneux, M. et al. (2021) *New Feminist Activism, Waves and Generations*.https:// www.unwomen.org/en/digital-library/publications/2021/05/discussion-paper-new -feminist-activism-waves-and-generations

Mossberger, K., J. Tolbert, and S. McNeal (2008) *Digital Citizenship: The Internet, Society, and Participation*, Cambridge, MA: MIT Press.

Nazneen, S. (2020) 'Feminist Methodologies', *Gender and Development Course Session/Gender Space*. https://web.microsoftstream.com/video/056f6fb7-0944 -4c10-afd6-a293b9f35ff5.

Nigerian National Broadband Plan (2020) 'Nigerian National Broadband Plan 2020– 2025', Federal Government of Nigeria, Abuja, https://www.ncc.gov.ng/documents /880-nigerian-national-broadband-plan-2020-2025/file.

Nip, J. Y. M. (2004) 'The Relationship Between Online and Offline Communities: The Case of the Queer Sisters', *Media, Culture & Society*, 26 (3): 409–28. https://doi.org /10.1177/0163443704042262.

Nyamu-Musembi, C. (2005) 'Towards an Actor-Oriented Perspective on Human Rights', in N. Kabeer (ed.), *Inclusive Citizenship: Meanings and Expressions*, 149–66, London: Zed Books.

Odutola, A. (2020) 'CBN Receives Order to Freeze Bank Accounts of 20 #ENDSARS Sponsors', *Nairametrics*, 7 November, accessed 9 July 2021.

Ojebode, A. (2018) 'How Bring Back Our Girls Went from Hashtag to Social Movement, While Rejecting Funding from Donors', *FP2P/Oxfam Blog*, 10 October, accessed 12 July 2021.

Ojebode A. (2011) 'Nigeria's Freedom of Information Act: Provisions, Strengths, Challenges', *African Communication Research*, 4 (2): 267–84. https:// d1wqtxts1xzle7.cloudfront.net/31731980/Nigerias_FOI--Ojebode-libre.pdf ?1392397200=&response-content-disposition=inline%3B+filename%3DNigeria _s_freedom_of_information_act_Pro.pdf&Expires=1671717538&Signature=UT2 BwCZUU3CquTecsPaEKo09BtGXjqVhNx1MGyLxtU8vKjZVAGhBsPpMzhM CpU5W1Mm2oRWt431Zif2lZNw9~XVgvfSmsfq2K-9nvKAm-ozM8obvu1Bs 3POxIOS7L88~y~BWvTQ1mDxjt9WmNaQxBuwmopCNHcrAw0MjvUB4O tV7MWg-8SgbxOH2AvWxaYTZ8GMIGI73r0CaimlK2yT78YD1Wt0rpT3X9uR bezrFpalDP~hlTVZTdnboEve5UgrnnUTgXD7vmwFzjTNYHOX0Mwo2XdmIs

dbAhoKpj2noehU38-YuxQqmfNeGK8eL242xFgdHem64e70drn-B~AWT0g__
&Key-Pair-Id=APKAJLOHF5GGSLRBV4ZA.

Ojebode, A. and W. Oladapo (2018) 'Using Social Media for Long-Haul Activism: Lessons from the BBOG Movement in Nigeria', Briefing, Partnership for African Social Governance Research.

Ojedokun, U. A., Y. O. Ogunleye, and A. A. Aderinto (2021) 'Mass Mobilization for Police Accountability: The Case of Nigeria's #EndSARS Protest', *Policing: A Journal of Policy and Practice*, 15 (3): 1894–903. https://doi.org/10.1093/police/paab001

Ojo, O. (2010) *Challenges of Sustainable Democracy in Nigeria*, Ibadan: John Archers Publishers.

Oke, L. (2015) 'Democracy, Women's Political Participation and the Policy Environment in Nigeria', *Developing Country Studies*, 5 (10). https://www.iiste.org/Journals/index.php/DCS/article/view/22466/22679.

Okoi, O. and M. Iwara (2021) 'The Failure of Governance in Nigeria: An Epistocratic Challenge', *Georgetown Journal of International Affairs*, 12 April, accessed 14 October 2021.

Okoli, A. and N. Stephen (2019) 'Boko Haram Insurgency and Gendered Victimhood: Women as Corporal Victims and Objects of War', *Small Wars & Insurgencies*, 30 (6–7): 1214–32.

Okunola, A. (2021) 'Nigeria's Feminist Coalition Wants Women in Positions of Power. But Why Is That Important?' Global Citizen website. https://www.globalcitizen.org/en/content/feminist-coalition-nigeria-women-power-equality/.

Okwori, J. and O. Abah (2009) *Democracy, Citizenship and Conflict in Nigeria: Towards Making Governance Work for the People*, TFDC Policy Briefing No.3, Brighton: Institute of Development Studies.

Oladapo, O. and A. Ojebode (2021) 'Nigeria Digital Rights Landscape Report', in T. Roberts (ed.), *Digital Rights in Closing Civic Space: Lessons from Ten African Countries*, Brighton: Institute of Development Studies, accessed 14 October 2021.

Oladapo, O. A. and B. R. Ojebuyi (2017) 'Nature and Outcome of Nigeria's #NoToSocialMediaBill Twitter Protest Against the Frivolous Petitions Bill 2015', in O. Nelson, B. R. Ojebuyi and A. Salawu (eds), *Impacts of the Media on African Socio-Economic Development*, 49–63, Hershey PA: IGI Global.

Olaoluwa, A. (2020) 'End Sars Protests: The Nigerian Women Leading the Fight for Change', *BBC News*, 1 December, accessed 17 July 2021.

Olowogboyega, O. (2020) 'Nigeria's SIM Card Registration Laws Are "Invasive", New Report Says', *TechCabal*, 10 January, accessed 15 October 2021.

Olugbemi, V. (2011) 'Women and Political Development in Nigeria Since 1960', in A. A. Agagu and R. F. Ola (eds), *Development Agenda of the Nigerian State*, 73–95, Akure: Lord Keynes Publishing Company.

Oluyemi, M. (2016) *Monitoring Participation of Women in Politics in Nigeria*. Presentation to Sixth Global Forum on Gender Statistics Finland. https://mdgs.un .org/unsd/gender/Finland_Oct2016/Documents/Nigeria_ppt.pdf.

Oluyemi, O. (2015) 'Monitoring Participation of Women in Politics in Nigeria', *National Bureau of Statistics*, accessed 19 December 2020.

O'Neil, C. (2017) *Weapons of Math Destruction: How Big Data Increases Inequality and Threatens Democracy*, London: Penguin Books.

Oriola, T. (2017) '"Unwilling Cocoons": Boko Haram's War Against Women', *Studies in Conflict & Terrorism*, 40 (2): 99–121.

Orisadare, A. (2018) 'An Assessment of the Role of Women Group in Women Political Participation, and Economic Development in Nigeria', *Frontiers in Sociology* 4 (32). https://www.frontiersin.org/articles/10.3389/fsoc.2019.00052/ full

Oyedemi, T. (2015) 'Internet Access as Citizen's Right? Citizenship in the Digital Age', *Citizenship Studies*, 19 (3–4): 450–64.

Oyedemi, T. D. (2020) 'The Theory of Digital Citizenship', in *Handbook of Communication for Development and Social Change*, 237–55, Singapore: Springer.

Oyedemi, T. T. D. (2012) 'The Partially Digital: Internet, Citizenship, Social Inequalities, and Digital Citizenship in South Africa', Doctoral Dissertations Available from Proquest. AAI3518402. https://scholarworks.umass.edu/ dissertations/AAI3518402.

Pateman, C. (1970) *Participation and Democratic Theory*, New York: Cambridge University Press.

Polletta, F. and J. M. Jasper (2001) 'Collective Identity and Social Movements', *Annual Review of Sociology*, 27: 283–305.

Pollock, S. and J. Sutton (1999) 'Women Click: Feminism and the Internet', in S. Hawthorne and R. Klein (eds), *CyberFeminism: Connectivity, Critique and Creativity*, Melbourne: Spinifex Press Pty Ltd.

Ragozzino, A. (2021) 'Hundreds of Nigerian Students Kidnapped . . . Again: Is Nigeria a Failed State?' Global Risk Insight website. https://globalriskinsights.com/2021/04 /hundreds-of-nigerian-students-kidnapped-again-is-nigeria-a-failed-state/.

Renfrow, D. (2016) *Intersectionality: Theory, Methodology, and Practice*, London: Routledge.

Reynolds-Stenson, H. (2017) 'Protesting the Police: Anti-Police Brutality Claims as a Predictor of Police Repression of Protest', *Social Movement Studies*, 17 (1): 48–63.

Ribble, M. (2015) *Digital Citizenship in Schools*, Arlington: International Society for Technology in Education.

Ribble, M., G. Bailey, and T. Ross (2004) 'Digital Citizenship: Addressing Appropriate Technology Behavior', *Learning & Leading With Technology*, 32 (1): 6–9.

Richardson, D. (2000) 'Claiming Citizenship? Sexuality, Citizenship and Lesbian/Feminist Theory', *Sexualities*, 3 (2): 255–72.

Roberts, N. (2004) 'Public Deliberation in an Age of Direct Citizen Participation', *The American Review of Public Administration*, 34 (4): 315–53.

Roberts, T. (2017) 'Participatory Technologies: Affordances for Development', in J. Choudrie, M. Islam, F. Wahid, J. Bass, and J. Priyatma (eds), *Information and Communication Technologies for Development*, 194–205, Cham: Springer International Publishing.

Roberts, T. (ed.) (2021) *Digital Rights in Closing Civic Space: Lessons from Ten African Countries*, Brighton: Institute of Development Studies (IDS), accessed 15 October 2021.

Roberts, T. and K. Hernandez (2017) 'The Techno-Centric Gaze: Incorporating Citizen Participation Technologies into Participatory Governance Processes in the Philippines', *Making All Voices Count Research Report*, Brighton: Institute of Development Studies.

Roberts, T. and K. Hernandez (2018) *Leaving No One Behind in a Digital World*, K4D Emerging Issues Report, Brighton: Institute of Development Studies.

Roberts, T. and K. Hernandez (2019) 'Digital Access Is Not Binary: The 5 'A's of Technology Access in the Philippines', *Electronic Journal of Information Systems in Developing Countries*, 85 (5): e12084, https://onlinelibrary.wiley.com/doi/full/10.1002/isd2.12084.

Roberts, T., A. Mohamed Ali, M. Farahat, R. Oloyede, and G. Mutung'u (2021) *Surveillance Law in Africa: A Review of Six Countries*, Brighton: Institute of Development Studies. https://opendocs.ids.ac.uk/opendocs/handle/20.500.12413/16893

Schou, J. and M. Hjelholt (2018) 'Digital Citizenship and Neo-Liberalization: Governing Digital Citizens in Denmark', *Citizenship Studies*, 22 (5): 507–22.

Schuck, P. (2002) 'Liberal Citizenship', in B. Turner and E. Isin (eds), *Handbook of Citizenship Studies*, 183–99, London: Sage Publishing.

Seidman, G. (1999) 'Gendered Citizenship: South Africa's Democratic Transition and the Construction of a Gendered State', *Gender and Society*, 13 (3): 287–307.

Simons, K. C. (2010) 'New Governance and the "New Paradigm" of Police Accountability: A Democratic Approach to Police Reform', *Catholic University Law Review*, 59 (2): 373–426.

Somolu, O. (2007) 'Telling Our Own Stories: African Women Blogging for Social Change', *Gender & Development*, 15 (3): 477–89. doi:10.1080/13552070701630640

Statista.com (2020a) *Number of Internet Users in Nigeria from 2018 to 2022, with Forecasts from 2023 to 2027*. Statista website. https://www.statista.com/statistics/183849/internet-users-nigeria/.

Statista.com (2020b).

Statista.com (2020c) *Number of Internet Users in Nigeria from 2017 to 2026*.

The Cable (2018) 'EXCLUSIVE: PDP Hires Trump's Lobbyist for $90k per Month', 2 November, accessed 15 October 2021.

Tommaso, M. (ed.) (2013) *Democracy and Gender Equality: The Role of the UN*, Discussion Paper, New York: International Institute for Democracy and Electoral Assistance/ Office of the Permanent Observer for International IDEA to the United Nations.

Touraine, A. (1995) *Critique of Modernity*, Oxford: Blackwell.

Tufekci, O. and Hashiru, M. (2019) 'Women Empowerment Through Political Participation in Rising Powers: Comparison of Turkey and Nigeria Cases', in M. İ. Yenilmez and O. B. Çelik (eds), *A Comparative Perspective of Women's Economic Empowerment*, 219–33, London: Routledge.

Tufekci, Z. (2017) *Twitter and Tear Gas: The Power and Fragility of Networked Protest*, New Haven: Yale University Press.

Turkle, S. (1995) *Life on the Screen: Identity in the Age of the Internet*, New York: Simon & Schuster Paperbacks.

Turkle, S. (2005) *The Second Self: Computers and the Human Spirit*, Cambridge, MA: MIT Press.

UN (2011) *Report of the Special Rapporteur on the Promotion and Protection of the Right to Freedom of Opinion and Expression, Frank La Rue, Human Rights Council, Seventeenth Session Agenda Item 3*, United Nations General Assembly.

UN Women (2019) 'It's Election Season in Nigeria, But Where Are the Women?' *UN Women Website*, 6 February, accessed 15 October 2021.

Universal Service Provision Fund (USPF) (2019) 'Clusters of ICT/Telephony Gap in Nigeria, 2019', accessed 15 October 2021.

Unwin, T. (2009) *Reclaiming Information & Communication Technologies for Development*, Oxford: Oxford University Press.

Uwalaka, T. and J. Watkins (2018) 'Social Media as the Fifth Estate in Nigeria: An Analysis of the 2012 Occupy Nigeria Protest', *African Journalism Studies*, 39 (4): 22–41. doi:10.1080/23743670.2018.1473274.

Uwazuruike, A. R. (2021) '#EndSARS: The Movement Against Police Brutality in Nigeria', *Harvard Human Rights Journal*, 34 (1). https://harvardhrj.com/2020/11/endsars-the-movement-against-police-brutality-in-nigeria/.

Van Dijk, J. A. G. M. (2006) 'Digital Divide Research, Achievements and Shortcomings', *Poetics*, 34 (4–5): 221–35. doi:10.1016/j.poetic.2006.05.004

Vanguard (2020) 'Five Demands from #EndSARS Protesters', 12 October, accessed 9 July 2021.

Vincent, D 2020. 'How Women Powered Nigeria's #EndSARS Movement.' *Elle Magazine*, November 18, accessed April 2021, https://www.elle.com/culture/career-politics/a34699000/endsars-nigeria-feminist-coalition/.

Waylen, G., K. Celis, J. Kantola, and S. L. Weldon (eds) (2016) *The Oxford Handbook of Gender and Politics*, Oxford: Oxford University Press.

World Bank (2022) 'Countries Data Bank', World Bank website. https://data.worldbank.org/country/NG.

YacobHaliso, O. and, T. Falola. Cham: Palgrave Macmillan. https://doi.org/10.1007/978-3-030-28099-4 Google Scholar.

Zachariadis, M., S. Scott, and M. Barrett (2013) 'Methodological Implications of Critical Realism for Mixed-Methods Research', *MIS Quarterly*, 37 (3): 855–79. http://www.jstor.org/stable/43826004.

Zukas, L. (2009) 'Women's War of 1929', in I. Ness (ed.), *The International Encyclopaedia of Revolution and Protest: 1500 to the Present*, Chichester: Wiley-Blackwell. https://onlinelibrary.wiley.com/doi/abs/10.1002/9781405198073.wbierp1604.

6

Digital citizenship and cyber-activism in Zambia

Sam Phiri, Kiss Abraham and Tanja Bosch

Introduction

Through a critical meta-analysis of existing research and using three case studies, this chapter explores and reflects on the forms of digital citizenship that have emerged in Zambia. In particular the chapter focuses on the state's responses to cyber-activism and argues that a new kind of digital citizenship is emerging. The chapter begins by outlining the Zambian political and digital context to provide background to the discussion. We then explore the three case studies: a 2004 incident in which an activist hacked a government website; the 2015 by-elections and 2016 elections; and the so-called bush protest of 2020. We argue that these cases highlight Virilio's (2006) conceptions of dromology and dromocracy, which see social change as a result of the speed with which social forces are pushing for change in society. Using this theoretical frame, we utilize the concept of citizenship as rights-claiming constituted by the exercise of performative actions and struggles with the state over control of digital space. This chapter argues that the space for digital citizenship is contested on three fronts which we explore in turn: technologies, tactics and laws.

The Zambian political and digital context

In the period following independence from British colonial rule, Zambia is considered to have experienced three broad political eras: the first republic

(1964–73), the second republic (1973–89) and following constitutional changes in 1989, the third republic has endured up to the present day. Thus, a whole new generation of Zambians, oblivious to past political circumstances, have grown up within the context of multiparty democratic practices.

At the advent of independence, Zambia initially operated as a democracy but soon became a one-party state, under the United National Independence Party (UNIP) which remained in power for nineteen years from 1972 until multiparty elections in 1991. Since then, Zambia has held nine presidential and general elections and enjoyed a relatively stable democracy and peaceful transfers of power between four political parties: UNIP, the Movement for Multiparty Democracy (MMD), the Patriotic Front (PF) and the current incumbent United Party for National Development (UPND). Despite the shift to democracy, the state has tightly controlled civic space by silencing independent media outlets, while the country has experienced growing rates of poverty and inequality, high levels of foreign debt and political scandals (Gavin 2021). Multiparty democracy is well established but 'opposition parties face onerous legal and practical obstacles to fair competition, and the government regularly invokes restrictive laws to curb freedom of expression and ban peaceful demonstrations and meetings', and political violence remains a problem (Freedom House 2021).

With respect to the media landscape, newspapers, radio and television (TV) stations were subject to strict government regulation since the 1960s, and 'when the internet was introduced in Zambia in 1994, concerns about press freedom, pluralism, and privatisation intensified' (Parks and Mukherjee 2017: 223). During the late 1990s, the government attempted to out-compete independent media by financing state media, but independent outlets, often online, have filled a gap by providing critical news and attracting significant readership (Parks and Mukherjee 2017: 223). 'Along with intimidation, sometimes the state uses arrests, detentions, and protracted legal proceedings against journalists who are marked as problematic' also confiscating their digital equipment, which is costly to replace (Parks and Mukherjee 2017: 223). According to an article in *Foreign Affairs* (Norris 2021), global regressions from the democratic ideals of the early 1990s started when elected political leaders undermined and gradually dismantled core institutions such as the judiciary, electoral management bodies, independent legislatures and the news media. The result is that political and civil liberties are limited in Zambia. The judicial arms of the state are restricted, media independence is violated, while the public end up confused, as citizens 'do not see the damage caused to democracy until it's too late' (Norris 2021). When people do, they respond in various ways, as we discuss later in this chapter.

Regarding internet access, Zambia has generally had very low internet usage, but usage increased slightly when a national information and communications technology (ICT) policy was adopted by the Zambian government in 2006. Of a total population of about eighteen million, 52 per cent (9.8 million) have access to the internet. This has been a nearly 50 per cent increase in internet usage over the past ten years. Of these, a fair number of people accessing the internet are youth, who constitute 37 per cent of the population (Zambia Government 2015: 2). If you were to ignore the youth-age barrier of fifteen years and incorporate children, then there are an estimated 8.4 million youth and children under the age of thirty-five years in Zambia (Country Meters 2019). As of January 2021, Zambia had a population of 18.65 million, with 44.9 per cent living in urban centres, while the rest (55.1 per cent) live in rural areas. Only 5.48 million of Zambia's population are internet users, and internet penetration stood at 29.4 per cent in January 2021.

In terms of social media, there were 2.6 million users in Zambia, equivalent to 13.9 per cent of the total population in January 2021 (Kemp 2021). Social media, and Facebook in particular, have emerged as the leading channels for digital citizenship in Zambia (Internet World Stats 2021), possibly as a result of Facebook's early experiment of providing variants of free basic access services for citizens of the Global South. This was a global initiative started in Zambia in 2014 (Schoon et al. 2020) and later extended to several African countries and countries in other regions. NapoleonCat (2021) reports that there are 2.9 million Facebook users in Zambia as of September 2021.

As of December 2020, there were more than 2.5 million Zambians with Facebook pages (Internet World Stats 2021). According to StatCounter (2021), a site that measures and tracks internet usage based on page views, between April 2020 and April 2021, Facebook had a 55.15 per cent market share of Zambia's social media space. Its highest point during that period was in March 2021, when Facebook took 69.45 per cent of the social media usage space in Zambia. Its main competitors had a much smaller share: Twitter's market share was 21.62 per cent, Pinterest's about 15 per cent, YouTube's about

6 per cent and Instagram's about 2 per cent. Clearly, more than half of the debates on social media are taking place on Facebook. Unlike in other parts of the continent, Twitter usage lags so far behind that its use can be considered inconsequential to Zambian digital citizenship.

Theoretical context: Citizenship, digital citizenship and political participation

The terms 'citizenship', 'digital citizenship' and 'political participation' are central to this chapter and so we explore them in detail in this section. We should note that citizenship is a contested concept. In the academic literature, it can be understood as political status, civic action or a contractual relationship. Citizenship can be understood as the relationship between an individual and a nation state (Pangrazio and Sefton-Green 2021); as the action of taking part in public affairs (Jones and Gaventa 2002); or a level of entitlement in a relationship between a person and the state (Youkhana 2015). At the broadest level, citizenship can simply be understood as participation in community affairs (Lindgren 2017).

Turner (1990) argues that citizenship should not be understood as a unitary term because there are in fact several approaches to the concept. These include dimensions of participation, the need for expansion of social rights, aspects of active or passive participation or indeed what individuals do in their private spheres. Further, Turner (1990: 194) argues that citizenship 'is no longer formally confined by the particularities of birth, ethnicity or gender' but is 'pushed along by the development of social conflicts and social struggles . . . as social groups compete with each other over access to resources'.

Turner's thoughts extend beyond the liberal conception of citizenship as a situation where the individual is subject to the nation state, where the individual is a member of the nation and where a person's rights and responsibilities are established within a geographical and political boundary (Caglar 2015). It also outstrips the narrower view that citizenship is a status bestowed upon individuals by the state, but with accompanying rights and obligations, to being a process of participation in political and civic life. This conception, however, has been questioned by Clarke et al. (2014), who have called for the destabilization, unbundling, disputation and decentralization of the concept.

In fact, other scholars argue that whereas citizenship may be granted, what should be in place is 'civic consciousness', which is deliberately nurtured by individuals themselves (Vlasenko et al. 2021) for the purposes of participation in community affairs and the struggle for social resources.

Further, citizenship should not be seen as something that is handed over to individuals from those in power. When viewed from the top down, citizens' rights become passive rights, an aspect which precludes that citizenship could in fact be a consequence of social struggles, as Turner (1990) argued.

These issues continue to be relevant in the consideration of digital citizenship. The battle for access to resources and the tussle over digital spaces are extended in the online world. The notion of digital citizenship should embrace the view that citizenship involves claiming one's rights with mobile and internet tools and in online spaces.

Mossberger, Tolbert and McNeal (2008: 1–2) define digital citizenship as 'the ability to participate in society online'. This includes aspects of inclusion, civic participation and economic opportunity. These three are the metrics demonstrating the ability to participate online and therefore of digital citizenship. They also help define digital citizens as 'those who use technology frequently [daily] . . . for political information to fulfil their civic duty, and [those] who use technology at work for economic gain' (Mossberger et al. 2008). Moreover, Vlasenko et al. (2021: 220) state that digital citizenship 'includes a wide range of activities, from creation, consumption, exchange, gaming, communication, learning and professional activities . . . [these activities] respond to new and everyday challenges related to education, work, employment, leisure, inclusion and participation in the life of a society, respect for human rights and intercultural differences'. Further, in Vlasenko et al.'s view (2021: 222), digital citizens should be 'able to actively, responsibly and constantly participate in community life using ICT'. Essentially, one aspect of citizenship is a form of political action in which individuals 'engage with the state and navigate their sense of belonging to a larger community' (Beaman 2016: 851); or indeed, as Isin and Ruppert (2015: 44) argue, digital citizenship is the 'capacity for making rights claims' and 'involves making rights claims through the internet'. Pangrazio and Sefton-Green (2021: 16) argue that citizenship goes beyond the practices of voting and civic activism, to the ideal of 'participating in online discussion'.

It is that active, responsible and constant participation in community life, through the internet, that, for the purposes of this chapter, is also referred to as political participation. In that respect, political participation is the act of people exercising their right of 'influencing issues of particular importance to themselves . . . through praxis' (Dahl 1996: 79) or, as Fuchs (2017: 69) argues, it is the reality of humans having the 'right to be part of decisions and to govern and control the structures that affect them'. Further, this form of participation is in line with concepts of cultural citizenship where social spaces and rights are actively claimed (Flores and Benmayor 1997: 15–17).

Digital citizenship milestones in Zambia

This section explores how Zambians have used the digital sphere for political activism as far back as 2004 and reflects on more recent manifestations of digital citizenship in the context of the 2021 elections. We also outline the legal and political context in which these contestations took place and reflect particularly on how the state responded to citizen occupation of cyberspace. We consider three significant cases: a 2004 incident of hacking; the 2016 elections; and the more recent 2020 'bush protest'.

One of the earliest expressions of digital activism in Zambia was in 2004, as an act of subversion when a young computer expert replaced President Frederick Chiluba's official portrait on the State House website with a cartoon. Shockwaves ran through the state structures. How could that happen under their noses and at that elevated space? The youth in question was hunted down, arrested but released soon after, as there was no adequate law under which to prosecute him. However, this incident, among others, seemingly alerted the state to the presence of internet-based civic activism. The state, soon after, enacted the aptly named Computer Misuse and Crimes Act (*The Sydney Morning Herald* 2004). This law, which was almost a cut-and-paste act of a similarly worded British law of 1990, prohibited unauthorized access to or modification of computer data. Offenders could face up to seven years in prison (Zambia Government 2004). Some years later, in 2014, the Zambia Information and Communications Technology Authority (ZICTA) launched the first cybercrime fighting lab at police headquarters in Lusaka. This lab consisted of three laptops, three external hard discs, two computer forensic machines and eight computers (Temwa 2016). It was aimed at fighting cybercrimes and becoming a 'platform for retrieval, analysis, and reporting of evidence contained on computer systems and computing devices' (ZICTA 2014). Then in March 2020, a fifteen-year-old schoolboy in the small town of Kapiri Mposhi was arrested for defaming the president. The youth, who went by the name 'Zoom' on Facebook, was accused of insulting the president when he wrote that 'we are better off as a country without Edgar Lungu' and that he could name a dog after the president (News24 2020).

Using sophisticated technology, cybercrime police traced, found and arrested the teenager. Earlier, in 2019, in response to what was perceived as increased abuse of the internet, the Zambian government formed the Special Joint Cybercrime Crack Squad (SJCCS), which brought together specialists from security agencies such as the police, national intelligence, the Drug Enforcement Commission and the Anti-Corruption Commission. According to the state, the SJCCS was meant to stop abuse and the illegal use of digital platforms among and against Zambians. Minister of Transport and Communications Brian Mushimba said the special security branch would 'reduce risks brought about by the digital revolution'. However, critics argued that the squad was an eavesdropping monster 'out to haunt citizens from enjoying their rights and freedoms' (Msoni 2019). Dataveillance, or 'digital surveillance' (Schleusener 2019), refers to the control, access, exploitation or denial of data, and the collection of personal data, bundling it together and using technologies to cross-reference that data so as to attribute general characteristics to individual citizens (Elmer 2003). All these are within the provisions of the new cybercrimes law (Chilufya-Musonda and Mwamulima 2021).

Following the rise of social media in Africa in the wake of the Arab Spring, and its role in mobilizing protests and enabling political change in North Africa, Zambian citizens similarly drew on these platforms during the 2016 elections (Willems 2016). Citizens used social media to access information on election results in real time; and as Mkandawire (2016) argues, digital media technologies, including social media, coexist with mainstream media in a new converged media landscape in Zambia. Civil society used Facebook and mobile phone SMS messaging 'to ensure transparency and credibility in the electoral process during the 2015 presidential by-election results reporting process' (2016: 96). Mkandawire thus argues that digital platforms have consolidated democracy in the electoral process by helping to validate the official elections results.

More recently, the so-called bush protest in 2020, which was driven by Zambian youth, can be seen as another expression of digital citizenship in which Zambians found innovative ways to protest. According to the Zambian government (2015), the youth comprise 36.71 per cent of a population of about eighteen million. Phiri (2019) has argued that Zambian youth have little faith in representative democracy and instead use social media platforms to directly engage with decision-makers, thus subverting the authority of Parliament. The growth of digital citizenship in Zambia can be attributed to this youth population, and this case clearly illustrates how the youth, and citizens in general, are challenging the state over the occupation of the public sphere. The protests were led by young activists, musicians and artists, some of whom had been associated with media networks for children's rights and civic activism from an early age (Namwawa 2021).

The bush protest comprised an offline protest in an undisclosed location that was broadcast live on social media platforms on 22 June 2020; it was dubbed the 'bush protest' because protesters wanted to avoid the use of lethal force by authorities by holding the protest away from the city. The youth had initially wished to petition the government; they intended to march through the streets of Lusaka before symbolically assembling at the Freedom Statue, in Independence Avenue, outside the country's largest government office building that hosts the ministry responsible for youth affairs. In Zambia, the Freedom Statue, which depicts a man breaking the chains above his head, was erected in October 1974 during the tenth anniversary of the country's independence from British colonial rule. It has come to represent national aspirations for political freedom and freedom of expression. But even with the best of intentions, the police banned the planned youth demonstration, citing Covid regulations, which did not allow for large gatherings (*Lusaka Times* 2020).

The purpose of the protest was to 'denounce bad governance and what they referred to as "oppression by the government and foreign investors". Among other demands, the protesters called on the government to curb corruption, be accountable, respect human rights, create job opportunities and include the youth' (CIVICUS 2020). Riot police were deployed all over the capital, Lusaka, as thirteen youth activists live-streamed themselves making speeches against corruption and poor governance, while more than half a million people tuned in online (Allison 2020).

Protesters set out ten demands, among them better job opportunities, an end to corruption, better education, constitutionalism, protection of human rights including the right to free assembly and free expression and access to information. The protest was triggered by a call made online by (among others) a 22-year-old University of Lusaka (UNILUS) political science student, Mumbi Namwawa, and singers like Kings Malembe (Zed Gossip 2020). The call was for President Lungu to create jobs, economic empowerment and political positions in the government for youth. Lusaka province minister Lusambo responded viciously, saying that the call was 'stinking nonsense . . . stupidity at its highest level, and rubbish', and that youth should stop lawlessness and the 'misbehaviour' of addressing the president through social media (Zambia Landscape 2020). Namwawa responded that the youth would respond to the ministerial insults with public demonstrations and called on youth across the country to join the protests. They applied for a permit, which was denied. Pilato, an activist musician, then called on the youth to 'use social media to the maximum', adding that 'we have the power in our hands and we have to use it for the collective good of our country. Let's go live on Facebook, let's post and make graphics to express ourselves' (Pilato 2020).

A chorus of counter-responses from state operatives followed: President Lungu said that he had 'information that some people are ganging up under the name of civil-society organisation to bring anarchy because they are saying the freedom of speech has been threatened by remarks attributed to Honourable Lusambo'. He warned that those 'plotting' to cause chaos and anarchy, and plunge the country into turmoil, would be dealt with within the law (Ask Muvi TV 2020) and called for their arrest. Lungu's personal lawyer and a Member of Parliament for the then governing Patriotic Front Party, Tutwa Ngulube, called on the police to 'break their bones' (Let's Talk About Zambia 2020).

On the day of the scheduled march, heavily armed troops in newly acquired riot gear, showing off the latest anti-riot trucks and ambulances, in a shock-and-awe operation, patrolled the Lusaka streets until nightfall. But the youth were nowhere to be seen; instead, they had left town, to a secret location in the bush, to broadcast their demands, online, to the rest of the world (Mwebantu 2020b). This unique countermove, shifting the protest online and garnering widespread support, represents a shift to digital citizenship. A form of 'pirate modernity' had occurred. In Sundaram's view, pirate modernity is the 'creative corruption of . . . media technologies that create their own spatiality and thereby reproduce non-legal economic practices, media objects, [and] software' to create forms which are different from the originals (Sundaram 2010: 12–15). It is a 'contagion of the ordinary', which distorts the very "orderliness" of the everyday life'; or as in this instance, the youth had fashioned for themselves an alternative communication infrastructure (Schoon et al. 2020: 6) by creatively circumnavigating police challenges, swiftly shifting away from offline forms of protest to cyberspace and thereby reaching more people within and outside Zambia.

Nonetheless, the police celebrated their victory – the march did not take place. But one of the protesters, B'Flow (2020), tweeted: 'One day the people will ask "Why were the police on the streets in Lusaka with guns on the 22nd June, 2020?" Then the story will be told about how the young people of the country mobilised the police to march on their behalf.' The youths had no permit to go onto the streets under the old precolonial Public Order Act and Covid guidelines. But who needs to worry about a permit and Covid guidelines in cyberspace?

Whereas the Public Order Act gives power to the police to regulate public processions, and Covid guidelines required that all gatherings of more than five people should be permitted by the Ministry of Health (*Lusaka Times* 2020), no such requirement is possible, or enforceable, in the digital sphere. As part of the Covid regulations that came into effect in March 2020, any gathering of more than five people who were not family members was prohibited. People who contravened this law were liable to six months' imprisonment (Zambia Government 2020). Such draconian rules are in tandem with those in Nigeria, Mozambique and Pakistan. These rules assist states in 'rolling back democratic progress by squeezing an already-constrained civic space still further', especially as the pandemic becomes an excuse for states to 'advance pre-existing anti-democratic projects of stifling dissent and manufacturing consent' (Anderson et al. 2021: 42).

However, Zambian Covid law, together with the police stance, is against the notions of political citizenship, which are 'grounded in the guarantee of legal and political protection from raw coercive power' (Fayomi and Adebayo 2018: 537). Nonetheless, out of fear of the state's panoptic gaze, (Foucault 1977), the 2020 youth assumed thereafter that they were under watch by the state, as Elmer (2003) could have warned. They thus never assembled in the bush again. Instead, they dispersed their protests through several individual internet-based platforms, including posting blank but black-painted message pages on Lungu's official State House site (Namwawa 2021).

Some young people (Namwawa 2021) felt that the youth-led movement, whose highlight was perhaps the bush protest, was a success because it may have brought certain results: offers of economic incentives to the youth; hastily arranged government meetings that some youths boycotted; high numbers of youth registering to vote; high youth voter turnout; and the subsequent victory of the opposition in the August 2021 elections.

Nigeria's Ayibakuro (2021) agrees with Namwawa (2021) that Zambian youth took action to bring democratic solutions to economic problems. Those actions included registering to vote in large numbers, massive turnout at the polls [and] the 'use of social media to mobilise, despite attempts by government to restrict same, especially on election day and a simple determination to engender change' that would impact on youth lives. The protest resulted in, among other things, a Youth Charter of 2020 in which young people demanded that they be acknowledged as the 'future of Zambia' whose burdens must be 'met in our lifetime' (Zambian Eye 2020).

Popular expressions of digital citizenship

As in other contexts, not all expressions of digital citizenship in Zambia are related to political activism. Facebook user analytics for one month (August 2020) show that Zambia's most popular Facebook sites were Mwebantu, with 4.2 million people reached in one week; Zambian Landscape, with 2.7 million; Zambian Watchdog, with 2.1 million; Zambian Weddings and Kitchen Parties, with 1.9 million; Chellah Tukuta Photography, with 1.8 million; Zed Diary, with 1.5 million; Milly Beauty Products, with 1.2 million; QFM Radio, with 1.1 million; and the opposition politician, now president, Hakainde Hichilema, with 1 million people reached in just seven days (Mwebantu 2020a). Further, most recent statistics suggest that the fastest-growing Facebook pages may be youth-oriented. For May 2021, these included Esther Chungu's page, with 30,792 new fans. Chungu is a youthful, gospel artist and TV presenter. She was closely followed by Hakainde Hichilema, the leader of the opposition UPND, with 24,516 new fans; Mwebantu, a news page, with 20,209 new followers; Pompi, a performance artist, with 15,383 new fans; and President Lungu, who gained 13,961 new followers in one month (Social Bakers 2021). Clearly, youth were in competition with popular politicians.

It is important to note that these pages reach people who constitute youth, most of whom were born and brought up within the new digital culture, which, according to Lindgren (2017: 4), is the summing-up of the 'equation of digital media + society'. This is a society that emerged after the explosion of the internet and social media, leading to the creation of 'networked publics' which are spaces 'open and designed for participation by everyone' (Hjorth and Hinton 2019: 19). While these Facebook pages are not designed for political activity, they represent a form of cultural citizenship, creating pathways of communication to form virtual communities (Bosch 2020). Glancing through the earlier factors concerning Zambian youth's occupation of various digital platforms, a question might arise as to whether such occupation is sufficient to constitute digital citizenship. However, in taking note of that concern, what should not be lost is that proponents of social media and the internet, or techno-fetishists (Fuchs 2017: 247), argue that the internet and digital channels are spaces favoured by societies across the world as they facilitate democratic participation. Thus, in Malaysia, for example, people's internet activity has led to the adoption of terms like 'online participation', 'digital democracy' and 'cyber-democracy' (Abdulla et al. 2021). In Zambia, though, a Zambian Governance Foundation report (Nyambe and Hamusunga 2017) reveals that 91 per cent of youth do not directly engage with decision-makers in any way because of limited participation opportunities. This may slowly be changing, as indicated by the examples cited earlier.

Unfortunately, it is that prospect of unlimited and uncontrolled participation in public affairs that has brought about new and perhaps predictable responses from mostly illiberal state structures, Zambia's included. There is a definite contestation over who should control the digital space in Zambia, as the state sees digital citizenship as a challenge to its authority, as demonstrated earlier. Popular culture in Africa is increasingly related to citizenship and identity claims, with people's everyday engagement with popular culture a central part of this. As Dolby (2006: 35) has argued, popular culture is a site of struggle and 'Citizenship thus is an active process that involves the core of people's daily existence, including the ways in which they interact with and use popular culture'. Cultural citizenship refers to the ways in which citizens experience their social context and how they relate to others in seeking a sense of belonging, with the internet – and, in this instance, Facebook – as a 'site of sociocultural and political agency' (Bosch 2020).

Discussion and analysis

In our analysis of these three cases, we use the framework of 'dromology' to analyse the interactions and emergent relationships between citizen and state, as both sides 'mutually prostheticise' (Bratton 2006) against each other for control of digital space through speedy actions. In doing so, usually, states employ dromological techniques to exercise power (Virilio 2006) over youth and the rest of the population.

Paul Virilio's (2006) conception of dromology argues that the real world is a result of social velocity and speed. Reality is not static; in fact, he argues that stasis is death. Thus, this view can be interpreted as meaning that there is nothing like civil development, or modernity, or the quiet democratization of society. Instead, what we have is the state of 'dromocracy', which sees social change as a result of the speed with which social forces are pushing for change in society.

In one respect, this involves a complex set of 'rights claims-making and performative citizenship, and [especially with regard to] the participation of young people in politics . . . [and] entails complex and often contradictory struggles over definition of social membership, over the categories and practices of inclusion and exclusion, and over different forms of participation in public life' (Sanghera et al. 2018). Whereas literally, dromology is the insatiable, uncontrollable and abnormal impulse to wonder and travel in the lust for new experiences (Sam 2013), dromocracy, in this chapter, may be an appellation for social change towards either more open societies or more closed societies. For 'success', change depends on the 'velocity of knowledge' spread through (among other things) the 'dictatorship of movement' (Orlet and Cardoso de Castro 2016), or sometimes effected through performative citizenship and rights-claiming.

According to Bratton (2006), modernity is a world in motion that is expressed in a political landscape governed by competing technologies of surveillance, mobilization, fortification and their interdependent administrations. It is a contest of shifting, restless logistics of differential governances while transforming the raw material of the world and rendering it into more appropriate forms. Further, within the context of citizenship, dromology requires us to see that the concept refers to states of inclusion or exclusion of individuals from either the nation state or, in our instance, the digital space. In other words, full citizens have rights either in the nation state, or they inhabit the nation's public sphere. If so, there has to be a dromological movement of 'being-ness' between the state of existing as an alien, or stranger without rights, to being a person with rights, responsibilities and privileges. In between those two irreconcilable states, there is the shadowy citizen, or 'denizen' (Cresswell 2010). Denizenship, in that regard, is the in-between state where the occupant has rights but at the same time is excluded from certain privileges. This conception accepts that the individual is in a state of mobility where the person becomes 'prosthetic' (Cresswell 2019) from being excluded, without rights and privileges, to being advantaged. The person is thus entangled in a pervading sense of motion, or movement. Such mobility is defined by Cresswell as the morass of a person being classified (represented), or in movement, or in the actual practice/act of citizenship.

This chapter further acknowledges that a fast, or dromological, movement towards the public's use of social media, the ubiquity of the internet and the speedy occupation of the digital space is happening before our eyes. As technological optimists could argue, this trend could lead to more open societies. It is also argued that a similar trend in reverse could lead to more closed societies. In that sense, dromocracy refers to the state of the 'rule of the fastest (the one who possesses the weapon of superior speed) or to the rule of speed itself (a form of power that can evade human control' (Collins 2008). This is irrespective of the direction the speeding arrow is pointed at.

But this drive does not exist in isolation. In Zambia, it is accompanied by a countervailing force. Bentham's concept of the public good, or social utilitarianism, has been misappropriated by the Zambian state through the use of many surveillance techniques and technologies. These include closed-circuit television (CCTV), speed cameras and the Smart City project, which has resulted in a $230 million country-wide secretive national surveillance infrastructure run by an unknown government department. This Chinese-built data-mining and information management system, initiated in 2015, will cover seventeen cities through a national broadband network consisting of

9,000 kilometres of optic cables. When completed, the national data collection and storage facility will be able to analyse large amounts of data to ensure 'secure, efficient and interoperable systems' between government departments (Huawei 2021). However, according to Briant (2021), the existence of such pervasive infrastructures leads to citizens realising that the idea of technologies being neutral is a myth.

Thus, this descriptive study sees citizens as engaged in a contest with the state where both sides 'mutually prostheticise' (Bratton 2006) against each other for the control of digital space through speedy actions. In doing so, usually, states employ dromological techniques to exercise power (Virilio 2006) over youth and the rest of the population. In Zambia's case, and building on Virilio's framework, we argue that youth activists momentarily gain advantage with the speed of adoption of new technologies and rights claims to digital spaces, but that the slow state arrives on the scene with more 'muscle' – i.e., tools, tactics, laws and power. Youth, who are early adopters of new technologies, may use speed to gain advantage but the government subsequently catches up with them and overtakes them through several means, including making SIM-card registration mandatory; banning of bulk SMS; passing laws that force mobile service providers to keep records of all transactions on their systems; and compelling the mobile telephone service companies to make such records available to the state (Roberts and Bosch 2021). All these actions facilitate the state's surveillance and arrest of youth activists.

Another key strategy utilized by Zambian citizens is described by Parks and Mukherjee (2017: 225) as platform-jumping, where users 'cross multiple platforms each day, shifting from analogue to digital, desktop to mobile, and audio to text-based systems as they participate in social and work-related communication and information exchanges'. When news or information is blocked, users platform-jump, tactically shifting their 'practices of sharing or consuming information from one platform to another in an effort to facilitate broader access to that information' (2017: 225). Examples of platform-jumping include scenarios where radio DJs post controversial material on social media instead of on-air. As in other African countries, blogging and vlogging have also emerged as a vehicle for social activists, though such content is not always political.

Yartey and Ha (2015) define self-broadcasting as a communication style in which an individual self-projects their identity, which may entail posting pictures, adding status messages or commenting on posts of others on Facebook and other platforms. We consider this to be a manifestation of digital citizenship.

One example is the Zambian YouTuber Joey Mukando, one of the leading self-broadcasters in Zambia. She has several websites, and on one site, there are 40,000 followers; on another she is followed by 13,000 people. On her most recent vlog, Mukando had 15,000 views while the vlog was shared 214 times. Kax Tee, on the other hand, on the vlog analysing and listing Zambia's top vloggers, had 8,970 subscribers and 32,747 followers. These are impressive numbers for individual youth bloggers when compared to social media 'likes' for state-owned news corporates. For example, government-owned newspapers like the *Times of Zambia* had 38,271 likes and 39,809 followers (*Times of Zambia* 2021). The more popular *Zambia Daily Mail* had 291,023 likes and 306,989 followers (*Zambia Daily Mail* 2021).

State responses to digital citizenship

The Zambian state has responded to these expressions of digital citizenship in a variety of ways, including a move to pass laws dealing with perceived cybercrimes. In 2004, the government campaigned for and swiftly passed (without much parliamentary debate) the Computer Misuse and Crimes Act, in response to the humiliation caused by the young computer expert who replaced President Chiluba's official portrait on the State House website with a cartoon. After these and similar occurrences, it has been observed that the state has a tendency to mount new legal structures, or even design counter-narratives, when such incidences occur.

After the drama of 2004, the struggle for civic spaces continued. In 2019, a special cybercrimes police force was quickly formed. In 2021, the government speedily enacted the Cyber Security and Cyber Crimes Act – a law that had been talked about for years. However, the haste and drama with which it was brought into force raised some eyebrows. It pointed to government's discomfiture with citizens' increased use of the internet and social media for information sharing. It was on the basis of this law that the state shut down sites like Facebook, Twitter and Instagram on polling day, in August 2021.

According to Bowmans (Chilufya-Musonda and Mwamulima 2021), the new cyber law legalized the state's interception of any form of communication where the government believed that a cybercrime was being committed or planned to be committed. It formed a special 'police', created a storage facility for intercepted communications, compelled internet service providers to install interception and storage facilities and software at their own expense and surrendered all intercepted communications to the government when requested.

In all this, citizens had no right to be informed that they were under intelligence scrutiny, or that their communications were being intercepted and transferred to a government storage facility. However, the June 2020 response by youth, of leaving Lusaka streets to conduct their protest campaign on the internet and in the bush, suggests an awareness that they were being watched.

Beyond that, the new law has also created new cybercrimes, including spreading of hate speech. However, there is a broad definition of what constitutes 'hate speech'. As Mwananyanda (2021) argues, hate speech is a 'notoriously difficult concept to define . . . [and] a lack of clarity leaves people unsure what expression is allowed or prohibited, leading to self-censorship'. It is that form of self-censorship which can be likened to Foucault's (1977) conception of the panoptic gaze, which Simon (2005) argues leaves people with a sense 'that there is nowhere to run and nowhere to hide'.

To illustrate this point, and in an unusual move, the normally reserved former president, when signing the bill into law, issued a statement indirectly confirming that the panoptic would be at play. Lungu said the new law would bring 'sanity in the way the internet was used' and end 'abuse by people who feel they can do or say whatever they want using the veil of cybersecurity' (*Lusaka Times* 2021). This is the same excuse that was used to justify the creation of the SJCCS (see previous discussion).

In response, several civil-society organizations challenged the law and took the issue to the constitutional court. They argued that the new law had a 'chilling effect' on media freedom and compromised the privacy of citizens. Moreover, the law fell short of international standards such as the African Union Convention on Cyber Security and Personal Data Protection (2014), also known as the Malabo Convention, to which Zambia is a signatory (MISA-Zimbabwe 2021).

As Mwananyanda (2021) argues: 'The speed with which this law was passed ... is highly concerning. Rather than provide security, this law could backfire against its promulgators in future, and history in Zambia is replete with examples of how laws meant to deal with dissent came back to bite those who had made them.'

Closing civic spaces for youth, either through coercive forces like the police or through legislative frameworks, and enticing them with free money are just some of the ways in which the state has responded to youth occupation of digital spaces in 2020. The state has used these and other means at its disposal, including economic avenues and political promises of a good future around the corner, to restrict civic spaces.

For instance, immediately after the 2020 youth protests, Zambia witnessed revitalization of dormant youth-centred programmes as a way of responding to youths' demands for economic empowerment and jobs. At the last count, there were seventeen such national projects under the then Ministry of Youth and Sport. Such projects were launched, or relaunched, or reinvigorated, through a $23 million Multi-Sectoral Youth Empowerment Programme to benefit 150,000 youths (Lungu 2021). The state, seemingly, strategically (re) introduced and channelled money through 'youth empowerment schemes' as a way of buying support (Mwebantu 2020c). However, the strategy proved ineffective. Just as happened in 1991 and 2011, the youth and other citizens took the money but voted against the governing party (Electoral Commission of Zambia 2021).

Clearly, a vigorous macro dialogue between the state and youth was taking place in Zambia through the two sides' actions. Primarily, this offline and online debate was around control of civic space. The speed with which the two opposing 'actors' responded over the years, but chiefly since 2004, could (in Virilio's view) determine the winner of this contest. As we have shown, each time youth claim their rights in the digital sphere, the state reverts to all means at its disposal to reassert its dominant position in that space. For a long time, this has been a tit-for-tat affair. What is not in doubt, though, is that this competition demonstrates that Zambia is in a state of dromological change.

Thus, we see the contestation over digital space as follows (Table 6.1).

As Table 6.1 shows, it is clear that the act of citizenship, and moreover, digital citizenship, is contested. From the youth perspective, citizenship is an act of placing demands upon the state through street marches and the

Table 6.1 State Versus Youth Dialogue over Cyberspace

Actors	Context	Intentions	Persuasive Aim	Actions
Youth	Citizenship	Political participation	Quest for civil rights and open spaces	Publication of Youth Charter Intended march across Lusaka streets
	Digital citizenship	Rights claims	Make internet an open and free public space	Blogging and self-broadcasting Vlogging in the 'bush' from outside Lusaka
The state	Citizenship	Minimization of digital spaces	Peace fostered by a strong, domineering state	Application of laws, institutions and systems to narrow civic spaces
		Unfettered power and control	Pursuit of peace, stability and security	Deployment of police to curtail protests
		Define public interest	Easy access to funds	Funding of numerous youth projects and programmes
	Digital citizenship	Controlled digital spaces	Protecting citizens from cybercrime and abuse	Enactment of cyber laws, Covid regulations and intensified surveillance
			Minimizing criticism of state actions	Creation of special Cyber Squad and surveillance infrastructure

publication of the Youth Charter. When that is not possible, youths resort to acts of digital citizenship through self-broadcasting, blogging and vlogging from the bush.

In response, and in line with republican conceptions of citizenship as a status bestowed upon individuals by the state (Clarke et al. 2014), the state functionaries apply the law, unleash the police and entice youth with financial incentives so as to stop public protests and narrow citizens' access to public spaces. With regard to digital citizenship, the state enacts special cyber laws, implements tough Covid regulations, and establishes special institutions such as the SJCCS, and unleashes them into cyberspaces.

Conclusion

We have positioned the digital sphere as a 'dromological society' (Virilio 2006), which is built on Castells's (2010) networked society of speed, information flows and crucial spaces. The internet, like cross-country road infrastructure, was made for the necessity of fast, frequent, long-range mobility (Dalakglou 2017). So, movement is at the centre of the occupation of digital spaces and was central to this study.

Clearly, citizenship consists of intertwined pull and push factors in a dialectical relationship between the state and youth. We have observed that the push for change was constantly made by youth, who wanted civic spaces to be opened up and to be expanded. They were inspired by the pull factors within the principles of democracy and the ideals for limited roles of the state. They pushed for dromological changes in society. On the other hand, the state experienced different pull and push factors: the push was inspired by the search for stability, peace and for state-guided civic spaces. The pull factors were embedded in the philosophies of illiberalism. Such ideas justified the state's increased access to political, economic, social, legal, surveillance and other resources – the panoptic project. However, the net result of this contestation is a country that is engrossed in a rapidly changing but constant state of social change and social movement, or dromocracy. The ultimate winner, or victor, is undetermined and thus undeclared. The fight, as we have described, is over the public sphere, including the digital space.

Bibliography

Abdullah, N. H., I. Hassan, M. F. Ahmad, bin, N. A. Hassan, and M. M. Ismail (2021) 'Social Media, Youths and Political Participation in Malaysia: A Review of Literature', *International Journal of Academic Research in Business and Social Sciences*, 11 (4): 845–57.

Allison, S. (2020) 'Audacious Zambian Protesters Outsmart the Police', *Mail & Guardian*, 26 June, accessed 20 October 2021.

Anderson, C. et al. (2021) *Navigating Civic Space in a Time of COVID: Synthesis Report*, Brighton: Institute for Development Studies, accessed 19 October 2021.

Ask Muvi TV (2020) 'President Lungu Defends Lusambo', *Facebook*, accessed 2 September 2021.

Ayibakuro, M. (2021) 'Zambia's Historic Youth Driven Vote', *PressReader*, accessed 28 September 2021.

Bauer, M., G. Gaskell, and N. C. Allum (2003) 'Quality, Quantity, and Knowledge Interests: Avoiding Confusions', in M. W. Bauer and G. Gaskell (eds), *Qualitative Researching with Text, Image and Sound*, 3–23, London: Sage.

Beaman, J. (2016) 'Citizenship as Cultural: Towards a Theory of Cultural Citizenship', *Sociology Compass*, 10: 849–57.

B'Flow (2020) @B'flow music.

Bosch, T. (2020) *Social Media and Everyday Life in South Africa*, London: Routledge.

Bratton, B. H. (2006) 'Introduction', in P. Virilio (ed.), *Speed and Politics*, 7–26, Cambridge, MA: MIT Press.

Briant, E. (2021) 'Canadian Military's Bungled Propaganda Campaigns Should Be a Lesson Across Nato', accessed 12 October 2021.

Caglar, A. (2015) 'Citizenship, Anthropology of', in J. D. Wright (ed.), *International Encyclopaedia of Social Sciences & Behavioural Sciences*, 3 (2): 637–42.

Calderisi, R. (2007) *The Trouble with Africa*, London: Yale University Press.

Castells, M. (2010) 'Globalisation, Networking, Urbanisation: Reflections on the Spatial Dynamics of the Information Age', *Urban Studies*, 37 (14): no page numbers. https://journals.sagepub.com/doi/10.1177/0042098010377365.

Chilufya-Musonda, B. and J. Mwamulima (2021) 'Zambia: The Cyber Security and Crimes Act, 2021 – Key Provisions and Implications for Service Providers and Private Citizens', *Bowmans*, 23 April, accessed 20 October 2021.

CIVICUS (2020) 'Youths Find Innovative Ways TO Protest in Zambia', CIVICUS Monitor website. https://monitor.civicus.org/updates/2020/10/26/youths-find -innovative-ways-protest-zambia/.

Clarke, J., K. Coll, E. Dagmino, and C. Neven (2014) *Disputing Citizenship*, Chicago: Policy Press.

Collins, J. (2008) 'Dromocratic Palestine', *Middle East Research and Information Project 248*, accessed 20 October 2021.

Constitution of Zambia (1996) *Constitution of Zambia*, accessed 9 June 2021.

Country Meters (2019) List of Countries and Dependent Territories of the World by Population (countrymeters.info), accessed on 30 October 2021.

Cresswell, T. (2010) 'Towards a Politics of Mobility', *Environment and Planning D: Society and Space*, 28 (1): 17–31, accessed 20 October 2021.

Cresswell, T. (2019) 'The Prosthetic Citizen: Forms of Citizenship for a Mobile World', accessed 26 August 2021.

Dahl, H. (1996) 'From Decision to Discourse: Notes on the Interplay Between Media and Democracy', in M. B. Andersen (ed.), *Media and Democracy*, 77–96, Oslo: University of Oslo Press.

Daka, H., W. J. Jacob, P. Kakupa, and K. Mwelwa (2017) 'The Use of Social Networks in Curbing HIV in Higher Education Institutions: A Case Study of the University of Zambia', *World Journal of AIDS*, 7 (2): 122–37.

Dalakglou, D. (2017) *The Road: An Ethnography of (Im)Mobility, Space, and Cross-border Infrastructures in the Balkans*. Manchester: Manchester University Press.

Deleuze, G. (1992) 'Postscript on the Societies of Control', *October*, 59: 3–7, accessed 20 May 2021.

Dolby, N. (2006) 'Popular Culture and Public Space in Africa: The Possibilities of Cultural Citizenship', *African Studies Review*, 49 (3): 31–47.

Electoral Commission of Zambia (2021) *2021 Presidential Election Results by Constituency*, accessed 20 October 2021.

Elmer, G. (2003) 'A Diagram of Panoptic Surveillance', *New Media & Society*, 5 (2): 231–47.

Eroukhmanoff, C. (2018) 'Securitisation Theory: An Introduction', accessed 29 August 2021.

Fayomi, O. O. and G. T. Adebayo (2018) 'Political Participation and Political Citizenship', in S. O. Oloruntoba and T. Falola (eds), *The Palgrave Handbook of African Politics, Governance and Development*, 537–51, New York: Palgrave Macmillan.

Fiske, J. (1993) *Power Play, Power Works*, London: Verso.

Fletcher, A. (2014) *A Short Introduction to Youth Rights*, Olympia, MA: The Freechild Project.

Flores, W. and R. Benmayor (1997) *Latino Cultural Citizenship: Claiming Identity, Space and Rights*, Boston: Beacon Press.

Fombad, C. M. (2020) 'Taming Executive Authorities in Africa: Some Reflections on Current Trends in Horizontal and Vertical Accountability', *Hague Journal on the Rule of Law*, 12: 63–91.

Foucault, M. (1977) *Discipline and Punish: The Birth of the Prison*, New York: Pantheon Books.

Freedom House (2021) 'Freedom in the World Report: Zambia', Freedom Hose website. https://freedomhouse.org/country/zambia/freedom-world/2021.

Fuchs, C. (2017) *Social Media: A Critical Introduction*, London: Sage.

Gane, N. (2012) 'The Governmentalities of Neoliberalism: Panopticism, Post-Panopticism and Beyond', *Sociological Review*, 60: 611–34.

Gavin, M. (2021) 'Warning Signs Appear Ahead of Zambian Elections', *Council on Foreign Relations Blog*, 29 July, accessed 20 October 2021.

Goodwin, C. and J. Heritage (1990) 'Conversation Analysis', *Annual Review of Anthropology*, 19: 283–307.

Grünberg, L. (2013) 'Adjusting Locally to a World Under Ubiquitous Surveillance', accessed 20 October 2021.

Hintz, A., L. Dencik, and K. Wahl-Jorgensen (2019) *Digital Citizenship in a Datafied Society*, Cambridge: Polity.

Hjorth, L. and S. Hinton (2019) *Understanding Social Media*, London: Sage.

Huawei (2021) 'New ICT Helps Build Smart Zambia', accessed 4 September 2021.

Internet World Stats (2021) 'Internet World Stats: Usage and Population Statistics, Zambia', accessed 26 May 2021.

Isin, E. and E. Ruppert (2015) *Being Digital Citizens*, London: Rowman & Littlefield.

Janse van Rensburg, A. H. (2012) 'Using the Internet for Democracy: A Study of South Africa, Kenya and Zambia', *Global Media Journal-African Edition*, 6 (1): 93–117.

Jones, E. and J. Gaventa (2002) *Concepts of Citizenship: A Review*, Brighton: Institute for Development Studies.

Kemp, S. (2021) 'Digital 2021: Zambia', DataPortal website. https://datareportal.com/reports/digital-2021-zambia?rq=Zambia.

Leach, J. (2003) 'Rhetorical Analysis', in M. W. Bauer and G. Gaskell (eds), *Qualitative Researching with Text, Image and Sound*, 207–26, London: Sage.

Let's Talk About Zambia (2020) *Break Their Bones . . . Facebook*, accessed October 2021.

Lindgren, S. (2017) *Digital Media & Society*, London: Sage.

Lungu, E. C. (2021) *Facebook Post*, accessed 8 June 2021.

Lusaka Times (2019) 'The Internet Is Worse Than Traditional Ceremonies', *Lusaka Times*, 4 November, accessed 19 June 2021.

Lusaka Times (2020) 'Police in Full Riot Gear Deployed All Over Lusaka to Stop Peaceful Protests', *Lusaka Times*, 22 June, accessed 23 May 2021.

Lusaka Times (2021) 'President Lungu Has Signed the Cyber Security and Cyber Bill into Law', *Lusaka Times*, 26 March, accessed 20 June 2021.

MISA-Zimbabwe (2021) 'Regional Communique: Zambia's Newly Enacted Cybercrime Law Challenged in Court', Media Institute for Southern Africa, 6 April, accessed 25 May 2021.

Mossberger, K., C. J. Tolbert, and R. S. McNeal (2008) *Digital Citizenship: The Internet, Society, and Participation*, Cambridge, MA: MIT Press.

Mouton, J. (2002) *How to Succeed in Your Master's and Doctoral Studies*, Pretoria: Van Schaik.

Msoni, N. (2019) 'Government Cyber Squad Aimed at Blocking Media, Internet', *Zambian Watchdog*, accessed 2 September 2021.

Mwananyanda, M. (2021) 'Free Speech? Zambia's New Internet Law Fails Basic Human Rights Scrutiny', *Daily Maverick*, 5 April, accessed 25 May 2021.

Mwebantu (2020a) 'Top Facebook Pages with High Engagement in Zambia with a Million Reach a Week, From 3 August 2020 to 9 August 2020', accessed 25 May 2021.

Mwebantu (2020b) 'Lusaka Police Studying Protest Videos, Pictures', accessed 2 September 2021.

Mwebantu (2020c) '*President Edgar Lungu Hands over Youth Empowerment Equipment*', accessed 2 September 2021.

Myers, G. (2003) 'Analysis of Conversation and Talk', in M. W. Bauer and G. Gaskell (eds), *Qualitative Researching With Text, Image and Sound*, 191–206, London: Sage.

Namwawa, M. (2021) Face-to-face Interview held in Lusaka, 1 September.

NapoleanCat (2021) 'Facebook Users in Zambia', NapoleanCat website. https://napoleoncat.com/stats/facebook-users-in-zambia/2021/09/.

News24 (2020) 'Zambia Arrests 15-year-old for Defaming President on Facebook', accessed 1 September 2021.

Nikku, B. K. and A. Azman (2017) 'Populism in the Asia: What Role for Asian Social Work?' *Social Dialogue*, 17 (5): 9–11, accessed 19 October 2021.

Noelle-Naumann, E. (1984) *The Spiral of Silence*, Chicago: University of Chicago Press.

Norris, P. (2021) 'Voters Against Democracy: The Roots of Autocratic Resurgence', *Foreign Affairs*, accessed 20 October 2021.

Nyambe, M. K. and G. Hamusunga (2017) *Youth Participation in Decision-Making Processes in Zambia: ZGF's Experience*, Lusaka: Zambian Governance Foundation, accessed 20 October 2021.

Orlet, J. and B. T. Cardoso de Castro (2016) 'Conceptions of Dromology in a Logically Conformed Society', accessed 20 October 2021.

Pangrazio, L. and J. Sefton-Green (2021) 'Digital Rights, Digital Citizenship and Digital Literacy: What's the Difference?' *Journal of News Approaches in Educational Research*, 10 (1): 15–27.

Parks, L. and R. Mukherjee (2017) 'From Platform Jumping to Self-Censorship: Internet Freedom, Social Media, and Circumvention Practices in Zambia', *Communication and Critical/Cultural Studies*, 14 (3): 221–37.

Phiri, C. (2020) 'President Lungu Is God Sent – Catholic Priest', *Zambia Reports*, 19 October, accessed 28 September 2021.

Phiri, S. (2019) 'Youth Participation in Politics: The Case of Zambian University Students', in J. Kurebwa and O. Dodo (eds), *Participation of Young People in Governance Processes in Africa*, 104–24, Dar es Salaam: Mkuki na Nyota Publishers.

Phiri, S. and Zorro (2021) 'Zambia Digital Rights Landscape Report', in T. Roberts (ed.), *Digital Rights in Closing Civic Space: Lessons from Ten African Countries*, 61–84, Brighton: Institute of Development Studies, accessed 20 October 2021.

Pilato (2020) 'Ladies and Gentlemen Word from the Organisers of the 22nd June Protest Were This Morning Summoned to Lusaka Central Police', accessed 2 September 2021.

Prior, H. R. (2014) 'Public Sphere and Panopticism: Considerations About Surveillance in Everyday Life', *Sphera Publica*, 1 (14): 23–38.

Prior, H. R. (2015) 'Democracy Is Watching You', *Revista Famecos: Midia, Cultura e Tecnologia*, 22 (1): 32–58.

Roberts, T. and T. Bosch (2021a) 'Concepts of Digital Citizenship', unpublished memo.

Roberts T. and T. Bosch (2021b) *Digital Citizenship or Digital Authoritarianism in OECD Development Co-operation Report 2021: Shaping a Just Digital Transformation*, Paris, Organisation for Economic Cooperation and Development. https://www.oecd-ilibrary.org/sites/ce08832f-en/1/3/2/9/index.html?itemI.

Sam, M. S. N. (2013) 'Dromomania', in *PsychologyDictionary.org What is DROMOMANIA? Definition of DROMOMANIA (Psychology Dictionary)*, accessed 30 October 2021.

Sanghera, G., K. Botterill, P. Hopkins, and R. Arshad (2018) '"Living Rights", Rights Claims, Performative Citizenship and Young People – The Right to Vote in the Scottish Independence Referendum', *Citizenship Studies*, 22 (5): 540–55, accessed 20 October 2021.

Schleusener, S. (2019) 'The Surveillance Nexus: Digital Culture and Society of Control', *Real: Yearbook of Research in English and American Literature*, 34 (1): 175–202.

Schoon, A., H. M. Mabweazara, T. Bosch, and H. Dugmore (2020) 'Decolonising Digital Media Research Methods: Positioning African Digital Experiences as Epistemic Sites of Knowledge Production', *African Journalism Studies*, 41 (4): 1–15, accessed 19 October 2021.

Silvia, A. (2012) 'Conversation Analysis and the Structure of Conversation', Jakarta, English Department, UIN Syarif Hidayatullash, Unpublished Presentation Paper.

Singh, P. (2018) 'Digital Citizenship: Issues and Challenges of Privacy in India', *International Research Journal of Commerce, Arts and Science*, 9 (3): 178–85.

Social Bakers (2021) 'Zambia Facebook Page Statistics', accessed 25 May 2021.

StatCounter (2021) 'Social Media Stats Zambia', accessed 27 May 2021.

Sundaram, R. (2010) *Pirate Modernity*, New York: Routledge.

Temwa, M. (2016) 'Cyber Security in Zambia', 24 August, accessed 28 September 2021.

The Sydney Morning Herald (2004) 'Zambian Parliament Passes Tough Cyber-Crime Law', 11 August, accessed 25 May 2021.

Times of Zambia (2021) 'Facebook Home Page', accessed 31 May 2021.

Turner, B. S. (1990) 'Outline of a Theory of Citizenship', *Sociology*, 24 (2): 189–217.

USAID. (2021) *Democracy, Human Rights, and Governance*, Zambia: U.S. Agency for International Development (usaid.gov), accessed 30 October 2021.

van Deursen, A., J. van Dijk, and E. Helsper (2014) *Investigating Outcomes of Online Engagement*, London: London School of Economics, accessed 28 May 2021.

van Dijck, J. (2014) 'Datafication, Dataism and Dataveillance: Big Data Between Scientific Paradigm and Ideology', *Surveillance & Society*, 12 (2): 197–208.

Virilio, P. (2006) *Speed and Politics*, Cambridge, MA: MIT Press.

Vlasenko, O. et al. (2021) 'Audit of Digital Civic Space in the Modern School: From Teacher to Creative Leader', *BRAIN: Broad Research in Artificial Intelligence and Neuroscience*, 12 (3): 214–35, accessed 19 October 2021.

Willems, W. (2016) 'Social Media, Platform Power and (Mis)Information in Zambia's Recent Elections', *Africa at LSE Blog*, 30 August, accessed 20 October 2021.

Willems, W. (2019) '"The Politics of Things": Digital Media, Urban Space, and the Materiality of Publics', *Media, Culture & Society*, 41 (8): 1192–209.

Wyche, S. and E. P. Baumer (2017) 'Imagined Facebook: An Exploratory Study of Non-Users' Perceptions of Social Media in Rural Zambia', *New Media & Society*, 19 (7): 1092–108.

Yartey, F. N. A. and L. Ha (2015) 'Smartphones and Self-Broadcasting Among College Students in an Age of Social Media', in A. Mesquita and C. Tai (eds), *Human Behavior, Psychology and Social Interaction in the Digital Era*, 95–129, Hershey PA: IGI Global.

Youkhana, E. (2015) 'A Conceptual Shift in Studies of Belonging and the Politics of Belonging', *Cogitatio*, 3 (4): 10–24.

Zambia Daily Mail (2021) 'Zambia Daily Mail Facebook Page', accessed 20 October 2021.

Zambia Government (2015) *National Youth Policy*, Lusaka: Ministry of Youth and Sport.

Zambia Government (2004) *Computer Misuse and Crimes Act No. 13 of 2004, The Zambia Computer Misuse and Crimes Act, 2004*, 3, ICT Policy Africa, accessed 5 October 2021.

Zambia Landscape (2020) 'Minister for Lusaka Lusambo Gives Youths 24 hrs to Apologise', accessed 2 September 2021.

Zambian Eye (2020) 'Zambian Youth Charter 2020: Youths Demand Accountable Leadership', *Zambia Eye*, 10 August, accessed 23 May 2021.

Zed Gossip (2020) 'Apparently, This Is What Kings Malembe Malembe Said, Which has Irked ba Bowman Lusambo, Lusaka Province Minister', accessed 2 September 2021.

ZICTA (2014) *2014 Annual Report*, Lusaka: Zambia Information and Communications Technology Authority, accessed 28 September 2021.

7

Digital citizenship and political accountability in Namibia's 2019 election

Mavis Elias and Tony Roberts

Introduction

In 2012 only 10 per cent of urban Namibians and 1 per cent of rural Namibians had internet access. Over the past decade, the percentage of citizens using the internet has grown substantially, but it remains the case that only half the population use the internet (World Bank 2022; Kemp 2022). During the national election of 2019, citizen's use of the internet in political engagement was a significant factor, with Namibians using social media to criticize unemployment levels, hold corrupt politicians to account and call for people to vote against the ruling SWAPO regime (Nakale 2019). This chapter analyses the emergence of digital citizenship and asks the question of how Namibian citizens used social media to hold politicians accountable during the 2019 election.

According to Mossberger, Tolbert and McNeal (2008: 2), 'Digital citizens are those who use technology frequently, who use technology for political information to fulfil their civic duty, and who use technology at work for economic gain.' The use of mobile and internet technologies is steadily increasing. The number of mobile phone subscriptions in Namibia has exceeded the number of citizens since 2017 (Statista 2021), and the percentage of citizens using the internet increased from 14 per cent to more than 40 per cent between the national elections of 2014 and 2019 (World Bank 2021). As this chapter will illustrate, the use of electronic petitions, electronic government portals and social media for civic engagement in political life has also grown significantly over the same period.

Although there is a burgeoning literature on digital citizenship and on digital governance, to date this has focused disproportionately on experiences in the Global North. There has been relatively little research on digital citizenship in Africa and none on digital citizenship for political accountability in Namibia. This chapter addresses that gap. The absence of existing literature presents a challenge as there is little data on which to build. This chapter therefore draws on grey literature, including media reports, social media posts and key informant interviews to provide a foundation upon which other scholars can build.

Background: The Namibian political context

Namibia is located in South-West Africa with a 1,572 kilometre coastline extending north from South Africa. It is sparsely populated with just 2.5 million people occupying a territory of 825,418 square kilometres. Namibia emerged from German colonial rule and from racial segregation under the apartheid South African regime to hold its first democratic elections in 1989 (Namibia Statistics Agency 2013; Saunders 2018). The South-West African People's Organization (SWAPO) has won every presidential election since liberation in 1989, resulting in more than three decades of uninterrupted one-party rule (Melber 2020). SWAPO enjoyed between an overwhelming majority (74–80 per cent) in national elections from 1995 until 2014 (Melber 2021).

However, the 2019 national election saw the first ever fall in support for SWAPO, with its percentage of the popular vote falling from 80 per cent to 65 per cent (Nakale 2020). Although still a commanding majority, the elections marked a significant fall in public support, with some analysts noting youth disengagement with establishment politics as explaining declining support (Tjipueja 2019).

Older voters who lived under apartheid remain loyal to SWAPO which delivered independence from external domination. However, for the 'born free' generation (those born after 1989), the high levels of youth unemployment and government corruption are compelling issues. Tjipueja (2019) highlighted that 52 per cent of the votes cast in the 2019 election were cast by people under the age of thirty-four (up from 44 per cent in 2014) and 30 per cent were 'born free'. This generation of Namibians is also more active on social media, including Facebook, Instagram and Twitter (WeAreSocial 2019).

The number of Namibian citizens with internet connectivity increased from 80,000 in 2000 to one million by the elections of 2019, by which time both citizens and politicians were using a range of digital technologies in political discourse from e-government platforms to social media (O'Dea 2021). In a country where party politics was stagnant for decades and in which the main press and TV channels were either state-owned or state-regulated, social media provided a novel and relatively vibrant platform to participate in discussions of Namibian politics. In the run-up to the 2019 election some Namibians used digital technologies to air their concerns about unemployment, participate in political discourse and call government to account for its record on unemployment and corruption (Shihomeka 2017). Prior to the 2019 election, the youth unemployment rate stood at 46 per cent. The gerontocratic party structure of SWAPO was seen as failing to represent young citizens, and issues of corruption had resulted in a lack of trust in the political system and disengagement from electoral politics (Mathekga 2021; Melber 2021; Nakale 2020).

Literature review

The chapter focuses on the intersection between the study of digital technologies, citizenship and governance, as illustrated in Figure 7.1. The intersection of the three elements is the focus of this chapter: the use of digital technologies to enable participatory digital governance such that citizens' voices are influential in holding politician powerholders to account. This section reviews the existing literature on digital citizenship and digital governance to inform an analysis of online participation and accountability during Namibia's 2019 election.

Digital citizenship is the ability to participate in society using digital tools and using online platforms (Mossberger et al. 2008). Not all citizens have the digital devices, connectivity or literacies needed to achieve digital citizenship, though. Roberts and Hernandez (2019) offer the five 'A's of availability, affordability, awareness, abilities and agency as a framework to analyse this

Figure 7.1 Intersecting areas of research. *Source*: Authors.

uneven digital access among citizens. Digital citizens, according to Mossberger et al. (2008), are 'those who use technology [daily] for political information to fulfil their civic duty, and who use technology at work for economic gain'. Oyedemi (2020) characterizes digital citizens as those who can regularly and flexibly apply technology in social, cultural, economic and political life, and he connects digital citizenship to issues of rights, equality and social justice. Isin and Ruppert (2015: 44) argue that the capacity for making rights claims is central to citizenship and that 'becoming digital citizens' involves citizens making those rights claims using digital tools or over the internet. This chapter includes an analysis of Namibian citizens' access to and use of digital tools to claim the right to accountable, corruption-free government.

The advent of social media led to a great deal of literature on the emancipatory potential of digital technologies for circumventing establishment control of media and government (Shirky 2008; Ekine 2010). In their review of the digital citizenship literature, Hintz, Dencik and Wahl-Jorgensen (2019: 31) note that 'the overarching focus in studies of digital citizenship is on users' action and digital agency' with the result that 'the concept of digital citizenship has an intrinsic connection with citizen empowerment' (2019: 31). However, particularly since the Cambridge Analytica scandal and the Snowden revelations about state surveillance, scholarship has turned to explore how state and corporate use of digital technology has closed the space of digital citizenship (Hintz et al. 2019; Roberts and Mohamed Ali 2021). Hintz et al. (2019: 40) conclude that 'Digital citizenship is thus constituted, partly, through the enactment of users but also, partly, through data analysis by the state and the private sector'.

Governance refers to the way power is exercised in the management of a country's social and economic resources (World Bank 1991). 'Good governance' and 'participatory democracy' are normative views about how governance should be improved by, among other things, increasing transparency, accountability and extending the inclusion of citizens in governance (UNESCAP 2009). The global consensus that all states should commit to achieving 'more responsive, inclusive, participatory, and representative decision-making at every level' is enshrined in the Sustainable Development Goals (SDGs) as target 16.7 (United Nations Development Programme 2015).

Digital governance was hailed with the promise that the application of mobile and internet technologies to the objectives of participatory governance would enable more open, transparent and accountable governance. It was argued by multilateral agencies and politicians that through measures such as payroll automation, making budgets transparent online and enabling more interactive policy discussion between citizens and powerholders, corruption could be reduced, decision-making made more participatory and government more responsive (UNCTAD 2020). Sæbø, Rose and Skiftenes Flak (2008: 4) define digital participation as 'the extension and transformation of participation in societal democratic and consultative processes mediated by information and communication technologies (ICT), primarily the Internet'. Practical examples are the use of government websites, discussion forums, blogs, wikis, chat rooms, geographical information systems, decision support systems, voting systems and podcasts (Sæbø, Rose and Molka-Danielsen 2010). The use of social media platforms such as Twitter, WhatsApp, Instagram and Facebook has gained popularity to allow for interactive many-to-many communication, enabling the public to participate in public discourse and officials to garner public opinion on policy issues (United Nations 2020).

Advocates of digital governance point to its benefits, such as when Afghanistan moved to paying police officers directly to their mobile phones, which resulted in a 30 per cent decrease in salary misappropriation (Leber 2012). 'Civic tech' innovations include the creation of apps that enable citizens to monitor government budgets and project implementation, actively participate in inclusive decision-making and call officials to account. Examples include FixMyStreet, which allows citizens to report and discuss neighbourhood issues with local government, and crowdsourced platforms like Publish What You Pay, which enables citizens to track procurement and project contracts. Broader participatory budgeting and participatory democracy platforms like Decidim allow citizens to participate in governance and 'reprogram democracy' in municipalities, including Yacatan, Helsinki and Barcelona.[1] Some countries (including Ukraine) have established an online asset declaration system for elected politicians to create transparency and combat corruption (Cela 2018). However, research shows that technologies alone are insufficient to deliver the kind of trusting civic relationships necessary to meet wider governance and democratic objectives (McGee et al. 2018). In his review of digital development programmes, Toyama (2015) concluded that technology can amplify existing human capacity and intent but that it can never substitute for their absence. This means that when there is no political will or insufficient capacity, even the most sophisticated technology is unlikely to deliver good governance.

Affordances are a concept from technology design science that can help analyse how particular technologies make new actions possible. Affordances are the particular 'action possibilities' that a specific technology enables or allows (Norman 1988). From this perspective, social media affords digital citizens the new action possibility of self-publishing a text message, blog or video message and transmitting it instantly to a global audience – something previously only possible for media moguls. Citizens can use these new affordances to share videos of cats or to call out government corruption. Politicians can use the affordances of digital technologies to provide real-time transparency online on government finances, or they can use them to conduct mass surveillance (Zuboff 2019). The point here is that the action possibilities of digital technologies are not technologically determined; they are determined by the political choices and agency of politicians and citizens (MacKensie and Wajcman 1985). As Krantzberg (1967) argued, technology itself is neither good nor bad, nor is it ever neutral.

Critiques of digital governance argue that marginalized citizens are excluded from digital governance and that social media disproportionately

---

[1]   https://decidim.org/

amplifies already relatively privileged voices (Tufekci 2014). Social media has also served as a platform for xenophobic and misogynist voice and amplified political disinformation and anti-democratic forces, as exemplified by the Cambridge Analytica scandal in the 2016 election that brought Donald Trump to power and the mobilization to breach the Capitol building when he lost the 2020 election (Farivar 2021).

Technology access

To address the critique of digital exclusion it can be helpful to incorporate a tool for foregrounding hierarchies of technology access into any assessment. Roberts and Hernandez (2019) have provided a simple model for thinking through barriers–enablers of technology exclusion–inclusion. They argue that the introduction of digital technologies into social processes always excludes someone. The five 'A's – availability, affordability, awareness, abilities and agency – is a simple heuristic device to guide assessment through a five-stage reflection about potential barriers and enablers to technology access. They can be visualized as five concentric circles (see Figure 7.2).

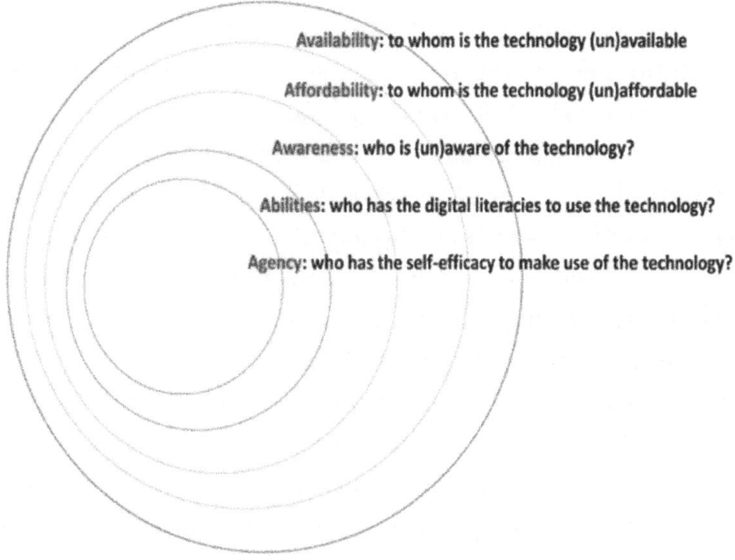

Figure 7.2 The five 'A's of technology access. *Source*: Roberts.

In any population there are some citizens for whom there is no internet *availability* because the cellular or internet connectivity does not reach where they live. In those geographies where there is a signal, there is a smaller group of people who cannot *afford* to have unlimited data. Among those who can afford technology access, there is a smaller group of people who lack *awareness* about its availability or its relevance to their priorities. Where there is availability, affordability and awareness, a lack of *abilities* can be a barrier to use (including digital and language literacies). *Agency* can be a barrier where social norms and values mean that use of a particular technology is discouraged for people of a particular gender, age or status. At the time of the 2019 election in Namibia, only 31 per cent of the population were internet users and 70 per cent of Twitter users were men, so dimensions of access are critical to understanding the potential and limits of digital citizenship.

Citizen Control

Another dimension commonly used to analyse civic engagement is the extent to which a process is initiated and controlled by citizens or the state. Citizen-led or 'bottom-up' processes include organizing petitions and citizen assemblies to aggregate opinion and focus collective action to strengthen claim-making on powerholders (European Parliament 2011; Kneuer 2016; Porwol, Ojo and Breslin 2016). Government-led or top-down processes include consultations and focus groups to solicit opinion and validate policy directions (Kneuer 2016; Porwol, Ojo and Breslin 2016). This distinction enables analysis of the origin and location of power in processes (Kneuer 2016). Assessing initiatives using these tools can provide insights into why some secure uptake and others fail to gain widespread interest from citizens as they can be perceived to be unrepresentative, monopolized by special interests and fail to generate trust among the general public (Sæbø et al. 2010).

The categories of bottom-up and top-down are not mutually exclusive, and well-functioning systems often include both. Porwol et al. (2016) developed an integrated model for participatory digital governance (or 'e-participation'). Their model usefully incorporates both top-down government-led initiatives and bottom-up digital citizenship, as illustrated in Figure 7.3.

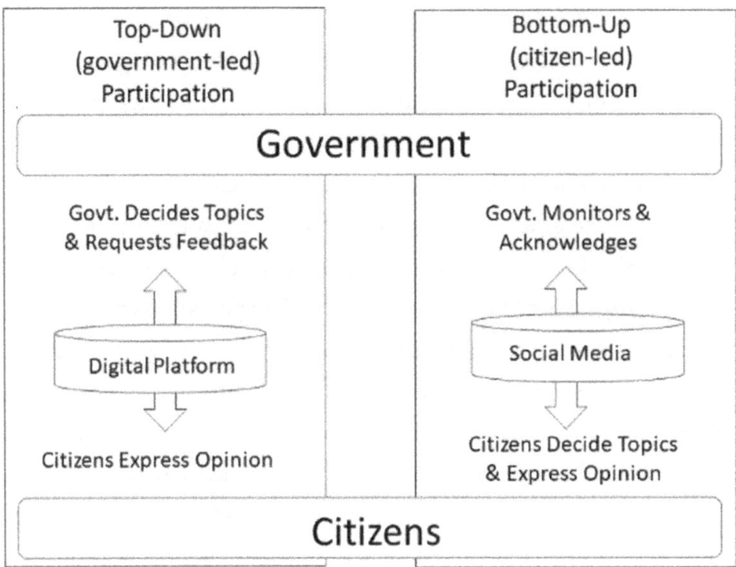

Figure 7.3 Top-down versus bottom-up participation. *Source*: Authors adapted from Porwol et al. 2016.

Elements of accountability

Schmitter (2007: 4) defines political accountability as 'a mutual exchange of responsibilities and potential sanctions between citizens and rulers, made all the more complicated by the fact that in between the two are usually a varied and competitive set of representatives'. Public oversight institutions such as anti-corruption commissions, ombudsmen, complaint offices and human rights commissions manage to influence accountability through what is called 'horizontal accountability' and refer to the relatively equal relationship between the state's institutions of checks and balances (McGee and Gaventa 2011). However, in the Namibian context, these public oversight institutions lack 'clout' and trust from citizens due to political and bureaucratic corruption which is enhanced by the proximity of public oversight officials to political candidates and 'wrongdoers go[ing] unpunished because of political considerations dictated by the ethno-social system of patronage' (Bertelsmann Stiftung's Transformation Index (BTI) 2012: 6).

Vertical accountability refers to the relationship between citizens and their elected representatives in democracies. The 'deepening of democracy' is a school of thought that advocates for extending citizen participation in governance beyond elections, and involves the study of rights-claiming, including demands for political accountability (McGee and Gaventa 2011). A report by McGee et al. (2018) synthesized findings from more than forty research projects focused on using digital technologies to amplify citizen voice and test the working assumptions and expectations about the roles that technologies can play in enhancing government accountability and responsiveness. The report found that not all citizens have access to digital technologies or the agency to use them in political engagement, but for those that do, they can provide new spaces for engagement between the citizen and state. The report also found that transparency and access to information were not sufficient to generate accountability and that the kind of trusting relationships and interactions necessary for accountability were rarely developed online (McGee et al. 2018).

Fox (2007: 663) noted the widespread 'hope that transparency will empower efforts to change the behaviour of powerful institutions by holding them accountable'. However, he questioned the assumption that increased transparency and access to information necessarily enhances accountability, as did other scholars (McGee and Gaventa 2011; Kneuer 2016), concluding that not only is it necessary for collective action to aggregate citizen 'voice' and influence, but they also need mechanisms that provide them with the 'teeth' to secure accountability (Fox 2015).

As a means to assess accountability, the Organisation for Economic Co-operation and Development (OECD) suggests three constituent elements of accountability: transparency, answerability and enforceability, which it defines as follows (OECD 2014: 33):

- **Transparency:** citizens have access to information about commitments that the state has made and whether it has met them.
- **Answerability:** citizens are able to demand that the state justifies its action.
- **Enforceability:** citizens are able to sanction the state if it fails to meet certain standards.

These three concepts are incorporated into the conceptual framework used in this chapter to assess Namibian citizens' use of digital technologies to secure accountability during the 2019 elections.

Conceptual framework

To incorporate the advantages of each method, in this chapter we use a model for assessing the use of digital that draws on the five 'A's (Roberts and Hernandez 2019), Porwol et al. (2016) and the OECD (2014). The model uses the five 'A's to assess digital inclusion – that is, who has the necessary access and ability to use the digital tools in question. The integrated model for e-participation is used to assess the top-down and bottom-up mechanisms for translating access and agency into digital citizenship, and the tripartite OECD framework of transparency, answerability and enforceability is used to assess the extent to which digital citizenship translates into political accountability. The model is illustrated in Figure 7.4.

Digital citizenship in Namibia

This section presents evidence of growing levels of digital citizenship before the 2019 election. It considers different digital tactics adopted by citizens but begins with some examples of digital governance. These examples of the digital agency of government are presented based on the argument of Hintz et al. (2019) that digital citizenship is constituted by the activities of the state and corporations as well as by the agency of citizens themselves. Governments, digital platforms companies and media houses play a key role in establishing the environment for digital citizenship. Government policy and practice establish a hostile or enabling environment for digital citizenship. Most of the popular social media platforms are run by private corporations, and mainstream media still plays a critical role in what elements of discourse from social media cross over to the dominant political discourse.

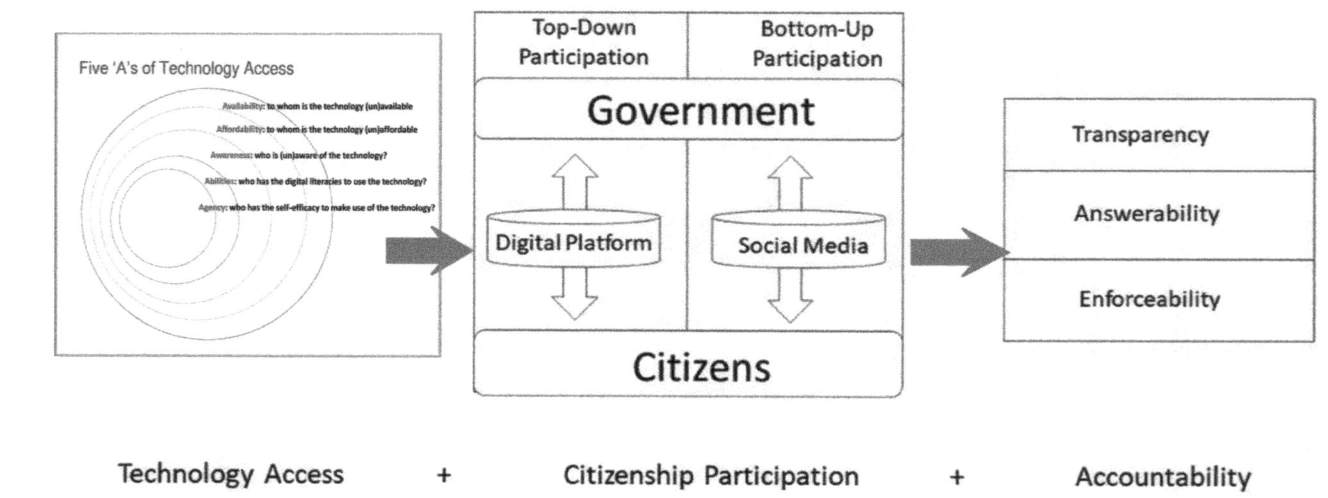

Figure 7.4 DiCaf framework. *Source*: Authors adapted from Roberts and Hernandez 2017; Porwol et al. 2016; OECD 2014.

A number of digital government initiatives have been adopted by Namibian ministries, including the addition of digital government services to run alongside in-person service delivery. The Namibian Ministry of Regional and Local Government, Housing and Rural Development (MRLGHRD) published its first digital governance strategy in 2008 (MRLGHRD 2008). The strategy included the objective of making all government services available electronically by December 2015. The city of Windhoek was one of the first to allow the general public to download government information, access forms and lodge complaints on its website. The Integrated Tax Administration System (ITAS) is an example of a national government service that is now available online, allowing citizens to access their tax account 24 hours a day, 365 days a year, making it easier for digital citizens to access information and process returns from their home or workplace and to receive real-time notifications of their tax status (Namibia Revenue Agency 2021). The government provides some financial incentives for online submission (Schlettwein 2019). The Ministry of Finance publicises ITAS on its Facebook page, where citizens can also comment and complain about services. The United Nations' e-Participation Index is a global ranking of governments' progress in fostering civic engagement and participatory governance through digital technologies. Namibia was ranked 112 of 193 countries in 2020 (UN 2021).

The Namibian National Assembly adopted a social media use policy and communication plan in 2017, in recognition of its growing importance in civic engagement (Ministry of Information and Communication Technology 2016). The policy and plan called for government offices to establish accounts on all of the main social media platforms. A study by Shihomeka (2017) on new media and political engagement in Namibia recorded the expanding political significance of digital engagement but noted that most of the population remained excluded from digital citizenship as they had no internet connectivity. Shihomeka also noted how elected officials' use of social media in Namibia is heightened during election periods and decreases afterwards, and how rural populations are under-represented in online participation (Shihomeka 2017). SWAPO's use of social media to influence digital citizenship around the election is considered in the section alongside the campaigns of other actors.

Namibian election 2019

Citizen use of digital technologies expanded significantly prior to the 2019 election. In 2011, only 10 per cent of all Namibians and only 1 per cent of the rural population had access to the internet (NSA 2011), but by the 2019 election, 31 per cent of the population were active internet users, with 630,000 active on Facebook and 46,000 on Twitter (WeAreSocial 2019; Kemp 2019). The main campaign issues were discussed and debated online by digital citizens (Mwenye et al. 2019). This section presents some of the key issues that animated online discussion during the election period, in order to analyse the technologies and tactics employed.

Namibia's 2019 election witnessed a significant amount of digital campaigning designed specifically to increase voter turnout and to influence the outcome. Digital campaigning is understood to mean strategically coordinated collective activities that engage a specific topic to a targeted audience using digital technologies to achieve predefined goals and objectives (Aichholzer and Rose 2020). Digital campaigning can be led by political parties or independent institutions or be citizen-led.

During the 2019 election, the Commonwealth Observer Group noted that citizens made extensive use of social media platforms to participate in political discourse (Mwenye et al. 2019). The main hashtags used to aggregate election content on Twitter were #ElectionYear19, #NamVotes19, #NamibiaVotes19 and #NamibiaVotes2019. The Electoral Commission of Namibia (ECN) ran a non-partisan digital campaign under the hashtag #IWillVote. Their campaign was run on Facebook and Twitter to support voter education and awareness to secure a high turnout on election day (ECN 2019a) and included messages encouraging engagement in the campaign and voter turnout.

The ruling party, SWAPO, ran its online re-election campaign under the banner #WeHaveHeardYou to communicate that it had heard citizens' concerns about unemployment and corruption and that it could be trusted to be responsive to them after the election. Campaign tweets featured marketing photographs of candidates and high-quality designs. The main opposition party, the Popular Democratic Movement (PDM), which eventually polled in second place, aimed to tap into electoral discontent under the hashtag #ChangeIsComing, encouraging digital citizens to vote for them. The issues that garnered most attention online prior to the election were youth unemployment and government corruption.

Contentious election issues

The next section discusses the topics that dominated online digital citizenship in the election period: declaration of assets by politicians, the Fishrot corruption scandal, youth unemployment and missing election voting machines.

Declaration of assets by parliamentarians

As a means of combating financial corruption, some countries maintain a public register on which they require elected officials to regularly declare their assets (OECD 2011). In 2015, President Geingob declared his assets and urged all members of Parliament to do the same, saying, 'Declaration of assets is an indicator of transparency and accountability, and if you do things legitimately then what do you have to hide? Accountability and transparency help to develop trust' (Weylandt 2016: 3). However, media investigations suggested that members of Parliament were dishonest in their declaration of assets, with many declaring nil or negligible assets (Likela 2020). Journalists assessed these declarations to be untruthful and to 'make a mockery' of transparency and accountability (New Era 2015). The asset registry in Namibia was not made available online, calling into question the government's commitment to transparency. The issue became the subject of significant debate on social media, with some citizens welcoming the declaration of assets by the president and First Lady as an advance for democratic accountability. Other digital citizens echoed the critique of journalists and used social media to call for accountability from other parliamentarians by submitting truthful declarations of assets in accordance with their government's own policy.

Fishrot scandal

Two weeks before the 2019 Namibian election, WikiLeaks published 30,000 emails, contracts, spreadsheets and PowerPoint presentations implicating six senior SWAPO officials in a $10 million corruption scandal involving a valuable fishing concession dubbed the 'Fishrot' scandal (Links 2020; Bonga 2021). The leaked documents alleged collusion between the Fishrot 6 to provide fishing quotas to the Icelandic commercial fishing conglomerate Samherji in exchange for financial kickbacks over a four-year period (Gibson 2020; Kleinfeld 2019). Namibian citizens used social media hashtag #Fishrot campaigns and electronic petitions to call for action. One petition on change.org gathered almost 20,000 signatures (Iyaloo 2019; Wentworth 2019). Mainstream media covered the story extensively and referred to social media comments in their coverage, bringing pressure to bear on the government to make itself accountable (Slinger 2019; Pflughoeft and Schneider 2020). Two government ministers were forced to resign. Digital citizens used social media to call for the public to vote against corruption, reminding them that they had the power to deliver change at the polls.

Ahead of election day, the presidential press secretary held a press conference and tried to diminish the damage caused by the revelations, calling it disinformation designed to influence the election outcome and tarnish the reputation of Namibia (Links 2019). Criminal charges have since been brought against ten people, including former Minister of Justice and the former Minister of Fisheries, who were scheduled to stand trial in the Windhoek High Court in 2022.

Youth unemployment and the electorate

Youth unemployment, which stood at 46 per cent prior to the election (NSA 2018), was a major issue in online debates. The Commonwealth Observer Group, which monitored conditions on the ground ahead of polling, reported that there was a significant level of voter apathy among young voters due to high unemployment (Mwenye et al. 2019). Despite this reported apathy, the majority of those voting (52 per cent) on election day were aged eighteen to thirty-two years. Almost a third (30 per cent) were 'born frees' aged twenty-nine or under (Tjipueja 2019). Digital citizens articulated their growing discontent about the lack of employment opportunities, levels of homelessness and poor health services, with some using social media to discourage citizens from voting for SWAPO, as a means of protest.

Missing voting machines

Shortly before election day, *The Namibian* newspaper reported that three electronic voting machines were missing after having been lent to the ruling SWAPO party by the Electoral Commission of Namibia in 2017. The newspaper article accused the ECN of concealing relevant information from the public and only being transparent when the story broke (Namibia Fact Check 2019; Smith 2019). The missing voting machines created public mistrust in the Electoral Commission and in the authenticity of election outcomes. Citizens took to social media to air their grievances, highlighting their distrust and demanding an honest account of who the machines were lent to and when. In a video shared on Facebook by *The Namibian*, the Independent Patriots for Change (IPC) candidate Panduleni Itula challenged the use of the voting machines in the elections. An online petition was launched, calling for the removal of the machines; it gained 2,786 signatures (Go Petition 2019).

Discussion

In this section, we analyse the examples of digital citizenship presented earlier, using the five 'A's framework adopted at the outset and illustrated in Figure 7.2 to answer the main research question: How did Namibian citizens use social media to hold politicians accountable during the 2019 election?

Access

Citizenship processes that rely on digital tools always exclude some parts of the population (Roberts and Hernandez 2019). At the time of the election, only a quarter of Namibians had the mobile devices and connectivity necessary to be digital citizens (WeAreSocial 2019). The five 'A's of technology access are one means of analysing hierarchies of inclusion (Roberts and Hernandez 2019).

Availability

Availability of cellular broadband is a barrier or enabler of digital citizenship. Fourth-generation (4G) mobile data speeds that are needed to engage in the kinds of digital citizenship mentioned earlier, on Twitter, Instagram and Facebook, were not available in many rural areas of Namibia in 2019.

Affordability

Affordability of 4G mobile data connectivity excluded some people from digital citizenship and limited the length of time others were able to take part in online debate.

Awareness

Awareness of which discussions were taking place when and on what social media platforms also affected who participated in digital citizenship.

Abilities

Abilities refer to the various literacies (technical, political and language) that exclude or include individuals' participation in particular aspects of digital citizenship.

Agency

It is also clear that social norms (including gendered norms) affect whether people have **agency** to take part in online political discourse. In Namibia, 71 per cent of online participants in 2019 were male (WeAreSocial 2019). This echoes Tufekci's (2014) point that if we rely on social media for digital citizenship, we must be conscious that urban, male, middle-class voices will be over-represented at the expense of rural women, who remain largely silenced.

Citizenship mechanisms

Prior to the 2019 election, the Namibian government was making progress expanding digital government services and using social media to interact with citizens. It had implemented several top-down government digital services such as online information access and a tax account portal. However, there were no interactive digital spaces, nor was there parliamentary asset transparency or any decision-making platforms along the lines of Decidim. Unlike South Africa and Kenya, Namibia has chosen not to become a member of the Open Government Partnership which supports government to increase transparency and accountability by, among other things, making national budget and expenditure records available.[2]

Rhetorically, the Namibian president pledged that his government 'is committed to promote effective governance and to execute its mandate, on the principles of accountability and transparency' (Geingob 2017: 1). In his 2019 New Year's Eve message, the president declared that 2019 would be the 'year of accountability', proclaiming his belief that transparency plus accountability will result in improved levels of trust (NBC 2019). Although the president had been transparent in making his own personal assets public and had urged other members of his government to do the same, the register of assets remains incomplete and has never been shared online, making it practically impossible for most citizens to access the records. More systematic transparency declarations by elected officials and real-time publishing of government finances on the internet are political and technical options that remain available to the Namibian government in the years ahead. The technology exists to make government data open and transparent, but in Namibia, as elsewhere, it is generally more difficult to mobilize the political will for this. And as Toyama (2015) concluded, technology can only amplify existing human capacity and intent.

Citizen-led mechanisms of digital citizenship include using online petitions and social media fora to influence narratives, to make accountability claims on government and to call on other citizens to vote in particular ways. WikiLeaks posted evidence on the internet, journalists posted their stories on Facebook and Twitter, and digital citizens contributed their critique and analysis across all the main social media platforms, causing the Fishrot corruption scandal

---

[2]   https://www.opengovpartnership.org/

to trend locally and spread virally through the diaspora. This put significant pressure on the government in the critical two weeks before the election. The government responded using its own social media channels, in an attempt to diffuse the criticism and promise action. This created a vibrant interaction of bottom-up and top-down information exchange that was successful in securing the accountability of politicians, in as much as ministers resigned and are due to appear in the High Court.

The affordances of social media for interactive many-to-many communication provide a channel for digital citizenship that is not entirely framed by political parties and establishment media. It is, however, mediated by commercial platforms whose opaque algorithms manipulate what appears in a digital citizen's social media feed in ways that are secret. So, although social media expands the space of digital citizenship and enhances citizens' agency and freedoms of expression, the affordances of the platform and its algorithms also shape and limit citizen agency in ways that are not transparent. Nevertheless, Namibian digital citizens were able to exercise their democratic right in the run-up to the election to raise issues of public concern on social media, organize electronic petitions and engage in a form of bottom-up digital citizenship not previously enabled by traditional media or political parties.

Online petitions are a hybrid tool for digital citizenship because citizens initiate them bottom-up to make demands, but they are designed to elicit government responsiveness. Once a petition has been submitted, the formal procedures of acknowledging or acting on its demands are organized top-down by government officials (Aichholzer and Rose 2020). Within the case context of the e-petitions submitted in the Fishrot corruption scandal, for example, no government institution provided a response, which raises questions about the government's commitment to accountability. Online petitions are an effective means for digital citizens to aggregate opinion, create a campaign focus, generate a contact list and articulate a collective demand for accountability. However, as Fox (2015) concluded about many social accountability mechanisms, even when they are successful in aggregating 'voice', they often lack the 'teeth' necessary to generate responsive, accountable government.

Digital campaigning can be bottom-up (citizen-led) or top-down (government-led) (Aichholzer and Rose 2020). SWAPO's top-down campaign led with the #WeHaveHeardYou slogan, which was intended to position the party as listening to complaints, suggestions and input from citizens and being responsive. However, the SWAPO digital campaign was a unidirectional 'communique' rather than interactive 'communication': encouraging party voting without any evidence of having listened and taken tangible action in response to citizens' demands. While SWAPO uses the language of transparency and accountability, concrete evidence of each is difficult to find. The next section continues a systematic analysis using the OECD element of the conceptual framework.

Transparency

Transparency within domestic accountability implies that citizens and institutions have access to information about commitments made by the state (the government and its agencies) and the extent to which these commitments have been honoured (Loquai and Fanetti 2011).

In the Fishrot case, transparency was provided by a whistle-blower who provided WikiLeaks with files exposing corruption between the Icelandic company where he worked and the Namibian government. After WikiLeaks released the files over the internet, they were made available to local journalists in Namibia who covered the story, spurring citizen comment, calling for the president to sack the accused and make good on his policy of 'zero tolerance for corruption'. When local newspaper *The Informante* (2019) added the news that SWAPO had accepted resignations from ministers Shangala and Esau and withdrawn the two from the National Assembly, the post received 954 likes and 338 comments, some demanding they be brought to court. It is impossible to precisely measure the influence of digital citizenship in this sequence of events, but it is reasonable to say that it was not insignificant. As Aichholzer and Rose (2020) note, government accountability is often elicited when there is a cross-fertilization between transparency and increased citizen engagement in making demands on government.

Answerability

Answerability within domestic accountability implies that government, its agencies and public officials are obligated to provide information to justify their actions and decisions to the public and supervising institutions (Loquai and Fanetti 2011).

The digital citizenship campaign around the missing electronic voting machines is a case in point. The disappearance of the machines was not explained, nor were they recovered. Citizens' demands for responsiveness went unheeded. The Electoral Commission's 'tight-lipped' response to the missing voting machines fell short of optimal transparency. The issue only came to light due to investigative journalism bringing to the public's attention a matter that the ECN had been aware of for some months. This suggests that horizontal accountability was not functioning and that the relevant public oversight institutions lack distance from the executive or 'clout'. In this case, the vertical accountability demands from citizens and independent media did not elicit answerability. The ECN did feel it necessary to provide some justification to manage public perception in the form of a guarded press release, but only after the issue was brought to light by the media. However, it did not answer any of the central questions about where the machines went, why and who was responsible. The government did provide some information, but this did not amount to a justification of their actions. It fell short of genuine answerability; nobody was ever held accountable.

The case in which digital citizens *were* able to elicit answerability was the #Fishrot scandal. Responding to social media demands for the sacking of ministers implicated in the scandal, the government was forced to publicly answer the demands. A press statement was published on the Namibian Presidency (2019) Twitter page, which stated that the president accepted the resignation of the 'Fishrot' accused – the then Justice Minister Sacky Shanghala and then Fisheries Minister Bernhardt Esau (Immanuel 2019; Namibian Presidency 2019). The statement said that the presidency 'has taken practical steps to promote effective governance, prioritising the fight against corruption, promoting greater transparency and accountability' (NAMPA 2019: 2). Controversially, the presidency thanked the accused ministers 'for their patriotism and contribution to the work of Government', which drew much criticism from the general public. Some felt this fell well short of 'zero tolerance for corruption' and sounded more like what McGee and Gaventa (2011) have called patronage and accommodation of corruption.

There is no evidence that online petitions resulted in answerability. The petitions were not acknowledged, responded to or mentioned elsewhere.

Enforceability

Enforceability within domestic accountability 'refers to the willingness and power of citizens or the institutions that are responsible for accountability to sanction the offending party or remedy the contravening behaviour' (Loquai and Fanetti 2011: 6).

Even the president of Namibia seems to lack either the willingness or power to enforce sanctions on parliamentarians who refuse to make transparent their assets. The Electoral Commission of Namibia lacks either the willingness or the power to enforce transparency or accountability for the stolen electronic voting machines. Although national elections offer a mechanism for enforcing a change of government, many Namibians have become disaffected by party politics, but digital citizenship affords an opportunity to make claims and demand accountability.

Conclusion

This chapter set out to understand how digital citizenship contributed to political accountability prior to the 2019 national election in Namibia. The most contentious episodes of online debate were analysed through a conceptual framework of technology access, citizenship mechanisms and elements of accountability.

The study documents increased digital citizenship in the 2019 election, the use of online petitions and social media engagement in politics (primarily on Facebook and Twitter). Political parties and government agencies ran their own online campaigns, while WikiLeaks and local journalists provided some transparency on issues not revealed by existing agencies or oversight mechanisms. This transparency enabled digital citizens to run hashtag campaigns to amplify contentious issues and demand accountability. This was made possible by increasing levels of internet access, but the majority of the population remain excluded from digital citizenship.

The analysis found that while digital citizenship is increasingly important in Namibian political accountability, it is early days; only one-third of the population can engage as digital citizens, and they are not demographically representative of the whole population. The analysis found that although the Namibian government is extending digital services, it is not yet doing so in a way that contributes to its stated objectives of accountability and zero tolerance for corruption. Increased digital citizenship has been used to call for accountability from government, especially around youth unemployment and government corruption. Despite rhetorical support for transparency and accountability, the government has chosen not to make government data open or to put the assets declarations of parliamentarians online. On the eve of the election, the ruling party provided answerability in the face of the Fishrot revelations by announcing the resignation of top SWAPO officials. In other cases, government officials have remained tight-lipped, and answerability has not been forthcoming.

Although the affordances of social media technologies have amplified digital citizens' claims-making in online spaces, they have had only limited success in translating increased 'voice' into 'teeth'. Accountability requires mechanisms that have the power of enforceability. This can be provided by well-functioning horizontal accountability mechanisms providing transparency, answerability and enforceability. Alternatively, it can come in the form of vertical accountability when voters enforce a change of government.

Digital citizenship is destined to play a greater role in Namibia's national elections in 2023 and 2027. The 'born frees' are an ever-expanding segment of Namibia's population. This generation is under-represented in Parliament, worst affected by unemployment and are early adopters and heaviest users of digital technologies. The number of young people forming their political consciousness online and using social media to enact their digital citizenship is growing. Youth unemployment is rising, and the Fishrot court case is scheduled to play out in court before the 2023 election. The outcomes of Namibia's next elections will not be determined by digital technologies, but they will be used to amplify the agency and claims-making of digital citizens as well as the government.

Bibliography

Aichholzer, G. and G. Rose (2020) 'Experience with Digital Tools in Different Types of e-Participation', in L. Hennen et al. (eds), *European E-Democracy in Practice*, 93–140, Cham: Springer, accessed 20 October 2021.

AXABA!! (2019) 'If You Vote SWAPO Today, You Shall Have Reaffirmed Continued Sale of Our Country and Its Resources. You Shall Have Voted for Another 5 Years of Poverty, Youth Unemployment, Homelessness, Poor Health Services. SWAPO and Both Their Candidates Is BAD for Namibia! [Tweet]', *@ExellentJy*, 27 November, accessed 20 October 2021.

Bonga, W. (2021) 'Corruption Prevalence in SADC Regional Bloc', *Journal of Research in Humanities and Social Science*, 9 (1): 8–16, accessed 20 October 2021.

BTI (2012) *Namibia Country Report*, Bertelsmann Stiftung's Transformation Index, accessed 20 October 2021.

Cela, B. (2018) *Electronic Asset Declarations for Public Officials – Two Years After Its Launch. A Panacea Against Corruption?* UNDP Ukraine, accessed 20 October 2021.

ECN (2019a) 'Media Statement: Missing Electronic Voting Machines (EVMs) [Tweet]', *@ECN_Namibia*, 20 October, accessed 20 October 2021.

ECN (2019b) 'Are You Looking Forward to the Presidential and National Assembly Elections? We Want to Hear From You Leading Up to the Elections. #NamibiaVotes19 #ElectionYear19 [Tweet]', *@ECN_Namibia*, 22 November, accessed 20 October 2021.

Ekine, S. (ed) (2010) *SMS Uprising: Mobile Activism in Africa*, Cape Town: Pambazuka Press.

Emmanouilidou, L. (2020) *Arab Uprisings: What Role Did Social Media Really Play?* The World from PRX. https://www.pri.org/stories/2020-12-17/arab-uprisings -what-role-did-social-media-really-play.

European Parliament. (2011) *E-public, e-participation and e-voting in Europe – Prospects and Challenges*: Final Report, Publications Office. https://data.europa.eu /doi/10.2861/13630.

Everything Namibian (2019) 'The Country is Messed up and we are Heading for Dark Times. Youth Unemployment is at 43% With More Jobs Being Lost and Many Other Issues. We Will Only Hear the Real Truths After Elections! We Need Youth Advisor @daisrym to Report Back Monthly to the Youth! [Tweet]', *@Our_Namibia*, 15 August. https://twitter.com/Our_Namibia/status /1161880436085284864.

Farivar, M. (2021) 'Who Were the US Capitol Rioters?', *Voice of America News*, 12 February, accessed 20 October 2021.

Fox, J. (2007) 'The Uncertain Relationship Between Transparency and Accountability', *Development in Practice*, 17 (4–5): 663–71, accessed 20 October 2021.

Fox, J. (2015) 'Social Accountability: What Does the Evidence Really Say?', *World Development*, 72: 346–61, accessed 20 October 2021.

Geingob, H. G. (2017) *Talking Points for H.E the President, Dr. Hage G. Geingob Year End Press Conference*, 13 December, accessed 20 October 2021.

Gibson, D. (2020) 'Namibia's "Fishrot" Scandal: From Start to Present', *Undercurrent News*, 6 January.

Go Petition (2019) 'No to EVM's – Presidential & National Assembly Elections 2019', *Go Petition*, 6 November, accessed 20 October 2021.

Hintz, A., L. Dencik, and K. Wahl-Jorgensen (2019) *Digital Citizenship in a Datafied Society*, Cambridge: Polity Press.

Immanuel, S. (2019) 'Esau, Shanghala Forced to Resign', *The Namibian*, 13 November, accessed 11 August 2021.

Informanté (2019) *Informanté – Posts. Facebook*, 2 December, accessed 20 October 2021.

Isin, E. and E. Ruppert (2015) *Being Digital Citizens*, London, Rowman & Littlefield.

Iyaloo, S. (2019) *Sign the Petition: Justice Brought and the Fishrot Culprits Punished.* https://www.change.org/p/namibian-justice-brought-and-the-fishrot-culprits -punished-f59ae2b7-3161-419b-9eda-fefaf8bb8466.

Kemp, S. (2019) Digital 2019: Namibia, *DataReportal – Global Digital Insights*, accessed 20 October 2021.

Kemp, S. (2022) Digital 2022 Namibia, DataPortal. https://datareportal.com/reports/ digital-2022-namibia.

Kleinfeld, J. (2019) *Anatomy of a Bribe: A Deep Dive into an Underworld of Corruption*, accessed 20 October 2021.

Kneuer, M. (2016) 'E-Democracy: A New Challenge for Measuring Democracy', *International Political Science Review*, 37 (5): 666–78, accessed 20 October 2021.

Krantzberg, G. (1967) 'Rules for the Evaluation of Technology', *Journal of Technology Education*, 1 (1): 8–15.

Leber, J. (2012) 'Cashing Out of Corruption: Are 15 Million Mobile Phones Enough to Wage War on Graft in Afghanistan?', *MIT Technology Review*, 19 March, accessed 20 October 2021.

Le Blanc, D. (2020) *E-participation: A Quick Overview of Recent Qualitative Trends*, (UN Department of Economic and Social Affairs (DESA) Working Papers No. 163; UN Department of Economic and Social Affairs (DESA) Working Papers, Vol. 163). https://doi.org/10.18356/0f898163-en.

Legal Assistance Centre. (2019) *Information About Namibia's Law: Independent Candidates.* https://www.lac.org.na/news/probono/ProBono_27-INDEPENDENT _CANDIDATES.pdf.

Leterme, Y. (2019) 'The Impact of Digital on Elections and Democracy in West Africa', Kofi Annan Foundation, 24 April. https://www.kofiannanfoundation.org

/supporting-democracy-and-elections-with-integrity/annan-commission/the
-impact-of-digital-on-elections-and-democracy-in-west-africa/.

Likela, S. (2020) 'Venaani Tears into Assets Register System', *The Namibian*, 25 July, accessed 20 October 2021.

Lindner, R. and G. Aichholzer (2020) 'E-Democracy: Conceptual Foundations and Recent Trends', in L. Hennen, I. van Keulen, I. Korthagen, G. Aichholzer, R. Lindner, and R. Ø. Nielsen (eds.), *European E-Democracy in Practice*, 11–45, Springer International Publishing. https://doi.org/10.1007/978-3-030-27184-8_2.

Links, F. (2019) 'FALSE: Reporting on Fishrot and Kora Scandals Is Not Disinformation', *Namibia Fact Check*, 25 November, accessed 18 December 2020.

Links, F. (2020) 'FALSE: Al Jazeera's 'Fishrot' Documentary Was Not Aired Before the 2019 Elections', *Namibia Fact Check*, 29 July, accessed 20 October 2021.

Loquai, C. and E. Fanetti (2011) 'Support to Domestic Accountability in Developing Countries: Taking Stock of the Approaches and Experiences of German Development Cooperation', European Centre for Development Policy Management, Discussion Paper 111, Maastricht. https://ecdpm.org/application/files/4216/5547/2401/Support-Domestic-Accountability-Developing-Countries_German-2011.pdf.

Macintosh, P. A. (2004) 'Characterizing e-participation in Policy-making', 37th Annual Hawaii International Conference on System Sciences, 5–8.

MacKensie, D. and J. Wajcman (1985) *The Social Shaping of Technology*, Milton Keynes: Open University Press.

Mathekga, R. (2021) 'Historical Resentment Lives On in Namibia', *Geopolitical Intelligence Services*, accessed 20 October 2021.

McGee, R., F. Feruglio, H. Hudson, C. Anderson, and D. Edwards (2018) *Appropriating Technology for Accountability: Messages from Making All Voices Count*, Making All Voices Count Research Report, Brighton: Institute of Development Studies, accessed 20 October 2021.

McGee, R. and J. Gaventa (2011) 'Shifting Power? Assessing the Impact of Transparency and Accountability Initiatives', *IDS Working Paper*, 2011 (383): 1–39, accessed 20 October 2021.

Melber, H. (2020) 'Namibia's Parliamentary and Presidential Elections: The Honeymoon Is Over', *The Round Table*, 109 (1): 13–22.

Melber, H. (2021) 'Namibia's Regional and Local Authority Elections 2020: Democracy Beyond SWAPO', *Journal of Namibian Studies: History Politics Culture*, 29: 73–83, accessed 20 October 2021.

Ministry of Information and Communication Technology (2016) *Social Media Policy and Implementation Plan, 2016/17-2019/20*, Windhoek: Government of the Republic of Namibia, accessed 20 October 2021.

Mossberger, K., C. J. Tolbert, and R. S. McNeal (2008) *Digital Citizenship: The Internet, Society, and Participation*, Cambridge: MIT Press.

MRLGHRD (2008) *Sub-national e-Government Strategy*, Ministry of Regional and Local Government, Housing and Rural Development. https://www.npc.gov .na/downloads/policies%20by%20year/2008/Sub-national%20e-Government %20Strategy.pdf.

Mwenye, M., D. Amdany, H. Hogger, and B. Waite (2019) 'Namibia Presidential and National Assembly Elections: The Commonwealth', accessed 20 October 2021.

Nakale, A. (2019) 'Social Media Dominate Campaign Trail', *New Era Live*, https:// neweralive.na/posts/social-media-dominate-campaign-trail.

Nakale, A. and K. Tjitemisa (2020) 'Swapo Loses Some Ground', *New Era*, 27 November, accessed 20 October 2021.

Namibia Fact Check (2019) 'Anatomy of a Misinformation Episode', *Namibia Fact Check*, 30 October, accessed 20 October 2021.

Namibia Revenue Agency (2021) *ITAS for Namibia | About Us*. https://www.itas.mof .na/about.html.

Namibian Presidency (2019) 'MEDIA ALERT Https://t.co/YJrzm8SIBz [Tweet]', *@NamPresidency*, 13 November. https://twitter.com/NamPresidency/status /1194612880232124417.

NAMPA (2019) *Ministers Sacky Shanghala and Bernhardt Esau Resign After Kickback Exposé*, NBC. https://nbc.na/news/ministers-sacky-shanghala-and-bernhardt-esau -resign-after-kickback-expos%C3%A9.26714.

NBC (2019) *President Geingob Declares 2019 the Year of Accountability* – NBC. https://www.youtube.com/watch?v=rTeanZkfphg.

Ndjavera, M. (2021) *Youth Unemployment Expected to Reach 50%*, Truth, for Its Own Sake. https://neweralive.na/posts/youth-unemployment-expected-to-reach -50.

New Era Newspaper (2021) *About New Era Publication Corporation – Truth, for Its own Sake*. https://neweralive.na/about-us.

New Era Newspaper (2015) *MPs Make Mockery of Asset Declaration – Truth, for Its own Sake*. https://neweralive.na/posts/mps-make-mockery-of-asset-declaration.

Norman, D. (1988) *The Design of Everyday Things*, New York: Basic Books.

NSA (2011) *Namibia 2011 Population & Housing Census Main Report*, Windhoek: Namibia Statistics Agency, accessed 20 October 2021.

NSA (2013) *Profile Namibia: Facts, Figures, and Other Fundamental Information*. https://d3rp5jatom3eyn.cloudfront.net/cms/assets/documents/p19dpmrmdp1 bqf19s2u8pisc1l4b1.pdf.

NSA (2018) 2018 Labour Force Survey Report, Namibia Statistics Agency.

O'Dea, S. (2021) 'Namibia Mobile Cellular Subscriptions 2000–2019', Statista, 3 March. https://www.statista.com/statistics/501008/number-of-mobile-cellular -subscriptions-in-namibia/.

OECD (2011) *Asset Declarations for Public Officials: A Tool to Prevent Corruption*, OECD Publishing. http://dx.doi.org/10.1787/9789264095281-en.

OECD (2014) *Accountability and Democratic Governance: Orientations and Principles for Development*. https://www.oecd.org/dac/accountable-effective -institutions/For%20WEB%20Accountability%20and%20democratic %20governance%20Orientations%20and%20principles%20for%20development .pdf.

OnlySWAPO (2020) 'Its Time to go on the Campaign Trail and Here is Your Thread to let you Know who is Speaking Where and When. Comrades, Retweet for Awareness. #WeHaveHeardYou Https://t.co/ZjRBL17tJ0 [Tweet]', *@SWAPONamibia*, 29 October. https://twitter.com/SWAPONamibia/status /1321836264987848712.

Oyedemi, T. D. (2020) *The Theory of Digital Citizenship'*, *Handbook of Communication for Development and Social Change*, 237–55, Singapore: Springer.

Perez, J. (2019) 'Tomorrow We Decide Whether We Want Change, War or Fishrot to Repeat Itself #NamibiaVotes2019 [Tweet]', *@James_Gee_Perez*. https://twitter.com/ James_Gee_Perez/status/1199471698824847370.

Pflughoeft, B. R. and I. E. Schneider (2020) 'Social Media as E-Participation: Can a Multiple Hierarchy Stratification Perspective Predict Public Interest?' *Government Information Quarterly*, 37 (1): 101422, accessed 20 October 2021.

Porwol, L., A. Ojo, and J. G. Breslin (2016) 'An Ontology for Next Generation e-Participation Initiatives', *Government Information Quarterly*, 33 (3): 583–94, accessed 20 October 2021.

Roberts, T. and K. Hernandez (2017) *The Techno-Centric Gaze: Incorporating Citizen Participation Technologies into Participatory Governance Processes in the Philippines*, Making All Voices Count Research Report, Brighton: Institute of Development Studies, accessed 20 October 2021.

Roberts, T. and K. Hernandez (2019) 'Digital Access Is Not Binary: The 5 'A's of Technology Access in the Philippines', *The Electronic Journal of Information Systems in Developing Countries*, 85 (4): e12084. https://doi.org/10.1002/isd2 .12084.

Roberts, T. and A. Mohamed Ali (2021) 'Opening and Closing Online Civic Space in Africa: An Introduction to the Ten Digital Rights Landscape Reports', in T. Roberts (ed.), *Digital Rights in Closing Civic Space: Lessons from Ten African Countries*, 9–42, Brighton: Institute of Development Studies, accessed 20 October 2021.

Sæbø, Ø., J. Rose, and J. Molka-Danielsen (2010) 'eParticipation: Designing and Managing Political Discussion Forums', *Social Science Computer Review*, 28 (4): 403–26, accessed 20 October 2021.

Sæbø, Ø., J. Rose, and L. Skiftenes Flak (2008) 'The Shape of eParticipation: Characterizing an Emerging Research Area', *Government Information Quarterly*, 25 (3): 400–28, accessed 20 October 2011.

Sanford, C. and J. Rose (2007) 'Characterizing eParticipation', *International Journal of Information Management*, 27 (6): 406–21. https://doi.org/10.1016/j.ijinfomgt.2007 .08.002.

Saunders, C. (2018) 'SWAPO, Namibia's Liberation Struggle and the Organisation of African Unity's Liberation Committee', *South African Historical Journal*, 70 (1): 152–67. https://doi.org/10.1080/02582473.2018.1430846.

Schlettwein, C. (2019) *Media Statement on Tax and Procurement Matters by Hon. Calle Schlettwein, Minister of Finance*, Namibia Ministry of Finance, accessed 20 October 2021.

Schmitter, P. C. (2007) 'Political Accountability in "Real-Existing" Democracies: Meaning and Mechanisms', *Istituto Universitario Europeo*, 21. https://www.eui.eu /Documents/DepartmentsCentres/SPS/Profiles/Schmitter/PCSPoliticalAccount abilityJan07.pdf.

Shihomeka, S. P. (2017) 'Engaging Citizens: New Media and Political Engagement in Namibia', *ResearchGate*. https://www.researchgate.net/publication/320043534 _Engaging_citizens_New_media_and_political_engagement_in_Namibia.

Shirky, C. (2008) *Here Comes Everyone: The Power of Organising Without Organisations*, New York: Penguin.

Slinger, M. (2019) 'Why is the Head of State Attacking the Media at Political Rallies? The Journalists are Just Doing Their Work. Corruption Should be Exposed any Time Information Becomes Available Whether its Election Time or not. Unfortunately its Election Time for the #fishrot #NamibiaVotes2019 [Tweet]', *@Beaumpho*, 24 November. https://twitter.com/Beaumpho/status /1198460768515178496.

Smith, S. (2019) 'Namibia: Lost EVMs Raise Doubt on Election Credibility', *AllAfrica. Com*, October 23. https://allafrica.com/stories/201910230179.html.

Tjipueja, N. (2019) 'Final Election Results Announcement Speech', *Electoral Commission of Namibia*, accessed 20 October 2021.

Toyama, K. (2015) *Geek Heresy: Rescuing Social Change from the Cult of Technology*, New York: Public Affairs.

Tufekci, Z. (2014) 'Big Questions for Social Media Big Data: Representativeness, Validity and Other Methodological Pitfalls', in *Proceedings of the Eighth*

International AAAI Conference on Weblogs and Social Media, Association for the Advancement of Artificial Intelligence.

UN (2021) *United Nations E-Participation Index*. https://publicadministration.un.org/egovkb/en-us/About/Overview/E-Participation-Index.

UNCTAD (2020) *Progress Made in the Implementation of and Follow-up to the Outcomes of the World Summit on the Information Society at the Regional and International Levels*. Report of the Security-General.

UNDP (2015) *Sustainable Development Goals*, New York: United Nations Development Programme. https://www.undp.org/publications/sustainable-development-goals-booklet.

UNESCAP (2009) *What Is Good Governance?* United Nations Economic and Social Commission for Asia and the Pacific: 3.

United Nations (2020) *Digital Cooperation at the UN*, Geneva: United Nations Office of Information and Communications Technology. https://unite.un.org/blog/digital-cooperation-at-the-united-nations.

WeAreSocial (2019) 'Namibia Social Media Statistics 2019', accessed 20 October 2021.

Wentworth, K. (2019) *Sign the Petition: 'Fish Rot' Culprits Must be Trialed, and Serve Prison Terms if Found Guilty*. https://www.change.org/p/the-president-of-namibia-fish-rot-culprits-must-be-trialed-and-serve-prison-terms-if-found-guilty.

Weylandt, M. (2016) 'Asset Declarations in Namibia', Institute for Public Policy Research, 16.

World Bank (1991) *Managing Development – The Governance Dimension*, A Discussion Paper, Washington, DC: World Bank, accessed 20 October 2021.

World Bank (2022) *Individuals Using the Internet (% of Population) – Namibia. World Bank statistics website*. https://data.worldbank.org/indicator/IT.NET.USER.ZS?locations=NA&lang=de.

Zuboff, S. (2019) '"We Make Them Dance": Surveillance Capitalism, the Rise of Instrumentarian Power, and the Threat to Human Rights', in R. F. Jørgensen (ed.), *Human Rights in the Age of Platforms*, Cambridge, MA: MIT Press, pp 3–49.

8

Citizenship, African languages and digital rights

The role of language in defining the limits and opportunities for digital citizenship in Kiswahili-language communities

Nanjala Nyabola

Introduction

All over the world, digital has emerged as a key site for public life. In addition to the organic embrace of social media and messaging as low-cost spaces for political organization and mobilization, several governments have also compelled their citizens to shift more aspects of their political lives online. 'Digital first government' is a central pillar for governments as disparate as the UK, Estonia, Kenya and India. This demands renewed attention to the ways in which shifting relationships with power online change the quality and quantity of political participation.

Some of the concepts that underpin our capacity to participate in civic life in the analogue space map perfectly onto the digital space, but others do not. Ideas like citizenship, democracy, networks and deliberation are all intimately connected to our political lives. Yet they are also rooted in specific linguistic and historical contexts, and this raises the question of whether simply grafting them onto the digital retains their full power. Citizenship, for instance, is routinely deployed in conversations about technology and politics, although the questions it triggers about how closely the analogue translates to the digital are only now gaining more attention. In some ways, the analogue concept of citizenship maps perfectly onto the digital – for instance, when thinking about services delivered by the government online.

This chapter selects one aspect of defining who the citizen is – language – and uses it to explore some of the opportunities and limitations triggered by the emergence of the digital public sphere. The chapter argues that there are less apparent aspects of citizenship that affect our ability to effectively participate in these digital platforms or to call ourselves digital citizens. Yet language is inherently connected to the capacities of the digital citizen. The dominance of English as the language of digital citizenship contributes to the circumscription of the digital citizen's rights. Moreover, language can be a legalistic marker of citizenship, defining belonging in strict terms. Using the example of Kiswahili-language communities, this chapter explores the role that language plays in both the digital and the analogue public sphere in these language communities.

From analogue to digital citizenship

The idea of a citizen is foundational to social and political theory and behaviour, and yet definitions remain varied and elusive. Etymologically, the word 'citizen' has Latin roots from the word 'civitas', which means a city. The city state was the foundational unit of belonging in Western Europe, and from the fourteenth century, the word referred explicitly to 'freemen' or inhabitants of a city, rather than slaves or foreigners (Etymonline 2000). In contemporary terms, the word is used in three connected but not necessarily overlapping ways. The first is the legal sense provided by the framework of legal eligibility (Cohen 1999); the second is connected to participation – that is, the citizen is one who participates in the political space in a specific entity (Kymlicka 2000); and the third is more reflexive and focused on the individual's identity and sense of identity and belonging (Carens 2000). Each of these definitions connects the citizen to a political geography in a certain way, establishing either rules, norms or sentiments as the foundation of the relation between an individual and the political entity they inhabit.

Digital citizenship therefore is an emerging body of work that considers the ability of individuals and indeed institutions and inanimate entities (such as corporations or bots) to participate in the digital sphere. Mossberger et al.

(2008: 1) initially define digital citizenship as simply 'the ability to participate in society online', though this triggers questions about access and connectivity. But even with full access to the internet and devices, standards of exclusion and inclusion into a digital society can still exclude people from considering themselves digital citizens of a specific group. Roberts and Hernandez (2019) developed the five 'A's to analyse how availability, affordability, awareness, abilities and agency stratify who is able to make effective use of digital technologies and who is excluded and left behind (Hernandez and Roberts 2018).

In his seminal work *Citizen and Subject*, Mamdani (1996) argues that the bifurcated colonial state gives the best entry point for understanding the distinction between a citizen and a subject, where 'citizenship would be a privilege of the civilised [and] the uncivilised world would be subject to all around tutelage' (Mamdani 1996: 17). Whereas a citizen was entitled to the full menu of rights, a subject was only entitled to some civil rights but no political rights because 'a propertied franchise separated the civilised from the uncivilised' (Mamdani 1996: 17). This was always the distinction embedded in the classical notions of citizenship, where the landed elite were entitled to participate fully in the governance of the city, but slaves, women and other disenfranchised groups were never fully considered citizens.

A digital citizen therefore could be one who is entitled to participate in the digital space, or one who participates actively in the processes and systems of the digital space, or one who belongs or has an identity that is drawn from their presence on the digital sphere. Each of these definitions is once again founded on the notion of relation – specifically, the relation that the individual has to the digital space and to the powers that shape it. But the notion of digital citizenship carries with it a complication that is not reflected in the literature on geographical citizenship, in that our participation in the digital public sphere is moderated and affected by private corporations. As such, a legalistic definition of the digital citizen would necessarily be rooted in rules established by corporations rather than by states – for instance, by the terms and conditions we agree to before signing up to digital platforms. Still, in practice, norms and sentiments rather than laws have determined the definition of a digital citizen, and the basis of digital citizenship is regularly connected to the sense of identity and belonging individuals get from participating in digital spaces.

Taken together, these definitions suggest that a digital citizen is one who inhabits the digital public sphere and is able to contribute towards it meaningfully. Yet the definition of a digital public sphere is also affected by unique concerns connected to the nature of the digital itself. In Western political theory, the public sphere is often described as a unitary space where political ideas are generated, debated and adopted (Habermas 1974: 49). Habermas suggests that the public sphere is defined primarily through speech acts, in that we are constantly engaged in processes of defining our political actions through debating them with others and with powerholders (Habermas 1992: 31). For Habermas, the public sphere is produced by ideas, and in this sense, the digital public sphere is basically the functions of an analogue public sphere grafted onto a new arena of engagement (Habermas 1992: 31). A digital public sphere is therefore produced wherever people can engage with power and with other citizens to debate the ideas that will shape their shared polity (Nyabola 2018b: 40).

On the one hand, one feature shared by both the digital and analogue public spheres is exclusion. Not everyone who exists can equally participate in the digital public sphere, even though ideally, everyone who wants to participate in both the digital and the analogue public spheres should be able to. The archetypical polis was not designed for women, the poor, slaves or foreigners. Indeed, scholars from the Global South argue that we in fact inhabit multiple public spheres, their work influenced by Ekeh's foundational studies on the bifurcation of the identity of the colonized individual (Ekeh 1975: 92). Feminists would argue that the home is a form of public sphere for women where the politics of patriarchy established by society outside the home affect their lives in the domestic sphere. In Ekeh's bifurcated public sphere, deliberation in service of political – and political in the broadest sense – action remains the same, but each of these spheres serves a different function and negotiates with a different centre of power (Mustapha 2012: 31).

On the other hand, a feature that significantly distinguishes the digital and the analogue public spheres is the participation of corporations, where in most countries private capital cannot participate in the public sphere as a distinct entity from those who wield or possess it. However, corporations can and do engage meaningfully in the digital space – for example, particularly where limits and standards on corporate communication sufficiently sever the identity of the person behind the account from the account itself. Increasingly, brands are turning digital participation into a core site for their corporate action, speaking more and more directly with consumers online than they would ever engage with offline and imbuing their digital avatars with aspects of personality. At the same time, the digital is also full of inorganic users – bots, automated processes and coordinated inauthentic behaviour (See Keller et al. 2020). In so far as the idea of citizenship has never been premised on equal and universal participation of all individuals, then the proliferation of inorganic users in the digital public sphere challenges the notion of digital citizenship as a flat, cohesive structure.

Another major distinction is that digital citizenship is not attached to a specific geographic entity but to networks of connection and participation. A digital citizen could be active across various civics, including some that may be in tension with each other – for example, when one participates in forums that call for treasonous action while also participating in conversations about local or national issues. Similarly, digital citizenship has few legal barriers to qualification: the threshold and standards for participation are entirely established by tacit agreement between the members of the community. These are all the primary characteristics of digital citizenship, but as we demonstrate in this chapter, language is an intervening factor that makes all of these subsequent characteristics possible.

There are also qualitative elements that define digital citizenship. In practice, the idea of digital citizenship is often connected to the ethical obligations that flow from participating in these digital spaces. For technology companies especially, it can sometimes be easier to define who a digital citizen is not than who a digital citizen is. This includes, for example, standards for community participation in platforms or list serves. Kim and Choi (2018: 156) argue that such approaches to regulating belonging within digital communities emphasize normative aspects like acknowledging the rights of others or respecting intellectual property of others. But they also assert that this is a minimalist standard and that in addition to these, digital citizenship must also encompass numerous affirmative actions – things that people must do in order to be considered part of the community – and that digital citizenship includes cognitive, emotional and behavioural factors (2018: 157).

Even so, Ekeh's and Habermas's conceptions of the public sphere do map strongly onto the digital. Digital citizenship, as defined by norms and practices, maps closely onto their ideas of an analogue public sphere and therefore analogue citizenship, while differing in some significant ways. Moreover, participating in digital platforms produces new relations between the individual, the collective and power, for instance challenging pre-existing norms about ethnic identities (Nyabola 2018b: 41). Arguably, the mere act of participating in these spaces gives shape to them and that shape is a form of public sphere even if it is incomplete (Warner 2002). Warner (2002) argues that a public can also be valid even if it has a constrained audience, and merely the capacity to articulate a view in public for this public constitutes the kind of rational-critical debate that is necessary to creating a public sphere, if not *the* public sphere (Warner 2002). One key social phenomenon that shapes the nature of the public sphere is language, as it is the means of communication and therefore connection. To understand what futures are possible for digital citizens of African communities, it is important to look at the histories that precede them, and language offers a crucial entry point for conducting such an analysis.

Kiswahili in the digital age

African sociolinguistics has long recognized the value of language in political cultures. In his seminal work *Decolonising the Mind*, Ngugi wa Thiong'o said that 'the choice of language and the use to which language is put is central to a people's definition of themselves in relation to their natural and social environment, indeed in relation to the universe' (wa Thiong'o 1981: 9). Ngugi argues that language is the most important vehicle through which power – and colonial power especially – 'held the soul prisoner' (wa Thiong'o 1981: 13). Language is not just a means of communication; it is also a carrier of culture. Ngugi continues that language is the means through which relation is established and through which the boundaries of our social interactions are formed. Language also orders our production or our relation to our means of life: it organizes our relation to the natural world (wa Thiong'o 1981: 14). Finally, language – particularly when written – is also a system of signs (wa Thiong'o 1981: 14). Language acts as a carrier of our histories and our politics, and this suggests that what is not written or what is not possible to write can be just as important as what is. For example, a society that names female genitalia in the same vein as shame and dirt betrays its patriarchy. A language that has a rich history of description that cannot describe the violence that colonization enacts on the colonized betrays its injustice. To decolonise African intellectual thought, therefore, Ngugi urges the use of indigenous African languages, not only as a form of protest but as a means of reclaiming the African identity and cultural experience from the violence of colonization.

Languages are also a marker of belonging and identity, and even a technology for political action (Nyabola 2018b: 174). Mazrui and Mazrui (1993) discuss the functions of Kiswahili, Kenya's second official language after English, in public life in the country. The Swahili people are a network of communities found along the East African coast ranging from southern Somalia to northern Mozambique. They consist of several small, related Bantu groups as well as descendants of Arab immigration in the fifteenth and sixteenth centuries (Matveiev 1984: 455–80). The Swahili coast of Kenya was never formally colonized by the British, as it was administered separately as a protectorate, but after independence the coast united with the mainland. Similarly, Zanzibar in Tanzania, which was once the capital of the Sultanate of Oman, was never fully colonized and remains in union with the mainland of Tanganyika rather than fully incorporated into it.

Given the colonial history, unlike other indigenous languages in the region, Kiswahili – literally, the language of the Swahili people – is also an official language in both Kenya and Tanzania, with a combined population of over 100 million people. Mazrui and Mazrui therefore call Kiswahili 'preponderant' – that is, it has numerous speakers even where the ethnic group that developed it is not dominant in the African country where it is spoken – and argue that the language has major sociolinguistic value (Mazrui and Mazrui 1993: 176).

Because the Swahili people were historically traders, including contributing to the Indian Ocean slave trade (Clarence-Smith 1989), there was also a great deal of commercial contact between the coast and the hinterland that continues today, as borders in the region remain relatively open to petty traders. As a result, Kiswahili is also spoken in northern Malawi, Zambia and Mozambique, as well as in the Eastern Democratic Republic of Congo. In Uganda, Kiswahili is spoken because it is one of the official languages of the East African Community as well as the unofficial language of trade. People in Rwanda, Burundi and South Sudan also speak Kiswahili, as a result of their membership of the regional bloc, but long-running conflicts in the three countries also resulted in the emigration of tens of thousands of refugees into Kenya and Tanzania. With the advent of peace, many of these refugees returned to their home countries and brought the language with them. As of 2021, there were plans to teach Kiswahili in schools in South Africa and Namibia (Mirembe 2020). Kiswahili is also the only African language that is an official language of the African Union.

The use of Kiswahili in the region underscores Ngugi's observation that language is a carrier of the history and politics of a society, as well as the importance of doing more than simply providing translation in order to secure the protection of digital rights. In Kenya especially, Kiswahili is poorly taught and spoken and in its standard form only loosely integrated into public life, in part because of the language's complex history and association with violence. Officially Kiswahili is the language of commerce in East Africa as a direct consequence of British imperialism and the desire to 'solve' the problems of language diversity in the region (Mazrui and Mazrui 1993). The uptake of Kiswahili in non-Swahili communities of Kenya and Tanzania, therefore, happens at the intersection of two contradictory impulses – the organic uptake of the language by those who wished to trade with the Swahili Arab coastal communities and the inorganic imposition of the language through imperial force.

Kiswahili is also a complex language. Although the language is an official language and all Kenyans are forced to learn it in school, Standard Kiswahili or the formal register of Kiswahili is rarely used in informal contexts (Githiora 2018). There are several major dialects of Kiswahili spoken by the various Swahili communities – Kimrima, Kiunguja, Kipemba, Kimgao in Tanzania and nineteen recognized dialects in Kenya, including Kibajuni, Kiamu, Kimvita, Kipemba, Kimambrui and Kipate (Kipacha 2003). The language retains tremendous sentimental value in Kenya's public sphere as it enabled the coordination of the independence and resistance effort, but it is also rejected for its association with the military (Mazrui and Mazrui 1993: 289). In so far as there is a bifurcation in the colonial mindset, in Kenya and Tanzania (and indeed in Uganda, where Kiswahili is associated with the 1979 war between the two countries), it also has distinct historical associations that constrain its uptake and popularity.

Most Kenyans and Tanzanians would not recognize this complexity because the cultural significance of language is also shaped by contemporary forces such as youth culture and commerce. Indeed, Kiswahili has a bizarre status in Kenya, culminating in the development of Sheng', the actual lingua franca of Kenya, and what Githiora (2018) argues is an informal register of Kiswahili that allows Kenyans to reconcile all of these contradictions. Sheng' is an amalgam of the various languages spoken in urban Kenyan settings and reflects the multilingual identities that exist in these contexts. Githiora (2018) has argued that Sheng' is more than broken English; it is a variety of Kenyan Kiswahili spoken spontaneously in informal and formal registers depending on the audience at hand. Sheng' contains multiple registers and vocabularies that reflect underlying frictions of class, while the index language that forms the speaker's grammatical foundation also reflects whether they are urban (English) or rural speakers. Sheng' can be used to create a context of both exclusion and inclusion and is, for some, a rebellion against economic marginalization and degradation in the public sphere (Githiora 2018). There is no standard form of Sheng', only a constantly evolving language that reflects the creativity and needs of those who develop it (Mazrui 1995: 169).

The place of Sheng' in public life mirrors the contours of the digital public sphere in many ways. Language innovation and digital cultures share the characteristic of being primarily driven by youth culture. Sheng' is inexorably linked to youth culture and, indeed, the choice of words for different objects or events in Sheng' is often a generational marker. Erastus and Hurst-Harosh (2020) argue that the combination of language innovation and digital cultures has allowed young people to create distinct youth cultures and push the boundaries of African languages. They call these networks 'communities of practice' – a group of people who share a common mutual endeavour – reflecting the definition of a digital public sphere or a digital citizen as a member of a community united by a shared interest in a specific social or political aspect (Erastus and Hurst-Harosh 2020). The emergence of Sheng' in Kenya identifies urban youth as a distinct community of practice that is dealing with socio-economic concerns that are qualitatively different from those faced by (for example) rural agrarian communities.

Erastus and Hurst-Harosh (2020) also point out that patois like Sheng' and digital cultures also share the characteristics of hybridity and an ability to take what exists in the dominant culture and add to it, enriching their digital experiences with this mix of backgrounds. Their research in South Africa shows how vernaculars from various geographies can often collide in WhatsApp messages, for example, where young people fluidly combine

American slang with isiZulu and Afrikaans words in forms that would not be acceptable in any of these languages. The same happens in Nairobi and Dar es Salaam, where words taken from youth culture in the United States like 'baller' or 'slay queen' enter the popular slang discourse and into Kiswahili by extension with no local language translation. In many African urban spaces, the influence of US popular culture is ubiquitous although also modified by regional and local popular cultures, particularly with the international success of pop culture icons and the rise of transnational digital platforms such as East Africa Television (EATV) and Netflix.

Githiora argues that for young people in Africa, the rejection of standard forms of language is a form of rebellion, but also a reflection of the high level of mobility among African youth (Erastus and Hurst-Harosh 2020). Sheng', he argues, is an attempt to create a non-ethnic youth culture that reflects the need to navigate these parallel worlds. Kenya, for example, is characterized by high rural–urban migration, resulting in what researchers call a 'dual system' (Nyabola 2018). Many people leave ethnically homogenous communities to enter ethnically heterogenous communities in urban areas, and the emergence of slang is not simply a reflection of 'de-tribalization' or loss of ethnic identity but the creation of a new one, marked with a different shared language and a myth of common ancestry. This suggests that Sheng' might be a more organic language for Kenya's digital citizens than Kiswahili. Both Kenya and Tanzania have young populations (the majority of their citizens are under the age of thirty-five), and if youth culture is the driving force in shaping the use of technology, arguably it makes more sense to use the language that is in popular use.

But neither Sheng' nor Kiswahili are used in this way in Kenya. In fact, the default language of technology in Kenya remains English, reflecting an unwillingness or inability to build technology that sees local contexts and prioritizes local needs. De Sousa Santos argues that 'what does not exist is actually produced as non-existent, that is, an unbelievable alternative to what exists' (de Sousa Santos 2012: 52). By extension this means that the inability of the rules-based language approach that computers take to processing languages to handle Sheng' is interesting not just because of that inability but because of what it says about disinterest in trying. It adds to a broader impulse to make Sheng' non-existent. This resonates with the Kenyan government's deliberate effort to mute or even eliminate Sheng' in the country. In 1987, for instance, the vice chancellor of Kenyatta University, Kenya's second-largest university, called Sheng' a subversive element in Kenya's language education (Mazrui 1995: 168).

African language practice is, of course, highly diversified, heterogenous and fluid in a way that rules-based ICT systems struggle to understand. Kiswahili has a high regional profile, but the complexity of Kiswahili and its relationship to Sheng' underscores the need for more asserted efforts to bring not just the language but its linguistic context into the way in which we build technology. There is currently no capacity to type or translate text into or from Sheng', and existing translation or text-to-type features online often intertwine the two languages. This creates what de Sousa Santos (2012) calls a sociology of absence. By its very nature, the fluidity and the transgressive nature of Sheng' demand an ontological approach that can process language in a way that is dynamic and equally transgressive. Artificial intelligence is inherently static and conservative, reliant on pre-existing data. The inability of language learning to capture Sheng' is indicative of the ontology of Sheng' itself – rejecting rules, constantly evolving and rebuilding itself from what it cannibalizes off other languages.

Language, rights and digital citizenship

Understanding the place of African languages in the digital sphere is part of the broader challenge of decolonising technology. For example, Aiyegbusi (2018: 441) argues that because the domain of digital humanities is preoccupied with Western institutions and research funds, the questions that might intrigue African researchers are often left unexamined. Language is a major part of how African analogue publics are defined, where ethnic communities of the modern age are united by only two things – a shared language and the perception of a shared homeland. Yet, as stated, the default language of the African digital sphere to date is English, with French a distant second. Few apps or platforms begin with African language as the default imagined user. African users are routinely placed in a position to interact with the digital through translation. Even alternative keyboards that recognize the diacritics of specific African languages do not exist. So discursive work around what language use reflects in African digital publics is poorly understood.

Yet language is intimately connected to the capacities of the digital citizen. Language defines how digital citizens present themselves in the digital publics. For instance, African digital users routinely toggle between languages, in order to extend or constrain their reach at will. Code-switching – the practice of alternating regularly between languages in multilingual speakers (Auer 2013: 3) – is a typical feature of Africa's digital publics where the average African is trilingual in a European language, a national African language and a third mother language. Code-switching is also used as a means of subverting power by switching to languages that cannot be translated online, in order to gossip or speak negatively about powerful people in English- or French-speaking constituencies. Code-switching in this way, however, can also be used to disseminate hate speech to avoid machine-based content moderation, which still cannot process most African languages.

In addition, language is a key tool through which communities can define the limits of their digital communities – to both include and exclude. African digital communities also use language to extend the reach of their digital communities. In Kenya, Sheng' is increasingly important to digital discourse as more users from working-class backgrounds join the platforms (Githiora 2018: 132–3). There is also the regionalization of political discourse, where (for example) 67 per cent of the tweets sent out in defence of Ugandan politician Bobi Wine sent out from Kenya means that political concerns also begin to transcend digital national boundaries (Nyabola 2018a). The desire to communicate more with people in Tanzania also fuels an interest in Kiswahili in Kenya. Language is allowing these digital public spheres to redefine their constituencies.

Moreover, language can be a legalistic marker of citizenship, defining belonging in strict terms. Where there is a requirement to speak and engage in an official language in a political entity, the inability to speak the language can be used to exclude. As stated, the complex position of Kiswahili in Kenyan public life is indicative of its history of imperialism and conquest, as well as liberation from these two forces. The British colonial state in Kenya had a stated interest in eliminating African languages, except Kiswahili, but the successor independent state has been slow to embrace the protection of mother languages. In the colonial state, language was imposed violently as a marker of citizenship, where children were beaten as part of the process of forced assimilation, or in contemporary states where other languages are simply not available for use (Ong'uti, Aloka and Raburu 2016: 161–6). The contemporary state has not gone far enough to defend these languages and so as sub-national languages, they do not have the resources required to strengthen their presence both online and offline. This further complicates the discourse on the bifurcation of identity and digital citizenship for Kenyans online (Ong'uti, Aloka and Raburu 2016: 161–6).

Language also determines the contours of the civic space that digital citizens have to demand their rights. Ragnedda (2018) adds to the idea that digital participation or digital exclusion is a factor not merely of technical access but also due to social and political factors (Ragnedda: 151). Language is one of these key social factors that gives users the confidence to speak up in the digital public sphere in the knowledge that their ideas will be heard and handled properly. Indeed, rights are, in the simplest sense, the claims that a citizen is able to make from the political society they belong to regarding their protection or survival.

Therefore, where words do not exist to describe and therefore contextualize certain harms, digital citizens will find it hard to demand the protection of those rights. For example, until 2019, Kenya did not have a data protection law, which meant that both public and private entities collected, transmitted and even commercialized citizen data without consent or consequence. In 2019, the country passed a Data Protection Act in part because a court held that without such a law, the nationwide data collection drive for the single source of truth digital identity system was unconstitutional. Yet, Kenya's Data Protection Act has not yet been translated into Kiswahili, and until 2021 there was no effort to even provide a Kiswahili translation for the term 'data protection'. The dominance of English as the language of digital citizenship contributes to the circumscription of the digital citizen's rights.

Language and rights are intimately connected, and there are laws that recognize that. The International Covenant on Civil and Political Rights (ICCPR) not only recognizes language as one of the key avenues through which discrimination can be perpetrated, but in Article 14, it also states that people have a right to participate in courts in their chosen language (Office of the High Commissioner for Human Rights 1966). The ICCPR recognizes that without the guarantee of language, an individual is unable to participate fully in court processes, and they will risk greater injustice. Article 14 also insists that translations should be made available to those who are charged in criminal cases to protect them from such exclusion (Office of the High Commissioner for Human Rights 1966). Moreover, Article 27 the ICCPR also recognizes a right for religious and ethnic minorities to use their own languages (Office of the High Commissioner for Human Rights 1966). At least 173 countries have ratified and are state parties to the ICCPR, which means that its provisions are on the way to becoming domestic law in at least 173 countries.

But even beyond legalistic foundations, language can also be a method of enforcing norms on belonging and participation. This relates to the ability of the individual to show up online as their whole chosen (authentic?) self. Drahos (2017: 230) uses the example of a Chinese character simplification exercise that undermined the ability of Chinese internet users to exist online with their full chosen names. In the twenty-first century, the Chinese government has been pushing an initiative to simplify the language characters that can be used online, inadvertently marginalizing individuals whose names contain unusual characters (Drahos 2017: 231). Nor was the problem restricted to participating in social networks or digital dialogues. The digitalization of identities that accompanied this process also created problems in opening bank accounts, proving home ownership, or even the process of obtaining identity cards itself (Drahos 2017: 231). Indeed, the government encouraged affected individuals to change their names, in order to make the new language policy work. The social impact of the language initiative was a big part of its rights context, but it was not taken into consideration.

Given this significance of language, an increasing number of initiatives around the world (many led by indigenous language speakers themselves) recognize the importance of language in the digital space. The Global Coalition for Language Rights is a network of international organizations that supports global efforts to increase access to critical information and services, as well as equal digital representation for all languages, while including speakers of indigenous and under-represented languages in social and educational issues online (Global Coalition for Language Rights 2022). Wikimedia regularly hosts editing marathons to provide content for Wikipedia in Kiswahili (Wikipedia Editathon Arusha 2020). In 2020, the UN Human Rights Office launched the #WikiForHumanRights campaign on International Mother Language Day to 'enhance the quality of human rights content online in languages other than English' (Sauveur 2020). During this event, Tanzanian contributors added forty-one new articles on human rights in Kiswahili, including details on major human rights conventions (Sauveur 2020).

It is worth noting that in the digital age, the question of language, digital citizenship and digital rights is complicated by private corporations. The concept of 'rights' is generally used to refer to the relationship between states and individuals, which is in turn governed by a social contract. Given that corporations dominate the digital space, the idea of a social contract recedes in favour of the idea of a commercial contract, and in many contexts digital rights are increasingly narrowly defined as consumer rights because the penalties for failing consumers are a lot clearer than the political and social violations that occur. Recalling Ngugi's (1981) argument that language is also about semiotics or signalling, the shift in language from 'citizen' or 'voter' (a person that has civic duties and protections) to 'user' (one who merely has commercial ties) is significant.

This shift perhaps explains why African languages continue to be neglected in digital spaces. This notion of consumer rights is rooted in US capitalism and the idea that US citizens as consumers deserved highly specific protections of their rights before corporations and reflects the dominance of US corporations in the digital space (Larsen and Lawson 2013). The commercialization of the internet and the shift from viewing it as a purely public good to a commercial one do not see non-English-speaking communities as viable markets – disenfranchizing them by circumscribing their ability to function as digital citizens. The argument for investing in the inclusion of African language communities online is primarily a civic rather than a commercial one, and this contradicts the logic of profiteering that dominates the internet.

The danger is that consumer rights protect the user from the excesses of the free market but do not specifically address those rights violations that arise even within the bounds of properly conducted business. Thus, for example, consumer rights would be concerned that the process of distributing advertising on social media platforms was fair and not exploitative but would have little to say about how the content of these political advertisements affected political behaviour and outcomes. When consumer rights displace human rights as the foundation of digital rights, the language of digital rights increasingly takes on the language of consumer rights. Rather than appeal to criminal or civil legal action, users are encouraged to appeal to community standards or self-policing. The success or interest in including African – and, indeed, global indigenous – language communities into the internet could therefore be a strong indicator of the extent to which the contours of digital citizenship will be defined by civic and political rather than commercial concerns.

Conclusion

Ultimately, digital rights are human rights and specifically human rights that protect digital citizens from the excesses of power in the digital space. Language is therefore crucial to the full comprehension and expression of digital rights, as it enables the digital citizen to not only understand their place in the digital public sphere but also to participate fully to express their identity and to belong to a digital community. Offline, language is a key entry point through which citizens can make rights claims from geographical entities and through which states can deny those claims. States routinely use language as a method to delineate belonging or citizenship, as when the Swedish government proposed language testing as a method for 'reducing social differentiation' or of homogenizing the diversifying society (Milani 2008).

In the digital space, imposing English on Kiswahili-language speakers is a projection of power that undermines the rights of Kiswahili-language speakers because it circumscribes the possibilities of digital citizenship through an imperial language. But the liberatory power of Kiswahili should not be overstated either, as the language also occupies a complex political space in the region. Overlooking other African languages in favour of Kiswahili has historical precedent, and the championing of Kiswahili should not come at the expense of creating opportunities for other languages to find full expression online as well. Kenya's language families are defined primarily by two factors – a shared language and a myth of common origin. Language can be as much a tool for exclusion as inclusion in a country where identities have formed the basis for political exclusion and even violence (Lynch 2006: 50). This complicates the context of preservation and popularization of mother languages. Particularly as the successor state makes more concerted efforts to link ethnic identities to the allocation of resources, this heightens the contestation between groups and the potential for collision (Lynch 2006). Thus, without due attention, privileging Kiswahili over other languages can also be interpreted as the decision to mould Kenyan digital citizenship through national rather than sub-national identities.

Pretorius and Soria (2017: 895) remind us that 'the destiny of a language is primarily determined by its native speakers and their broader cultural context'. Thus, as the digital becomes a more prominent part of African public lives, then the question of the language of the digital future becomes more urgent. The proper representation of African languages in the corpus of possibility of the digital is not just about diversity and representation but also about advancing digital rights in a shared digital future.

Bibliography

Aiyegbusi, B. T. (2018) 'Decolonizing Digital Humanities: Africa in Perspective', in E. Losh and J. Wernimont (eds), *Bodies of Information*, 75–90, Minneapolis: University of Minnesota Press.

Anthonio, F., B. Andere, and S. Cheng (2020) 'Shutdown Victim Stories: Tanzania Is Weaponizing Internet Shutdowns', *Access Now*, accessed 15 September 2021.

Auer, P. (2013) *Code-Switching in Conversation: Language, Interaction and Identity*, London: Routledge.

Carens, J. H. (2000) *Culture, Citizenship, and Community: A Contextual Exploration of Justice as Evenhandedness*, Oxford: Oxford University Press.

Clarence-Smith, W. G. (ed) (1989) *The Economics of the Indian Ocean Slave Trade in the Nineteenth Century*, Oxfordshire: Routledge.

Cohen, J. (1999) 'Changing Paradigms of Citizenship and the Exclusiveness of the Demos', *International Sociology*, 14 (3): 245–68.

de Sousa Santos, B. (2012) 'Public Sphere and Epistemologies of the South', *Africa Development/Afrique et Développement*, 37 (1): 43–67.

Drahos, A. (2017) 'Ungeilivable: Language Control in the Digital Age', *The China Story Yearbook 2016: Control*, 299–336.

Ekeh, P. (1975) 'Colonialism and the Two Publics in Africa: A Theoretical Statement', *Comparative Studies in Society and History*, 17 (1): 91–112.

Erastus, F. K. and E. Hurst-Harosh (2020) 'Global and Local Hybridity in African Youth Language Practices', *Africa Development/Afrique et Développement*, 45 (3): 13–32.

Githiora, C. (2018) *Sheng: Rise of a Kenyan Swahili Vernacular*, Suffolk: Boydell and Brewer.

Global Coalition for Language Rights (GCLR) (2022) 'About Us: Global Coalition for Language Rights', GLCR website https://www.coalitionforlanguagerights.org/about.

Habermas, J. (1974) 'The Public Sphere: An Encyclopedia Article', *New German Critique*, 3: 49–55.

Habermas, J. (1992) *The Structural Transformation of the Public Sphere: An Inquiry into a Category of Bourgeois Society*, London: Polity Press.

Hernandez, K. and T. Roberts (2018) *Leaving No One Behind in a Digital World*, K4D Emerging Issues Report, Brighton: Institute of Development Studies, accessed 13 October 2021.

Keller, T., T. Graham, D. Angus, A. Bruns, N. Marchal, L.-M. Neudert, R. Nijmeijer, K. L. Nielbo, M. D. Mortensen, A. Bechmann, P. Rossini, B. Stromer-Galley, E. Anita, and V. V. de Oliveira. (2020). 'Coordinated Inauthentic Behaviour' and Other Online Influence Operations in Social Media Spaces'. Panel presented at AoIR 2020: The 21st Annual Conference of the Association of Internet Researchers. Virtual Event: AoIR. Retrieved from http://spir.aoir.org. *'COORDINATED INAUTHENTIC BEHAVIOUR' AND OTHER ONLINE INFLUENCE OPERATIONS IN SOCIAL MEDIA SPACES* Tobias R. Keller Digital Media Research Centre, Queensland University of Technology Timothy Graham Digital Media Research Centre, Queensland University of Technology Daniel Angus Digital Media Research Centre, Queensland University of Technology Axel Bruns Digital Media Research Centre, Queensland University of Technology Nahema Marchal Oxford Internet Institute, University of Oxford Lisa-Maria Neudert Oxford Internet Institute, University of Oxford Rolf Nijmeijer LUISS Guido Carli Kristoffer Laigaard Nielbo Aarhus University Marie Damsgaard Mortensen Aarhus University.

Kim, M. and D. Choi (2018) 'Development of Youth Digital Citizenship Scale and Implication for Educational Setting', *Journal of Educational Technology & Society*, 21 (1): 155–71.

Kipacha, A. (2003) 'Lahaja Za Kiswahili OSW 303', *ResearchGate*, accessed 21 October 2021.

Kymlicka, W. (2000) 'Citizenship in Culturally Diverse Societies: Issues, Contexts, Concepts', in W. Kymlicka and W. Norman (eds), *Citizenship in Diverse Societies*, 3-29, Oxford: Oxford University Press.

Larsen, G. and R. Lawson (2013) 'Consumer Rights: An Assessment of Justice', *Journal of Business Ethics*, 112 (3): 515–28.

Lynch, G. (2006) 'Negotiating Ethnicity: Identity Politics in Contemporary Kenya', *Review of African Political Economy*, 33 (107): 49–65.

Mamdani, M. (1996) *Citizen and Subject: Contemporary Africa and the Legacy of Late Colonialism*, Princeton: Princeton University Press.

Matveiev, V. (1984) 'The Development of Swahili Civilization', in D. T. Niane (ed.), *General History of Africa Vol IV: Africa From the Twelfth to the Sixteenth Century*, 587–601, Paris: UNESCO.

Mazrui, A. M. (1995) 'Slang and Code-Switching: The Case of Sheng in Kenya', *Afrikanistische Arbeitspapiere: Schriftenreihe Des Kölner Instituts Für Afrikanistik* 42: 168–79.

Mazrui, A. M. and Mazrui, A. (1993) 'Dominant Languages in a Plural Society: English and Kiswahili in Post-Colonial East Africa', *International Political Science Review/Revue Internationale de Science Politique*, 14 (3): 275–92.

Milani, T. M. (2008) 'Language Testing and Citizenship: A Language Ideological Debate in Sweden', *Language in Society*, 37 (1): 27–59.

Mirembe, R. (2020) 'Kiswahili in Namibia Classes by 2021', *The East African*, 5 July 2020, accessed 15 September 2021.

Mossberger, K., C. J. Tolbert, and R. S. McNeal (2008) *Digital Citizenship: The Internet, Society, and Participation*, Cambridge, MA: MIT Press.

Mustapha, A. R. (2012) 'The Public Sphere in 21st Century Africa: Broadening the Horizons of Democratisation', *African Development*, 37 (1): 27–41.

Nyabola, N. (2018a) '#FreeBobiWine and Today's Pan-Africanism for the Digital Age', *African Arguments*, 23 August, accessed 15 September 2021.

Nyabola, N. (2018b) *Digital Democracy, Analogue Politics: How the Internet Era Is Transforming Kenya*, London: Zed Books.

Office of the High Commissioner for Human Rights (1966) 'International Covenant on Civil and Political Rights', accessed 16 October 2021.

Ong'uti, C. O., P. J. O. Aloka, and P. Raburu (2016) 'Factors Affecting Teaching and Learning in Mother Tongue in Public Lower Primary Schools in Kenya', *International Journal of Psychology and Behavioral Sciences*, 6 (3): 161–6.

Online Etymology Dictionary (2000) *Citizen*, accessed 15 September 2021.

Pretorius, L. and C. Soria (2017) 'Introduction to the Special Issue', *Language Resources and Evaluation*, 51 (4): 891–5.

Ragnedda, M. (2018) 'Tackling Digital Exclusion: Counter Social Inequalities Through Digital Inclusion', in Glenn W. Muschert et al. (eds), *Global Agenda for Social Justice: Volume One*, 1st ed., 151–8, Bristol University Press, https://doi.org /10.2307/j.ctv47wfk2.23.

Roberts, T. and K. Hernandez (2019) 'Digital Access is not Binary: The 5 'A's of Technology Access in the Philippines', *Electronic Journal of Information Systems in Developing Countries*, https://onlinelibrary.wiley.com/doi/full/10.1002/isd2.12084.

Sauveur, L. (2020) '#WikiForHumanRights: Promoting Knowledge of Human Rights in a Multilingual World', *UN Human Rights*, 21 February, accessed 15 September 2021.

wa Thiong'o, N. (1981) *Decolonising the Mind: The Politics of Language in African Literature*, Harare: Zimbabwe Publishing House.

Warner, M. (2002) 'Publics and Counterpublics', *Public Culture*, 14 (1): 49–90.

Wikipedia (2020) 'Wikipedia Editathon Arusha 2020', accessed 30 August 2021.

Index